Becoming Myself

ALSO BY IRVIN D. YALOM

BECOMING MYSELF

A Psychiatrist's Memoir

Irvin D. Yalom

BASIC BOOKS

New York

Basic Books
Hachette Book Group
1290 Avenue of the Americas, New York, NY 10104
www.basicbooks.com

Printed in the United States of America

First Edition: October 2017
First Trade Paperback Edition: May 2019

Published by Basic Books, an imprint of Perseus Books, LLC, a subsidiary of Hachette Book
Group, Inc. The Basic Books name and logo is a trademark of the Hachette Book Group.

The publisher is not responsible for websites (or their
content) that are not owned by the publisher.

Print book interior design by Jack Lenzo

Library of Congress Cataloging-in-Publication Data
Names: Yalom, Irvin D., 1931- author.
Title: Becoming myself : a psychiatrist's memoir / Irvin D. Yalom.
Description: New York : Basic Books, [2017] | Includes bibliographical references and index.
Identifiers: LCCN 2017016637 | ISBN 9780465098897
(hardback) | ISBN 9780465098903 (ebook)
Subjects: LCSH: Yalom, Irvin D., 1931---Mental health. | Psychiatrists--
United States--Biography. | Psychotherapy--Biography. |
BISAC: PSYCHOLOGY / Psychotherapy / General. |BIOGRAPHY & AUTOBIOGRAPHY
/ Personal Memoirs. | PSYCHOLOGY / Developmental / Adulthood & Aging.
Classification: LCC RC339.52.Y35 A3 2017 | DDC 616.89/14092--dc23
LC record available at https://lccn.loc.gov/2017016637

ISBN: 978-1-5416-9899-4 (paperback)

LSC-C

10 9 8 7 6 5 4 3 2 1

To the memory of my parents, Ruth and
Benjamin Yalom, and my sister, Jean Rose.

CONTENTS

CHAPTER ONE

THE BIRTH OF EMPATHY

I awake from my dream at 3 a.m., weeping into my pillow. Moving quietly, so as not to disturb Marilyn, I slip out of bed and into the bathroom, dry my eyes, and follow the directions I have given to my patients for fifty years: close your eyes, replay your dream in your mind, and write down what you have seen.

I am about ten, perhaps eleven. I am biking down a long hill only a short distance from home. I see a girl named Alice sitting on her front porch. She seems a bit older than me and is attractive even though her face is covered with red spots. I call out to her as I bike by, "Hello, Measles."

Suddenly a man, exceedingly large and frightening, stands in front of my bicycle and brings me to a stop by grabbing my handlebars. Somehow I know that this is Alice's father.

He calls out to me: "Hey, you, whatever your name is. Think for a minute—if you can think—and answer this question. Think about what you just said to my daughter and tell me one thing: How did that make Alice feel?"

I am too terrified to answer.

"Cummon, answer me. You're Bloomingdale's kid [My fa-
ther's grocery store was named Bloomingdale Market and many
customers thought our name was Bloomingdale] and I bet you're a
smart Jew. So go ahead, guess what Alice feels when you say that."

I tremble. I am speechless with fear.

"All right, all right. Calm down. I'll make it simple. Just tell
me this: Do your words to Alice make her feel good about herself
or bad about herself?"

All I can do is mumble, "I dunno."

"Can't think straight, eh? Well, I'm gonna help you think.
Suppose I looked at you and picked some bad feature about you
and comment on it every time I see you?" He peers at me very
closely. "A little snot in your nose, eh? How about 'snotty'? Your
left ear is bigger than your right. Supposed I say, 'Hey, "fat ear"'
every time I see you? Or how about 'Jew Boy'? Yeah, how about
that? How would you like that?"

I realize in the dream that this is not the first time I have
biked by this house, that I've been doing this same thing day after
day, riding by and calling out to Alice with the same words, try-
ing to initiate a conversation, trying to make friends. And each
time I shouted, "Hey, Measles," I was hurting her, insulting her.
I am horrified—at the harm I've done, all these times, and at the
fact that I could've been so blind to it.

When her father finishes with me, Alice walks down the
porch stairs and says in a soft voice, "Do you want to come up
and play?" She glances at her father. He nods.

"I feel so awful," I answer. "I feel ashamed, so ashamed. I
can't, I can't, I can't . . . "

Since early adolescence, I've always read myself to sleep, and
for the past two weeks I have been reading a book called *Our*
Better Angels by Steven Pinker. Tonight, before the dream, I had
read a chapter on the rise of empathy during the Enlightenment,

and how the rise of the novel, particularly British epistolary novels like *Clarissa* and *Pamela*, may have played a role in decreasing violence and cruelty by helping us to experience the world from another's viewpoint. I turned out the lights about midnight, and a few hours later I awoke from my nightmare about Alice.

After calming myself, I return to bed, but lie awake for a long time thinking how remarkable it was that this primeval abscess, this sealed pocket of guilt now seventy-three years old, has suddenly burst. In my waking life, I recall now, I had indeed bicycled past Alice's house as a twelve-year-old, calling out "Hey, Measles," in some brutish, painfully unempathic effort to get her attention. Her father had never confronted me, but as I lie here in bed at age eighty-five, recovering from this nightmare, I can imagine how it must have felt to her, and the damage I might have done. Forgive me, Alice.

CHAPTER TWO

SEARCHING FOR
A MENTOR

Michael, a sixty-five-year-old physicist, is my last patient of the day. I saw him for therapy twenty years ago, for about two years, and I had not heard from him since until a few days ago when he emailed to say, "I need to see you—this attached article has ignited a lot of things, both good and bad." The link led to an article in the *New York Times* describing how he had recently won a major international science prize.

As he takes his seat in my office, I am the first to speak.

"Michael, I got your note saying you needed help. I'm sorry you're distressed but I also want to say it's good to see you and wonderful to learn of your award. I've often wondered how you've been doing."

"Thank you for saying that." Michael looks around the office—he is wiry, alert, nearly bald, about six feet tall, and his gleaming brown eyes radiate competence and confidence. "You've redone your office? These chairs used to be over there? Right?"

"Yep, I redecorate every quarter-century."

He chuckles. "Well, you saw the article?"

I nod.

"You can probably guess what happened to me next: a flush of pride, all too brief, and then wave after wave of anxious self-doubting. Same old stuff—down deep I'm shallow."

"Let's go right into it."

We spend the rest of the session reviewing old material: his uneducated Irish immigrant parents, his life in the New York tenements, his poor primary education, the lack of any significant mentor. He spoke at length of how much he envied people who were taken in hand and nourished by an elder, whereas he had to work endlessly and get the absolute highest grades simply to be noticed. He had had to create himself.

"Yes," I say. "Creating yourself is a source of great pride, but it also leads to a feeling of having no foundations. I've known many gifted children of immigrants who have a sense of being lilies growing in a swamp—beautiful flowers but no deep roots."

He remembers my saying this to him years ago, and says he's glad to be reminded of it. We make plans to meet again for a couple of sessions and he tells me he feels better already.

I had always worked well with Michael. We connected from our very first meeting, and he had told me at points that he felt I was the only one who truly understood him. In our first year of therapy he talked a lot about his confused identity. Was he really the sterling student who left everyone behind? Or was he the bum who spent his spare time in the poolroom or shooting crap?

Once, while he lamented his confused identity, I told him a story about my graduation from Roosevelt High School in Washington, DC. On the one hand, I had been notified that I would be receiving the Roosevelt High School Citizenship Award at graduation. Yet, in my senior year, I had been conducting a small bookie venture handling bets on baseball: I was giving 10–1 odds that any three selected players on a given day would not get six hits between them. The odds were in my favor. I had been doing famously well and always had money to buy gardenia corsages for

Marilyn Koenick, my steady girlfriend. However, a few days before graduation I lost my bookie notebook. Where was it? I was in a frenzy and searched everywhere up to the very moment of graduation. Even when I heard my name called and started to stride across the stage, I trembled, wondering: Would I be honored as a sterling citizen of the Roosevelt High School 1949 class or expelled from the school for gambling?

When I told Michael that story, he guffawed and muttered, "A shrink after my own heart."

After writing notes on our session, I change into casual clothes and tennis shoes and take my bike out of the garage. At eighty-four, tennis and jogging are long behind me, but almost every day I ride on a bike path near my home. I start by pedaling through a park full of strollers and Frisbees and children climbing ultramodern structures, and then cross a rude wooden bridge over Matadero Creek and climb a small hill that grows steeper every year. At the crest I relax as I begin the long downhill glide. I love coasting with the rush of warm air streaming in my face. Only at these moments can I begin to understand my Buddhist friends who speak of emptying the mind and luxuriating in the sensation of simply being. But the calm is always short-lived, and today, in the wings of my mind, I sense the rustling of a daydream readying to go onstage. It is a daydream that I've imagined scores, perhaps hundreds, of times over my long life. It had been dormant for several weeks, but Michael's lament about the lack of mentors stirs it awake.

A man, carrying a briefcase and dressed in a seersucker suit, straw hat, white shirt, and necktie, enters my father's small, shoddy grocery store. I'm not in the scene: I see it all as if I'm hovering near the ceiling. I don't recognize the visitor but I know that he is influential. Perhaps he is the principal of my elementary school. It is a hot, steamy Washington, DC, June day and he takes out his handkerchief to wipe his brow before turning to address my father. "I have some important things to discuss with you concerning your son, Irvin." My father is startled and anxious; he has never before encountered such a thing. Never having assimilated into the American culture, my father and my mother were at ease only with kinsmen, other Jews who had emigrated with them from Russia.

Though there are customers in the store demanding attention, my father knows that this is a man not to be kept waiting. He phones my mother—we live in a small flat above the store—and, out of earshot of the stranger, tells her in Yiddish to rush downstairs. She appears a few minutes later and efficiently waits on the customers while my father leads the stranger into the tiny storage room in the back of the store. They sit down on cases of empty beer bottles and talk. Mercifully no rats or roaches make an appearance. My father is obviously uncomfortable. He would have much preferred for my mother to do the talking, but it would be unseemly to acknowledge publicly that it was she, not he, who ran things, who made all the important family decisions.

The man in the suit tells my father remarkable things. "The teachers in my school say that your son, Irvin, is an extraordinary student and has the potential to make an outstanding contribution to our society. But that would happen if, and only if, he were provided a good education." My father seems frozen, his handsome, penetrating eyes fixed on the stranger, who continues, "Now the Washington, DC, school system is well run and is quite satisfactory for the average student but it is not the place for your son, for a very gifted student." He opens his briefcase and hands my father a list of several private DC schools and proclaims, "I urge you to send him to one of these schools for the rest of his education." He takes a card out of his wallet and hands it to my father. "If you contact me, I'll do all I can to help him obtain a scholarship."

Upon seeing my father's bewilderment, he explains, "I'll try
to get some help to pay his tuition—these schools are not free
like the public schools. Please, for your son's sake, give this your
highest priority."

Cut! The daydream always ends at this point. My imagination
balks at completing the scene. I never see my father's response, or
his ensuing discussion with my mother. The daydream expresses
my longing to be rescued. When I was a child I didn't like my
life, my neighborhood, my school, my playmates—I wanted to be
rescued and in this fantasy I am, for the first time, recognized as
special by a significant emissary of the outside world, the world
beyond the cultural ghetto in which I was raised.

I look back now and see this fantasy of rescue and elevation
throughout my writing. In the third chapter of my novel *The Spinoza Problem*, Spinoza, while strolling to the home of his teacher,
Franciscus van den Enden, loses himself in a daydream that re-
counts their first meeting a few months earlier. Van den Enden,
an ex-Jesuit classics teacher who operated a private academy, had
wandered into Spinoza's shop to buy some wine and raisins and
had become astonished at the depth and breadth of Spinoza's
mind. He had urged Spinoza to enter his private academy so as to
be introduced to the non-Jewish world of philosophy and literature. Though the novel is, of course, fiction, I attempted as much
as possible to stay close to historical accuracy. But not in this passage: Baruch Spinoza never worked in his family store. There *was*
no family store: his family had an export-import business but no
retail outlet. I was the one who worked in the family grocery store.

This fantasy of being recognized and rescued abides within
me in many forms. Recently I attended a performance of the play
Venus in Fur by David Ives. The curtain opens on a backstage scene
showing us a weary director at the end of a long day of auditioning
actresses for a lead role. Exhausted and highly dissatisfied with all
the actresses he has seen, he is preparing to leave when a brash,

highly flustered actress enters. She is an hour late. He tells her he is finished for the day, but she begs and wheedles for an audition. Aware that she is obviously unsophisticated, profane, uneducated, and entirely inappropriate for the role, he refuses. But she is an excellent wheedler; she is savvy and persistent and finally, to get rid of her, he gives in and grants her a brief audition in which they begin to read the script together. As she reads, she is transformed, her accent changes, her speech matures, she speaks like an angel. He is stunned; he is overwhelmed. She is what he has been looking for. She is more than he could have dreamed of. Could this be the bedraggled, vulgar woman he met only thirty minutes earlier? They continue to read the script. They do not stop until they have brilliantly performed the entire play.

I loved everything about the performance, but that first few minutes, when he appreciates her true quality, resonated most deeply with me: my daydream of being recognized was enacted upon the stage and I could not contain the tears streaming down my face, as I rose, the first one in the theater, to applaud the actors.

CHAPTER THREE

I WANT HER GONE

I have a patient, Rose, who lately had been talking mostly about her relationship with her adolescent daughter, her only child. Rose was close to giving up on her daughter, who had enthusiasm only for alcohol, sex, and the company of other dissipated teenagers.

In the past Rose had explored her own failings as a mother and wife, her many infidelities, her abandoning the family several years ago for another man and then returning a couple of years later when the affair had run its course. Rose had been a heavy smoker and had developed crippling advanced emphysema, but, even so, she had for the past several years tried hard to atone for her behavior and devoted herself anew to her daughter. Yet nothing worked. I strongly advocated family therapy, but the daughter refused, and now Rose had reached her breaking point: every coughing fit and every visit to her pulmonary doctor reminded her that her days were limited. She wanted only relief: "I want her gone," she told me. She was counting the days until her daughter would graduate from high school and leave home—for college, a job, anything. She no longer cared which path her daughter would take. Over and again she whispered to herself and to me: "I want her gone."

I do all I can in my practice to bring families together, to heal rifts between siblings and between children and parents. But I had grown fatigued in my work with Rose and lost all hope for this family. In past sessions I had tried to anticipate her future if she cut her daughter off. Would she not feel guilty and lonely? But that was all to no avail, and now time was running out: I knew that Rose did not have long to live. After referring her daughter to an excellent therapist, I now attended only to Rose and felt entirely on her side. More than once she said, "Three more months till she graduates from high school. And then she is out. I want her gone. I want her gone." I began to hope she would get her wish.

As I took my bicycle ride later that day, I silently repeated Rose's words—"I want her gone. I want her gone"—and before long I was thinking of my mother, seeing the world through her eyes, perhaps for the very first time. I imagined her thinking and saying similar words about me. And now that I thought about it, I recalled no maternal dirges when I finally and permanently left home for medical school in Boston. I recalled the farewell scene: my mother on the front step of the house waving goodbye as I drove away in my fully packed Chevrolet, and then, when I vanished from view, stepping inside. I imagine her closing the front door and exhaling deeply. Then, two or three minutes later, she stands erect, smiles broadly, and invites my father to join her in a jubilant "Hava Nagila" dance.

Yes, my mother had good reason to feel relieved when I, at twenty-two, left home for good. I was a disturber of the peace. She never had a positive word for me, and I returned the favor. As I coast down a long hill on my bicycle, my mind drifts back to the night when I was fourteen and my father, then age forty-six, awoke in the night with severe chest pain. In those days, doctors made home visits, and my mother quickly called our family doctor, Dr. Manchester. In the quiet of the night, we three—my father, my mother, and I—waited anxiously for the doctor to arrive. (My sister, Jean, seven years older, had already left home for college.)

THE AUTHOR WITH HIS MOTHER AND SISTER, CA. 1934.

Whenever my mother was distraught, she reverted to primitive thinking: if something bad happened, there must be someone to blame. And that someone was me. More than once that evening, as my father writhed with pain, she screamed at me, "You—you killed him!" She let me know that my unruliness, my disrespect, my disruption of the household—all of this—had done him in.

Years later, when on the analytic couch, my description of this event resulted in a rare, momentary outburst of tenderness from Olive Smith, my ultraorthodox psychoanalyst. She clucked her tongue, tsk, tsk, leaned toward me, and said, "How awful. How terrible that must have been for you." She was a rigid training analyst in a rigid institute that valued interpretation as the singular effective action of the analyst. Of her thoughtful, dense, and carefully worded interpretations, I remember not a one. But her reaching out to me at that time, in that warm manner—that I cherish even now, almost sixty years later.

"You killed him, you killed him." I can still hear my mother's shrill voice. I remember cowering, paralyzed with fear and with fury. I wanted to scream back, "He's not dead! Shut up, you idiot." She kept wiping my father's brow and kissing his head as I sat on the floor curled up in a corner until, finally, finally, about 3 a.m., I heard Dr. Manchester's big Buick crunching the autumn leaves in the street and I flew downstairs, three steps at a time, to open the door. I liked Dr. Manchester very much, and the familiar sight of his large round smiling face dissolved my panic. He put his hand on my head, tousled my hair, reassured my mother, gave my father an injection (probably morphine), held his stethoscope to my father's chest, and then let me listen as he said, "See, Sonny, it's ticking away, strong and regular as a clock. Not to worry. He's going to be all right."

That night I witnessed my father drawing close to death, felt, as never before, my mother's volcanic rage, and made a self-protective decision to shut the door on her. I had to get out of this family. For the next two to three years I barely spoke to her—we lived like strangers in the same house. And, most of all, I recall my deep, expansive relief at Dr. Manchester's entrance into our home. No one had ever given me such a gift. Then and there I decided to be like him. I would be a doctor and pass on to others the comfort he had offered me.

My father gradually recovered, and though he had chest pain thereafter with almost any exertion, even walking a single block, and immediately reached for his nitroglycerin and swallowed a tablet, he lived another twenty-three years. My father was a gentle, generous man whose only fault, I believed, was his lack of courage in standing up to my mother. My relationship with my mother was an open sore all my life, and yet, paradoxically, it is *her* image that passes through my mind almost every day. I see her face: she is never at peace, never smiling, never happy. She was an intelligent woman, and though she worked hard every day of her life, she was entirely unfulfilled and rarely uttered a pleasant, positive thought. But today, on my bicycle rides, I think about her in a different way: I think of how little pleasure I must have given her while we lived together. I am grateful I became a kinder son in later years.

CHAPTER FOUR

CIRCLING BACK

From time to time I reread Charles Dickens, who has always had a central place in my pantheon of writers. Recently an extraordinary phrase in *A Tale of Two Cities* caught my eye: *"For, as I draw closer and closer to the end, I travel in a circle nearer and nearer to the beginning. It seems to be one of the kind of smoothings and preparings of the way. My heart is touched now by many remembrances that had long fallen asleep . . . "*

That passage moves me tremendously: as I indeed draw closer to the end, I, too, find myself circling more and more to the beginning. My clients' memories more often trigger my own, my work on their future calls upon and disturbs my past, and I find myself reconsidering my own story. My memory of early childhood has always been fragmented, probably, I've always believed, because of my early unhappiness and the squalor in which we lived. Now, as I move into my eighties, more and more images from early life intrude upon my thoughts. The drunks sleeping in our vestibule covered with vomit. My loneliness and isolation. The roaches and the rats. My red-faced barber calling me "Jew Boy." My mysterious, tormenting, and unfulfilled sexual throbbings as a teenager.

Out of place. Always out of place—the only white kid in a black neighborhood, the only Jew in a Christian world.

Yes, the past is drawing me in and I know what "smoothings" mean. Now, more than ever before, I imagine my dead parents watching and taking great pride and pleasure in seeing me speak before a crowd. At the time my father died, I had written only a few articles, technical pieces in medical journals that he couldn't understand. My mother lived twenty-five years longer and, though her poor grasp of English, and, later, her blindness, made it impossible for her to read my books, she kept them stacked by her chair and stroked them and clucked over them to visitors in her retirement home. So much is incomplete between my parents and me. There are so many things we never discussed about our life together, about the tension and unhappiness in our family, about my world and their world. When I think of their lives, picture them arriving at

THE AUTHOR'S FATHER AND MOTHER, CA. 1930.

Ellis Island, penniless, without an education, without a word of English, my eyes tear up. I want to tell them, "I know what you went through. I know how hard it was. I know what you did for me. Please forgive me for being so ashamed of you."

Looking back at my life from my eighties is daunting and sometimes lonely. My memory is unreliable, and there are so few living witnesses to my early life. My sister, seven years older, has just died, and most of my old friends and acquaintances are gone, too.

When I turned eighty, a few unexpected voices from the past awakened some memories. First there was Ursula Tomkins, who found me via my webpage. I had not thought of her since we attended Gage Elementary School together in Washington, DC. Her email read, "Happy 80th birthday, Irvin. I've read and enjoyed two of your books and asked our Atlanta library to get some of the others. I remember you from Miss Fernald's fourth grade class. I don't know if you remember me—I was pleasingly plump with red frizzy hair and you were a beautiful boy with coal-black hair!"

So Ursula, whom I remembered well, thought I was a beautiful boy with coal black hair! Me? Beautiful? If only I had known! Never, not for a moment, had I ever thought of myself as a beautiful boy. I was shy, nerdish, lacking in self-confidence, and never imagined that anyone found me attractive. Oh, Ursula, bless you. Bless you for telling me I was beautiful. But, why, oh why, didn't you speak up earlier? It might have changed my entire childhood!

And then, two years ago, there was a phone message from the deep past that began: "THIS IS JERRY, your old chess buddy!" Even though I had not heard his voice in seventy years, I recognized it immediately. It was Jerry Friedlander, whose father owned a grocery store on Seaton and North Capitol Streets, just a block from my father's store. In his message he told me that his granddaughter, in a clinical psychology course, was reading one of my books. He remembered that we had played together regularly for two years when I was twelve and he fourteen, a time I remember only as a wasteland of insecurity and self-doubt. Since I remembered so very little from those years, I jumped at the opportunity for feedback and pumped Jerry for any impressions he had of me (after, of course, sharing my impressions of him).

"You were a nice guy," he said. "Very gentle. I remember that in all our times together we never had an argument."

"Give me more," I said greedily. "I've such hazy images from then."

"You played around some but, for the most part, you were really serious and scholarly. In fact I'd say *very* scholarly. Whenever I came over to your place, your head was buried in a book—oh yeah, that I remember well—Irv and his books. And always reading hard stuff and good literature—way over my head. No comic books for you."

That was only partly true—in fact, I had been a major aficionado of Captain Marvel, Batman, and Green Hornet. (Not Superman, though: his invulnerability drained all suspense from his adventures.) Jerry's words reminded me that during those years I often bought used books from a bookstore on Seventh Street just a block from the library. As I reminisced, an image of a large, rust-colored, arcane book on astronomy drifted into view. No matter that I couldn't understand much of the optics discussed: that book fit another agenda entirely—I left it around in plain sight for my sister's attractive girlfriends to find, hoping to awe them with my precociousness. Their pats on the head or occasional hugs or kisses were quite delicious. I hadn't known that Jerry noticed the book too—he had been an unintended target hit by friendly fire.

Jerry told me that I generally won our chess games, but that I was not a gracious loser: at the end of one marathon game, which he had won in a hard-fought endgame, I pouted and insisted that he had to play my father. And so he did. He came to my home the next Sunday and beat my father as well, though he was certain my father had let him win.

This anecdote staggered me. I had a good, if distant, relationship with my father, but I cannot imagine having looked to him to avenge my loss. My recollection was that he taught me to play chess, but by the time I was about eleven I was beating him routinely and looking around for stronger opponents, especially his brother, my uncle Abe.

I always had an unstated grievance toward my father—that he never, even once, stood up to my mother. In all the years that my mother disparaged and criticized me, my father never disagreed with her. He never once took my side. I was disappointed by his passivity, his unmanliness. So I was puzzled: How could I have called upon him to redeem my failure with Jerry? Perhaps my memory erred. Perhaps I was more proud of him than I had thought.

That possibility gained credence as Jerry proceeded to describe his own life odyssey. His father had not been a successful businessman, and, on three occasions, business failures had forced the family to move, each time downward, to less comfortable quarters. Moreover, Jerry had to work after school and during summers. I realized that I was far luckier: though I often worked in my father's store, it was never a requirement but always for my own pleasure—I felt grown-up waiting on customers, adding their bills, collecting money, and giving them change. And Jerry had worked summers, whereas my parents had sent me to two-month summer camps. I had taken my privileges for granted, but my conversation with Jerry made it clear that my father had done many things right. Obviously he had been a diligent, intelligent businessman. It was his (and my mother's) hard work and business acumen that had made my life easier and my education possible.

After I hung up with Jerry, other forgotten memories of my father seeped in. One rainy evening when the store had been crowded with customers, a huge, menacing man had grabbed a case of liquor and run out into the street. Without hesitation, my father had taken off in pursuit, leaving my mother and me alone in a store packed with customers. Fifteen minutes later my father returned, carrying the case of liquor—the thief had tired in two

THE AUTHOR'S FATHER IN HIS GROCERY STORE, CA. 1930.

or three blocks, dropped his booty, and taken off. It was a gutsy thing for my father to have done. I'm not sure I would have been up to the chase. I *must* have been proud of him—how could I not have been? But, strangely, I hadn't let myself remember. Had I ever sat down and considered, truly considered, what his life had been like?

I know that my father started work at five in the morning, buying produce from the Washington, DC, southeast produce market, and that he closed the store at 10 p.m. on weekdays and midnight on Friday and Saturday. His only day off was Sunday. I occasionally accompanied him to the produce market, and it was hard, grueling work. Yet I never heard him complain. I remember talking with a man I called "Uncle Sam," my father's best friend even in childhood back in Russia (I referred to everyone in the circle who had emigrated together from Cielz, their shtetl in Russia, as uncle or aunt). Sam had told me about my father sitting for hours in the tiny cold attic of his house and writing poetry. But all that ended when he was conscripted into the Russian army as a teenager in World War I to help build railroad tracks. After the war, he came to the United States with the help of his older brother, Meyer, who had emigrated earlier and opened a small grocery store on Volta Street in Georgetown. His sister Hannah and his younger brother, Abe, followed. Abe came alone in 1937 and planned to bring his family over shortly, but it was too late: the Nazis killed everyone left behind, including my father's older sister and her two children and his brother Abe's wife and four children. But, of all this, my father's lips were sealed; never once did he speak to me of the Holocaust, or, for that matter, of anything else from the old country. His poetry, too, was a thing of the past. I never saw him write. I never saw him read a book. I never saw him read anything but the daily Jewish newspaper, which he would grasp as soon as it arrived and scan. I realize only now that he was looking for any information it might hold about his family and friends. Only once did he allude to the Holocaust at all. When I was about twenty, he and I went out to lunch together, just the two of us. This was rare: even though he'd sold the store by this time, it was still hard to pry him away from my mother. He never initiated a conversation. He never searched me out. Maybe he was uncomfortable with me, though he wasn't at all shy or inhibited with his clan of men—I enjoyed seeing him laugh with them and tell jokes as they played pinochle. Perhaps we failed one another: he never inquired about my life or my work, and I never told him that I loved him. Our lunch discussion remains clear in my mind. We spoke together as adults for an hour and it was quite wonderful. I recall asking him if he believed in God, and he replied, "After the Shoah, how can anyone believe in God?"

I know that it's now time, past time, to forgive him for his silence, for being an immigrant, for his lack of education and his inattention to the trivial disappointments encountered by his only son. It's time to put an end to my embarrassment at his ignorance and time to remember his handsome face, his gentleness, his graceful

THE AUTHOR WITH HIS FATHER, 1936.

interactions with his friends, his melodious voice singing the Yiddish songs he learned as a child in the shtetl, his laughter as he played pinochle with his brother and friends, his graceful sidestroke as he swam at Bay Ridge beach, and his loving relationship with his sister Hannah, the aunt I most adored.

CHAPTER FIVE

THE LIBRARY, A–Z

For a great many years until my retirement I biked back and forth to Stanford every day from my home, stopping many days to admire the Rodin statues of the Burghers of Calais, or the gleaming mosaics on the chapel dominating the Quad, or to browse at the campus bookstore. Even after retirement I continued to bike around Palo Alto, running errands or visiting friends. But lately I've lost confidence in my balance, and so I avoid biking in traffic and limit my riding to bike paths for thirty or forty minutes at sundown. Though my routes have changed, the experience of biking has always been one of liberation and contemplation, and lately when I ride, the experience of the smooth, swift motion and the breeze in my face invariably transports me into the past.

Aside from an intense ten-year affair with a motorcycle during my late twenties and early thirties, I've been faithful to bicycling since I was twelve, when, after a long, hard campaign of begging and wheedling, my parents gave in and bought me a flashy red American Flyer for my birthday. I was a persistent beggar and discovered at an early age a supremely effective technique, a technique that never failed: simply make a linkage between my

THE AUTHOR AT AGE TEN.

desired object and my education. My parents were not forthcoming with money for any type of frivolity, but when it came to anything even remotely related to education—pens, paper, slide rules (remember those?), and books, especially books—they gave with both hands. Hence, when I told them I would use the bicycle to visit the grand Washington Central Library at Seventh and K Streets more often, they could not refuse my request.

I kept my side of the bargain: every Saturday, without fail, I filled my bicycle leatherette saddlebags with the six books (the library limit) I had digested since the previous Saturday and took off on the forty-minute ride for new ones.

The library became my second home and I spent hours there each Saturday. My long afternoons served a dual purpose: the library put me in contact with the larger world I longed for, a world of history and culture and ideas, and at the same time it eased my parents' anxiety and gave them the satisfaction of knowing that they had begotten a scholar. Also, from their standpoint, the more time I spent indoors reading, the better: our neighborhood was a dangerous one. My father's store and our second-floor apartment were located in a low-income neighborhood of segregated Washington, DC, a few blocks from the border of the white neighborhood. The streets were rife with violence, theft, racial skirmishes, and drunkenness (much of that fueled by liquor from my father's store). During the summer school vacations, they were wise to keep me off the dangerous streets (and out of their hair) by sending me, at considerable expense, from the age of seven onward, to summer camps in Maryland, Virginia, Pennsylvania, or New Hampshire.

The enormous reception hall on the library main floor inspired such awe that I tiptoed as I moved through it. In the very center of the first floor stood a massive bookcase housing biographies, in alphabetical order by subject. Only after I had circled it a great many times did I work up the nerve to approach the officious librarian for guidance. Without a word, she shushed me with a forefinger over her lips and pointed to the great marble circular stairway leading to the children's section on the second floor where I belonged. Crestfallen, I followed her instructions, but nevertheless, each time I came to the library I continued to case the biography bookcase, and at some point I developed a plan: I would read one biography a week, beginning with a person whose name started with "A," and work my way through the alphabet. I started with Henry Armstrong, a lightweight boxing champion of the 1930s. From the B's I remember Juan Belmonte, the gifted matador of the early nineteenth century, and Francis Bacon, the Renaissance scholar. There was C for Ty Cobb, E for Thomas Edison, G for Lou Gehrig and Hetty Green ("The Witch of Wall Street"), and so on. In the J's I discovered Edward Jenner, who became my hero for having eliminated smallpox. In the K's I met Genghis Khan, and for weeks I wondered whether Jenner had saved more lives than Genghis Khan had destroyed. The K's also housed Paul de Kruif's *Microbe Hunters*, which inspired me to read many books about the microscopic world; the following year,

I worked on weekends as a soda jerk at Peoples Drug Store and saved enough money to buy a polished brass microscope, which I own to this day. The N's offered me Red Nichols, the trumpet player, and introduced me also to a weird dude named Friedrich Nietzsche. The P's led me to Saint Paul and Sam Patch, the first to survive a plunge over Niagara Falls.

I recall ending my biography project at the T's, where I discovered Albert Payson Terhune. I got sidetracked in the weeks that followed devouring his many books about such extraordinary collies as Lad and Lassie. Today I know I suffered no harm from this haphazard reading pattern, no harm from being the only child of ten or eleven in the world who knew so much about Hetty Green or Sam Patch, but still, what a waste! I yearned for some adult, some mainstream American mentor, someone like the man in the seersucker suit who would enter my father's grocery store and announce that I was a lad of great promise. Looking back now, I feel tenderness for that lonely, frightened, determined young boy, and awe that he somehow made his way through his self-education, albeit haphazardly, without encouragement, models, or guidance.

CHAPTER SIX

THE RELIGIOUS WAR

Sister Miriam was a Catholic nun referred to me by her confessor, Brother Alfred, whom I had seen in therapy many years before, after the death of his tyrannical father. Brother Alfred had written me a note:

> Dear Dr. Yalom, (sorry but I still cannot refer to you as Irv—another year or two of therapy would be needed for that.) I hope you can see Sister Miriam————. She is a loving, generous soul but is encountering many obstacles to serenity.

Sister Miriam was an attractive, engaging, but somewhat discouraged middle-aged woman, dressed without any sartorial mark of her calling. Open and forthright, she moved into her issues quickly and without embarrassment. For her entire career in the church, she had received considerable gratification from her hands-on charitable work with the poor, but because of her keen intelligence and executive abilities, she had been asked to assume higher and higher administrative posts in her order. Though she was highly effective in these positions, her quality of life had diminished. She had little time for her own prayers and meditation, and now, almost daily, she had conflicts with other administrators jockeying for more power. She felt stained by her rage toward them.

I liked Sister Miriam from the very beginning, and as we continued to meet weekly I felt ever greater respect for this woman who, more than anyone I had ever known, had truly dedicated her life to service. I was resolved to do everything I could to be of help. She was exceptionally intelligent and extraordinarily devout. She never inquired about my religious beliefs and, after several months of therapy, had grown to trust me enough to bring her private diary to the session and read aloud several passages. She disclosed her deep loneliness, her sense of ungainliness, and her envy of other sisters blessed with beauty and grace. When she read of her sadness for what she had forgone—marriage, a sexual life, and motherhood—she broke into tears. I ached for her as I thought of my cherished bonds with my wife and children.

Sister Miriam quickly pulled herself together and gave thanks for the presence of Jesus in her life. She spoke longingly of her early morning daily conversations with him, which had provided strength and consolation since her teenage years in the convent. Lately, her many administrative demands had made these early morning meditations all too rare, and she missed them greatly. I cared much for Sister Miriam and I was resolved to help her reinstate her morning connections with Jesus.

One day, after our session, while on my bicycle ride, I realized how rigorously I silenced my own religious skepticism whenever I sat with Sister Miriam. Never before had I personally encountered such sacrifice and dedication. Though I, too, thought of my therapy as a life of service to my patients, I knew that my giving could not be compared with hers; I gave on my own schedule and was paid for my services. How had she developed such selflessness? I thought of her early life and development. Her parents, poverty-stricken after a coal mining accident had disabled her father, had placed her, at age fourteen, into a convent school, and they had rarely visited her again. Her life from that time forward had been

heavily regulated with prayers, intense Bible studies, and catechism, morning, noon, and night. There was precious little time
for play, for fun, or for social activities, and, of course, no contact
with males.

After our sessions, I often reflected upon the ruins of my
own religious education. Young Jewish males in the Washington,
DC, of my day were exposed to an old-world doctrinaire approach
that, in retrospect, seemed almost designed to drive us away from
religious life. To the best of my knowledge, not a single one of
my peers has retained any religious sentiment. My parents were
ethnic Jews: Yiddish-speaking, meticulously adherent to kosher
dietary laws, with four different sets of dishes in the kitchen (for
dairy and meat during the year, and different sets for Passover),
observant of the High Holidays, and ardent Zionists. They and
their relatives and friends formed a tight group and almost never
developed a friendship with a non-Jew or reached out in any way
to join mainstream America.

Yet despite their strong Jewish identity, I saw little evidence
of true religious interest. Aside from the *de rigueur* synagogue
attendance on the High Holidays, fasting on Yom Kippur, and
avoiding leavened bread during Passover, none took religion seriously. Not a single one had a ritual of daily prayer, laying tefillin,
reading the Bible, or lighting candles on the Sabbath.

Most of the families operated small businesses, mostly grocery or liquor stores or delicatessens that they closed only on Sundays and on Christmas, New Year's Day, and the major Jewish
holidays. The High Holiday scene at the synagogue remains vivid
in my mind: my father's male friends and relatives all clustered in
the same row downstairs, and the women, including my sister and
mother, upstairs. I remember sitting next to my father, playing
with the fringes of his blue and white prayer shawl, inhaling the
scent of mothballs from his rarely worn High Holiday suit, leaning over his shoulder as he pointed to the Hebrew words being
chanted by the cantor or the rabbi. Since they were all nonsense

syllables to me, I concentrated as hard as I could on the English translation on the opposing page, which teemed with accounts of violent battles and miracles and exhaustingly endless glorification of God. Not a single line with any relevance to my own life. After a respectable period of time at my father's side, I darted outside into the small courtyard where all the children gathered to talk, play, and flirt.

Such was my religious exposure during my early years. It remains a mystery why my parents never, not once, attempted to teach me to read Hebrew or to impart important Jewish religious tenets. But as my thirteenth birthday and my Bar Mitzvah approached, things changed and I was sent to Sunday religious classes, where I was uncharacteristically unruly in class and persisted in asking such irreverent questions as, "If Adam and Eve were the first humans, then who did their children marry?" Or, "If the practice of not eating milk with meat was to avoid the possibility of the abomination of the calf being cooked in its mother's milk, then, Rabbi, why should the rule extend to chickens? After all," I reminded everyone annoyingly, "chickens give no milk." Eventually the rabbi got fed up with me and expelled me from the school.

But that wasn't the end of it. There was no getting out of a Bar Mitzvah. My parents sent me to a private tutor, Mr. Darmstadt, a straight-backed, dignified, and patient man. The major Bar Mitzvah task facing every thirteen-year-old boy on his birthday is to chant, aloud, in Hebrew, that week's Haftarah (a selection from the Book of Prophets) before the entire synagogue congregation.

A serious problem arose in my work with Mr. Darmstadt: I could not (or would not) learn Hebrew! I was an excellent student in all other endeavors, always at the top of my class, but in this task I suddenly became entirely stupid: I couldn't remember the letters or the sounds or the melody of the reading. Finally, the patient and much-beleaguered Mr. Darmstadt gave up and informed my father it was impossible: I would never learn the Haftarah.

Hence, at my Bar Mitzvah ceremony, my father's brother, my uncle Abe, chanted the Bar Mitzvah section in my place. The rabbi asked me to read the few lines of blessings in Hebrew, but in rehearsal it was evident I could not learn even these, and at the ceremony, the rabbi, resignedly, held up cue cards for me to read with the Hebrew transliterated into English letters.

It must have been a day of great shame for my parents. How could it not have been? But I remember nothing pertaining to their shame—not an image, not a single word exchanged with my father or mother. I hope that their dismay was ameliorated by the excellent speech (in English) that their son gave at the evening dinner celebration. Lately as I review my life, I often wonder why my uncle, rather than my father, read my portion? Had my father been overcome with shame? How I wish I could ask him this question. And what of my work over several months with Mr. Darmstadt? I have almost complete amnesia of our lessons. What I do recall was my ritual of stepping off the trolley one stop before his home to snack at a Little Tavern hamburger stand—a chain in Washington, DC, each stand with a green tiled roof, offering three burgers for twenty-five cents. That they were forbidden made them all the more delicious: it was the first *traif* (non-kosher food) I had ever eaten!

If an adolescent like the young Irvin, in the midst of an identity crisis, were to request a professional psychiatric consultation with me today and tell me that he could not learn to read Hebrew (even though he was an excellent student) and had been expelled from his religious school (though at no other time did he have significant behavioral problems), and moreover, that he had his first non-kosher meal on his way to his Hebrew teacher, then I believe he and I would have a consultation that ran something like this:

> DR. YALOM: Irvin, all these things you've said about your Bar
> Mitzvah cause me to wonder if you may be unconsciously
> rebelling against your parents and your culture. You tell

me you are an excellent student, always at the top of your class, and yet, at this momentous time, the very moment when you are about to take your place as a Jewish adult, you suddenly develop an idiopathic pseudo-dementia and cannot learn to read another language.

IRVIN: With all due respect, Dr. Yalom, I disagree: it is *entirely* explicable. It is a fact that I am very bad with languages. It is a fact that I've never been able to learn another language and I doubt if I ever will. It is a fact that I have made all A's in school except for B's in Latin and C's in German. And it is a fact, also, that I'm tone deaf and cannot carry a tune. During class singing, the music teachers pointedly ask me *not* to sing but to hum softly. All my friends know this and know that there is no way I could chant the melody of a Bar Mitzvah reading or learn another language.

DR. YALOM: But, Irvin, let me remind you this is not a matter of *learning* a language—probably less than 5 percent of American Jewish boys understand the Hebrew text they read at their Bar Mitzvah. Your task was *not* to learn to speak Hebrew, nor to understand Hebrew: your only task was to learn a few sounds and read a few pages aloud. How hard can that be? It is a task that tens of thousands of thirteen-year-olds accomplish every year. And let me point out that many of them are not A students but B and C and D students. No, I repeat, this is not a case of acute focal dementia: I am certain there is a better explanation. Tell me more about your feelings about being Jewish and about your family and your culture.

IRVIN: I don't know how to start.

DR. YALOM: Just speak your thoughts aloud about being Jewish at thirteen. Don't censor your thoughts—just utter them as they enter your mind. It's what we therapists call *free association.*

IRVIN: Free association, huh. Just think out loud? Wow! OK, I'll give it a whirl. Being Jewish . . . God's chosen people . . . what a joke that is for me—*chosen?* No, the exact opposite . . . being Jewish has not had one single advantage for me . . . Continual anti-Semitic remarks . . . Even Mr. Turner, the blond, red-faced barber only three stores up from my father's, calls me "Jew boy" when he cuts my hair . . . And Unk, the gym teacher, shouts, "Move it, Jew boy," when I try, unsuccessfully, to climb up the rope hanging from the ceiling of the gym. And the shame at Christmas when other kids in school describe their presents—I was the only Jewish kid in my elementary school class and I regularly lied and pretended to have gotten presents. I know my cousins, Bea and Irene, tell classmates their Hanukkah gifts are Christmas gifts, but my folks are too busy in the store and don't do any gift giving at Hanukkah. And they frown at my having any non-Jewish friends, including, especially, the black kids, who they will not permit me to bring home even though I regularly go to their houses.

DR. YALOM: So, it seems obvious to me that you want nothing more than to get out of this culture and that your refusal to learn Hebrew for your Bar Mitzvah and your eating *traif* on your way to your Hebrew lessons are all saying the same thing, and saying it loudly, "Please. Please. Somebody get me out of here!"

IRVIN: It's hard to argue with that. And my folks must feel they are in a terrible dilemma. They want something different and better for me. They want me to succeed in the outside world, but, at the same time, they must fear the end of their own world.

DR. YALOM: Have they ever expressed that to you?

IRVIN: Not directly, but there are signs of it. For example, they speak Yiddish to one another but not to me or to my sister.

They speak a type of pidgin English-Yiddish (Yinglish we call it) to us, but definitely they do not want us to learn Yiddish. They are also very secretive about their life in the old country. I have learned almost nothing about their lives in Russia. When I try to find out the exact location of their shtetl in the old country, my father, who has a wonderful sense of humor, jokes that they lived in Russia, but sometimes when they couldn't bear the thought of another severe Russian winter, they called it Poland. And for World War II and the Nazis and the Holocaust? Not one word! Their lips are forever sealed. And that same silence reigns in the homes of all my Jewish friends.

Dr. Yalom: How do you explain that?

Irvin: Probably they want to spare us the horror. I remember the newsreels at the movies after V-E Day showing the camps and the mountains of corpses being moved by a bulldozer. I was in shock—I was entirely unprepared for this, and I'm afraid I'll never get those scenes out of my mind.

Dr. Yalom: Do you know what your parents want for you?

Irvin: Yes—to be educated and to be American. They knew little of this new world. When they arrived in the United States they had no secular education—I mean zero . . . except the course to become US citizens. Like most Jews I know, they are "people of the book," and I believe, no, *I know,* that they are pleased whenever they see me reading a book. They never never interrupt me when I'm reading a book. Yet, they show no signs of wanting an education of their own. I think they know that possibility has passed— they are so crushed by their hard work hours. They are exhausted every night. It must be so bittersweet for them: they work hard so that I can have the luxury of education, but they must know that each book, each page I read, tugs me farther and farther from them.

DR. YALOM: I'm still thinking of your eating those Little Tavern hamburgers—that was the first step. That was like the bugle signaling the beginning of the long campaign.

IRVIN: Yes, I waged a long war for independence, and the early skirmishes were all about food. Even before the Bar Mitzvah rebellion I ridiculed the orthodox food laws. Those laws are a joke: they make no sense, and what's more, they cut me off from being American. When I go to a Washington Senators baseball game (Griffith Stadium is only a few blocks from my father's store), unlike my friends, I can't eat a hot dog. Even an egg salad or grilled cheese sandwich at the drugstore down the street is forbidden, because, my father explains, the knife that cut the sandwich might have just been used to cut a ham sandwich. I protest, "I'll ask that it not be cut."

"No. Think of the plate that may have been used for ham," my father or mother says. "*Traif*—it's all *traif.*" Can you imagine, Dr. Yalom, hearing this when you're thirteen? It's insane! This vast universe—trillions of stars being born and dying, natural disasters occurring every minute on earth, and my parents insist that God has nothing better to do than to check drugstore knives for molecules of ham?

DR. YALOM: Really? That's the way you think at such a young age?

IRVIN: Always. I'm interested in astronomy and have made my own telescope and whenever I look at the night sky I'm blown away by how tiny and insignificant we are in the great order of things. It seems obvious to me that the ancients tried to deal with feelings of insignificance by inventing some god who considered us humans so important that he should turn his attention to surveying our every act. And it also seems obvious that we try to soften the fact of death by the invention of heaven and other fantasies and fairy tales that have one common theme: "We do not die"—we continue to exist by passing on to another realm.

DR. YALOM: You really have those thoughts at your age?

IRVIN: I've had them as far back as I can remember. I keep them to myself. But to be honest with you, I think of religions and the ideas of the afterlife as the world's longest-running con game. It serves a purpose—it provides religious leaders a comfortable life and it dampens mankind's fears of death. But it comes at such a price—it infantilizes us, it blocks our vision of the natural order.

DR. YALOM: Con game? So strident! Why so intent on offending several billion people?

IRVIN: Hey, hey, you asked me to free-associate. Remember? Usually I keep this, all of this, to myself.

DR. YALOM: Quite right. I *did* ask you to do that. You complied. And then I knock you for it. My apologies. And let me ask something else. You speak about fear of death and the afterlife. I'm wondering about your own personal experiences with death.

IRVIN: My first memory is the death of my cat. I was about ten. We always had a couple of cats in the store to catch mice and rats and I played with the cats a lot. One day, one of them, my favorite—I forget her name—was hit by a car, and I found her by the curb, still breathing. I ran into the store, took some liver out of the meat case (my father was a butcher also), and cut off a sliver and placed it right by the cat's mouth. Liver was her favorite food. But she wouldn't eat, and she soon closed her eyes for good. You know, I feel bad forgetting her name and calling her "cat"—we spent tons of warm wonderful hours together, she sitting on my lap, purring loudly, as I petted her while reading a book.

As for human death, there was a boy in my third grade schoolroom. I can't remember his name, but I think we called him "L.E." He had white hair—perhaps he was an albino—and his mother packed unusual sandwiches in his lunch box—for example, sandwiches of cheese and pickle—I had never heard of pickles in sandwiches before. It's so strange how certain odd things get fixed in your memory. One day he didn't come to school, and the next day the teacher announced that he had gotten sick and died. That was all. I recall no particular reaction—my own or anyone else's in the class. But there is one extraordinary thing about it: L.E.'s face remains so clearly in my mind. I can still visualize him—with an astonished look on his face and his very light blond hair standing straight up in a short crew cut.

DR. YALOM: And that's extraordinary because? . . .

IRVIN: It is extraordinary that his image is so clear. It's weird because I didn't know him very well. I think he was in my class only that one year. What's more, he had some kind of sickness and his mother drove him to and from school, and so we never walked home together or played. There were many other kids in that class whom I knew far, far better, and yet I can't remember any other faces.

DR. YALOM: And that means that? . . .

IRVIN: It must mean that death obviously caught my attention, but that I chose not to think about it directly.

DR. YALOM: Were there times you *did* think directly about it?

IRVIN: It's hazy in my mind, but I recall I was walking around in my neighborhood, after having played on the pinball machine at a five-and-dime store, and the idea just thundered down on me that I was going to die like everyone else, everyone who lives, or will ever live. That's all I remember, except I know that it was my first realization of my own death, and also that I couldn't hold it in my mind for very long, and, of course, I never spoke of it to anyone. Until now.

Dr. Yalom: Why "of course"?

Irvin: My life is very solitary. There's no one I can share those thoughts with.

Dr. Yalom: Does solitary mean lonely?

Irvin: Oh, yes.

Dr. Yalom: What comes to mind when you think of "lonely"?

Irvin: I think of riding my bike in the old "Soldiers Home," a large park about ten blocks from my father's store . . .

Dr. Yalom: You always say "my father's store" rather than "my home."

Irvin: Yes, good catch, Dr. Yalom. I just noticed that too. My shame about my home runs deep. What comes to mind— and I'm still free-associating, right?

Dr. Yalom: Right. Continue.

Irvin: What comes to mind is a Saturday night birthday party I attended when I was about eleven or twelve held at a very ritzy house, a house the likes of which I had never seen except in Hollywood films. It was the home of a girl named Judy Steinberg whom I had met and romanced at a summer camp—I think we even kissed. My mother drove me to the party but could not come to take me home, because Saturday night was the time the store was busiest. So, when the party was over, Judy and her mother drove me home. I felt such humiliation at the thought of them seeing my hovel of a home that I asked them to drop me off a few doors away at a modest but more presentable house and pretended that was where I lived. I stood on the front doorstep waving until they drove away. But I doubt that I fooled them. I cringe thinking about this.

Dr. Yalom: Let's return to what you were saying earlier. Tell me more about your solitary bicycle rides in the Soldiers Home Park.

Irvin: It was a marvelous park, several hundred acres and very deserted except for a few buildings for sick or very old

veterans. I think those bike rides are my very best childhood memories . . . coasting down long hills, wind in my
face, feeling free, and reciting poetry aloud. My sister had
taken a course in Victorian poetry at college. When she
finished the course, I took her textbook and pored over
it time and again, memorizing simple poems that had a
strong beat, like Oscar Wilde's "Ballad of Reading Gaol,"
or some poems in Housman's *Shropshire Lad*, like "Love-
liest of Trees, the Cherry Now," and "When I Was One
and Twenty," some verses from FitzGerald's translation
of *The Rubaiyat* of Omar Khayyam, Byron's "Prisoner
of Chillon," and poems by Tennyson. Kipling's "Gunga
Din" was one of my favorites, and I still have a phonograph record I made at a little recording shop near the
baseball stadium when I was thirteen. On one side was
my Bar Mitzvah speech (in English, of course), and on the
reverse side were my recitation of "Gunga Din" and also
Tennyson's "Charge of the Light Brigade." Yes, the more I
think about it, I'd say those moments, coasting downhill
chanting lines of poetry, have been my happiest times.

DR. YALOM: Our time is about up, but before we stop, let me
say that I appreciate the scope of the struggle you're facing. You're caught between two worlds: you neither know
nor respect the old world, nor do you yet discern the
gate to the new one. This generates a lot of anxiety, and
you're going to need a lot of psychotherapy to help you
with that. I'm glad you decided to come see me—you're
resourceful and I have a strong premonition you're going
to be all right.

CHAPTER SEVEN

A GAMBLING LAD

I t is 8 a.m. Wednesday morning. I've had breakfast and stroll down the gravel path to my office, stopping only briefly to say good morning to my bonsai and pluck out a couple of weeds. I know that those little weeds have a right to exist, but I can't have them sucking up water that the bonsai need. I feel very content because I have an uninterrupted four-hour stretch of writing ahead of me. I look forward to beginning, but, as always, can't resist checking out my email, promising myself that I will spend no more than thirty minutes on responses. The first message greets me:

Reminder: GAME TONITE at my house. Doors open at 6:15. Delectable and expensive food provided. Eat fast—game starts promptly at 6:45. Bring barrels of moolah! Kevan

My first reaction is to delete it, but I stop myself, and try to experience the wistful feeling passing through me. I started that poker game over forty years ago, but can no longer play, because my poor (and uncorrectable) vision makes the game too expensive: misreading the cards cost me at least one or two big pots every game. For a long time I resisted giving up the game. *Getting old is giving up one damn thing after another.* Now, even though I haven't played in about four years, the guys continue to send me the invitation as a courtesy.

I've given up tennis and jogging and scuba diving, but giving up poker was different. The others are more solitary, whereas poker was a social endeavor: these sweet guys were my playmates and I miss them greatly. Oh, once in a while we get together for lunch (flipping coins or playing a quick round of poker at the restaurant table to see who pays the bill), but it isn't the same: I miss the action and sense of engagement in risky stuff. I've always loved the thrill of betting, and now all that remains for me is to try egging my wife into bets, bets on entirely silly things: she wants me to wear a necktie to a dinner party and I respond, "I'll bet you twenty dollars there won't be a single man wearing a necktie at the party tonight." In the past she ignored it, but now, since I stopped playing poker, she humors me by occasionally accepting a bet.

This type of play has been part of my life for a very long time. How long? A phone call a few years back supplied some information. It was from Shelly Fisher, whom I hadn't spoken to since the fifth grade. He has a grandniece studying to be a psychologist, and on a recent visit he saw her reading one of my books, *The Gift of Therapy.* "Hey, I know that guy," he said. He found my sister's name in the Washington, DC, phone book and called her to get my number. Shelly and I had a long talk, reminiscing about walking together to school every day, going bowling, playing cards and step ball, and saving baseball cards. The following day, he called again: "Irv, yesterday you said you wanted feedback. Well I've just remembered one other thing about you: you had a gambling problem. You kept pressing me to play gin rummy with baseball cards as stakes. You wanted to bet on everything: I remember one day you wanted to bet on the color of the next car to drive down the street. And I remember what a kick you got out of playing the numbers."

"Playing the numbers"—I hadn't thought about that for years. Shelly's words stirred up an antique memory. When I was about eleven or twelve, my father converted his grocery store to a liquor store, and life became a little easier for my mother and father: no more spoiled goods to throw out, no more 5 a.m. trips to the wholesale produce market, no more sides of beef to be carved up. But things also became more dangerous: robberies were not infrequent, and on Saturday evenings an armed guard hid out of view in the back of our store. During the day the store was frequently filled with larger-than-life characters: among our regular customers were pimps, prostitutes, thieves, both sweet and sour alcoholics, and the bookies and numbers runners.

Once I helped my father carry an order of several cases of scotch and bourbon to Duke's car. Duke was one of our very best customers and I was fascinated by his style: ivory-headed cane, suave blue cashmere double-breasted overcoat, matching blue fedora, and his mile-long gleaming white Cadillac. When we got to the car parked on a side street, half a block away, I asked if I should put my case of scotch in the trunk and my father and Duke both chuckled. "Duke, why don't we show him the trunk?" my father said. With a flourish, Duke opened the Cadillac trunk and said, "Not much room here, Sonny." I looked in and my eyes popped. Seventy years later I still see the scene with striking clarity: the trunk was stuffed to the hilt with cash-stacks of bills of all denominations, tied with thick rubber bands, and several large burlap sacks bulging and overflowing with coins.

Duke was in the numbers racket—an enterprise endemic in my Washington, DC, neighborhood. Here's how it worked: every day, bettors in my neighborhood placed wagers (often as small as ten cents) with their "runners" on a three-digit number. If they guessed correctly, they "hit the number, glory be," and were paid sixty dollars for a ten-cent bet—600 to 1 odds. But, of course, the real odds were 1,000 to 1, so the bookies made a huge profit. The daily number could not be manipulated, since it was derived by a publicly known formula based on the total amount wagered on three designated horse races at a local track. Though it was obvious the odds were against them, the bettors had two things in their favor: the wagers were very small, and the ongoing "glory be" hope of receiving a sudden stroke of great good fortune relieved some measure of their lifelong, poverty-induced despair.

I knew firsthand about this daily anticipatory excitement inherent in betting on the numbers because I occasionally, and secretly, placed a small bet myself (despite my parents' admonitions), often with nickels or dimes I filched from the store cash register. (This recall of my petty theft makes me, even now, cringe with shame.) My father repeatedly pointed out that only fools would bet against such big odds. I knew he was right, but, until I got older, it was the only game in town. I made the bets through William, one of the two black men working in the store. I always promised him 25 percent of my winnings. William was an alcoholic and a lively, charming man, though not a paragon of integrity, and I never knew whether he truly placed my bets or simply pocketed my dimes or booked the bet himself. I never hit the number, and I suspect that, if I had, William, most likely, would have begged off by saying the numbers runner had not come that day or some similar concocted story. I finally abandoned the enterprise when I had the great good fortune of discovering baseball betting pools, craps, pinochle, and, above all, poker.

CHAPTER EIGHT
A BRIEF HISTORY
OF ANGER

My patient Brenda came to her session today with an agenda. Without even glancing at me, she entered my office, took her seat, opened her purse to remove her notes, and commenced to read aloud a prepared statement listing complaints about my behavior during our previous meeting.

"You said I was doing a poor job in our sessions and that your other patients came better prepared to talk about issues. And you implied you much preferred to work with your other patients. And you scolded me for not bringing in dreams or daydreams. And you sided with my last therapist and said that my refusal to open up had been responsible for the failure of all my previous therapies."

During the previous hour, Brenda had sat silently, as she often did, and volunteered nothing, forcing me to work much too hard: I felt as if I were trying to pry open an oyster. This time, as she read her list of accusations, I became increasingly defensive. Dealing with anger is not my strong suit. My reflex inclination was to point out her distortions, but I held my tongue for a number of reasons. For one thing, this was a propitious start to a session—a hell of a lot better than last week! She was opening up, unharnessing the sorts of thoughts and feelings that had kept her so tightly bound. Moreover, even though she had distorted my words, I knew I had, indeed, *thought* some of the things she accused me of saying, and most likely these thoughts had colored my words in ways I had not recognized. "Brenda, I entirely understood your annoyance: I think you're misquoting me a bit but you're right on: I *did* feel frustrated and somewhat baffled last week." I then asked, "If we have a similar session in the future what do you advise? What is the best question I could pose?"

"Why don't you just ask me what happened during the last week that made me feel bad?" she replied.

I followed her suggestion and posed the question: "What happened to make you feel bad this last week?" It led to a productive discussion of disappointments and slights she had experienced the past few days. Toward the end of the hour, I circled back to the beginning and inquired how it felt for her to have been so angry with me. She wept as she expressed gratitude for my taking her seriously, for assuming responsibility for my role in it, and for hanging in there with her. I think we both felt we had entered a new phase of therapy.

The session left me thinking about anger as I rode my bike over the creek toward my home. Though I was satisfied with the way I had handled this incident, I know I have more personal work to do in that area, and I would have been far more uncomfortable had I not liked Brenda so much, and known how hard it was for her to criticize me. I had no doubt, also, that I would have felt far more threatened had my patient been an angry male. I've always been uneasy in confrontation, personally and professionally, and have carefully avoided any administrative position that might require it—for example, a chairmanship, committee head, or deanship. Only once, a few years after I had finished my residency, did I agree to be interviewed for a chairmanship—at my alma mater, Johns Hopkins. Fortunately—for me and for them—they selected another candidate for the position. I've always told myself that avoiding administrative positions was a wise move because my real strength lay in clinical research, practice, and writing, but I have to admit now that my fear of conflicts, and my general shyness, played a significant role in it.

My wife, knowing I prefer only small social events of four or, at the most, six people, finds it hilarious that I became an expert in group therapy. But, in fact, my experience in leading therapy groups turned out to be therapeutic, not only for my patients but for me as well: it greatly increased my comfort in group situations. And, for a long time, I have felt little anxiety in addressing large audiences. But then, such performances are always on my own terms: I want no part of a spontaneous confrontational public debate: I don't think quickly in such situations. One of the advantages of old age is that audiences now treat me with great deference: it's been years, decades, since a colleague or a questioner in the audience has verbally challenged me.

I halt my bike ride for ten minutes to watch the Gunn High School tennis team practice, thinking back to my days on the Roosevelt High School tennis team. I played number six on the six-player team, but was a much better player than Nelson at the number-five slot. Whenever we played one another, however, he intimidated me with his aggressiveness and cursing, and, even more, by his halting play at crucial points and standing still in silent prayer for a few moments. The coach was unsympathetic and told me to "grow up and handle it."

I continue biking and think of the many attorneys and CEOs I've treated who thrive on conflict, and I marvel at their appetite for battle. I've never understood how they got to be that way, nor, of course, how I came to be so conflict-avoidant. I think of elementary school bullies who threatened to beat me up after school. I remember reading stories of kids whose fathers taught them how to box, and how I pined for such a father. I lived at a time when Jews never fought: they were the ones who got beaten up. Except for Billy Conn, the Jewish boxer—I lost a wad betting on him when he fought Joe Louis. And then found out, years later, that he wasn't Jewish after all.

Self-defense was no minor issue during my first fourteen years. My neighborhood was unsafe, and even short trips from home felt perilous. Three times a week I went to the Sylvan cinema, just around the corner from the store. Since each show was a double feature, I saw six films a week, usually westerns or World War II flicks. My parents unhesitatingly allowed me to go because they figured I was safe in the theater. I imagine that as long as I was in the library, at the cinema, or reading upstairs, they must have been relieved: at least for those fifteen to twenty hours each week, I was out of danger.

But peril was always there. I was about eleven and working in the store one Saturday evening when my mother asked me to get her a coffee ice-cream cone from the drugstore four doors down the street. Immediately next door was a Chinese laundry, then there was a barbershop with yellowed pictures of various types of haircuts in the window, next a tiny, cluttered hardware store, and finally, the drugstore, which, in addition to a pharmacy, had a small eight-stooled lunch counter serving sandwiches and ice cream. I got the coffee ice-cream cone, paid my dime (single-scoop cones were a nickel, but my mother always liked a double-decker), and walked outside, where I was surrounded by four tough young white guys a year or two older than me. It was unusual and risky for groups of whites to hang out in our black neighborhood, and generally a sign of trouble.

"Oh, who's that cone for?" snarled one, a boy with small, dull eyes, a tight face, a crew cut, and a red bandana tied around his neck.

"My mother," I muttered, looking furtively around for some escape route.

"Your mommy? Well, why not have a taste yourself?" he said, as he grabbed my hand and shoved the cone into my face.

Just at that moment, a group of black kids, friends of mine, turned the corner and walked down the street. They saw what was happening and surrounded us. One of them, Leon, leaned in and said to me, "Hey Irv, don't you go taking that shit off that jerk. You can handle him." Then he whispered, "Use that upper-cut I showed you."

Just at that moment I heard heavy footsteps pounding and saw my father and William, his delivery man, running up the street. My father grabbed my hand and yanked me away, back into the safe harbor of Bloomingdale Market.

Of course, my father did the right thing. I would have done the same thing for my son. The last thing any father would want was for his son to be in the center of some interracial street fight. And yet I often look back upon his rescue with regret. I wish I had fought the guy and showed him my pathetic uppercut. I had never stood up to aggressors before, and here, surrounded by friends who would protect me, was the perfect opportunity. The boy was about my size, though a bit older, and I would have felt so much better about myself if I had traded punches with him. What's the worst that could have happened? A bloody nose, a black eye—a small price to pay for once taking a stand and holding my ground.

I know that adult patterns of behavior are complex and never initiated by a single event, and yet, I persist in believing that my unease in dealing with open anger, my avoidance of confronta-tion, even heated debates, my reluctance to accept administra-tive positions entailing confrontation and dispute, all would have been different had my father and William not yanked me out of that fight one night so long ago. But I also understand that I grew up in an environment of fear: iron bars on the windows of the store, danger everywhere, and hovering over us all the story of the Jews of Europe hunted down and killed. Flight was the only strat-egy my father taught me.

As I describe this incident, another scene seeps into consciousness: My mother and I were going to the movies, and we entered the Sylvan just as the film was about to begin. She very rarely went to the movies with me, especially in the middle of a Saturday afternoon, but she adored Fred Astaire and often went to his films. I wasn't happy about going with her because she had no manners, was often discourteous, and I never knew what was going to happen. I was embarrassed when any of my friends met her. In the cinema she spotted two seats in a center row and plunked herself down. A boy sitting next to one of the vacant seats said, "Hey, lady, I'm saving this seat."

"Oy, the big shot. *He's* saving a seat," she answered in a loud voice to all those sitting nearby, whilst I tried to hide by pulling my shirt over my head and covering my face. Just then the boy's companion arrived and the two of them, scowling and muttering, moved over to a side row. Shortly after the film started I snuck a look at them and the boy caught my eye, shook his fist at me, and mouthed, "I'll get you later."

And *that* was the boy who smashed my mother's ice-cream cone into my face. Since he couldn't get back at my mother, he must have remembered and lay in wait for a long time until he could catch me alone. What a double-decker pleasure for him to have learned the cone was meant for my mother—he got us both with a single stroke!

This all sounds plausible and makes for a satisfying narrative. How powerful is our drive to fill gestalts and to fashion neatly composed stories! But was it true? Seventy years later I have no hope of excavating the "real" facts, but perhaps the intensity of my feeling in those moments, the desire to fight and the paralysis, has bound them together somehow. True? Alas, I am now uncertain whether it was truly the same boy and whether the time sequence was correct: for all I know the cone-smashing may have preceded the movie incident.

As I get older it becomes ever more difficult to verify answers to such questions. I try to recapture parts of my own youth, but when I check with my sister and cousins and friends, I'm shocked at how differently we remember things. And in my daily work, as I help patients reconstruct their early lives, I grow increasingly convinced of the fragile and ever-shifting nature of reality. Memoirs, no doubt this one as well, are far more fictional than we like to think.

CHAPTER NINE

THE RED TABLE

My office is a studio about 150 feet from my house, but the two structures are surrounded with so much foliage that one is barely visible from the other. I spend most of my day in the office, writing all morning and seeing patients in the afternoons. When I feel restless, I step outside and putter over the bonsai, pruning, watering, and admiring their graceful shapes and thinking of questions I should pose to Christine, a bonsai master and my daughter's close friend, who lives only a block away.

After my evening bike ride, or a walk with Marilyn, we spend the rest of the evening in our library, reading, talking, or watching a film. The room has large corner windows and opens up to a rustic redwood patio with lawn furniture and a large redwood hot tub surrounded by California live oak trees. The walls are lined with hundreds of books, and it's furnished in a casual, California style, with a leather "back rest" chair and a sofa with a loose-fitting red and white cover. Standing in one corner, in stark contrast to everything else, is my mother's garish, faux-baroque table, with a red leather top, four curved black and gold legs, and four matching chairs with red leather seats. I play chess and other board games with my children on that table just as seventy years ago I played chess on Sunday mornings with my father.

Marilyn dislikes the table—it matches nothing else in our home—and she'd love to get it out of the house, but she gave up that campaign long ago. She knows it means a great deal to me, and has agreed to keep the table in the room, but in permanent exile in the far corner of the room. That table is tied to one of the most significant events in my life, and whenever I look at it I am flooded with feelings of nostalgia, of horror, and of emancipation.

My early life is divided into two parts: before and after my fourteenth birthday. Until I was fourteen, I lived with my mother, father, and sister in our small, shoddy flat over the grocery store. The flat was directly above the store, but the entrance was outside the store, just around the corner. There was a vestibule where the coal man regularly delivered coal, and therefore the door was unlocked. In cold weather, it was not uncommon to find one or two alcoholics sleeping on the floor.

THE ENTRANCE TO THE FAMILY FLAT OVER
THE GROCERY STORE, CA. 1943.

Up the stairs were the doors to two flats—ours was the one overlooking First Street. We had two bedrooms—one for my parents and one for my sister. I slept in the small dining room on a davenport sofa that could be turned into a bed. When I was ten my sister went to college and I took over her bedroom. There was a small kitchen with a tiny table upon which I took all my meals. During my entire childhood I never, not once, had a meal with my mother or father (aside from Sundays, when we had dinner with the entire network of the family—between twelve and twenty people). My mother cooked and left food on the stove, and my sister and I ate our meals on the small kitchen table.

My friends lived in similar places, so it never occurred to me to wish for a nicer apartment, but ours had a unique and persistent horror: cockroaches. They were everywhere, despite the efforts of exterminators—I was (and am to this day) terrified of them. Every night my mother put the legs of my bed in bowls filled with water, sometimes kerosene, to stop them from climbing up into the bed. Still, they often fell from the ceiling into my bed. At night, once the lights were out, the house was theirs, and I could hear them scuttling on the linoleum floor of our tiny kitchen. I didn't dare to go to the bathroom at night to pee, but instead used a jar I kept by my bed. I remember once, when I was about ten or eleven, reading a book in our living room when a giant roach flew across the room and landed in my lap (yes, cockroaches *can* fly—they don't often do it but they sure can!). I screamed and my father ran over and knocked it to the floor and stepped on it. The sight of the squashed roach was the worst thing of all, and I ran to the toilet to throw up. My father tried to calm me, but he simply couldn't understand how I could be so upset over a dead bug. (My roach phobia is still there, in hibernation, but has long been irrelevant: Palo Alto is too dry for roaches and I haven't seen one in half a century—one of the great bonuses of California life.)

And then, one day, when I was fourteen, my mother told me, almost casually, that she had bought a house, and we were going to move very shortly. The next thing I recall is walking into our new home on a lovely, quiet street only a block from Rock Creek Park. It was a large handsome two-story, three-bedroom home with a knotty pine recreation room in the basement, a screened-in side porch, and a small lawn surrounded by a hedge. The move was almost entirely my mother's project: she purchased the house without my father ever taking time off from the store to see it.

When did we move? Did I see the movers? What was my first impression of the house? What was my first night there like? And what about the enormous pleasure of saying adieu forever to that roach-infested flat, to the shame, and filth, and poverty, and the alcoholics sleeping just inside our vestibule? I *must* have experienced all these things, but I recall very little. Perhaps I was too preoccupied and anxious about transferring to the ninth grade in a new school and making new friends. Memory and emotions have a curvilinear relationship: too much or too little emotion often results in paucity of memory. I do recall wandering through our clean house and our clean yard in wonderment. I *must* have been proud to invite friends into my home, I *must* have felt more peaceful, less frightened, better able to sleep, but these are mere assumptions. What I do remember most clearly from that whole period is a story my mother proudly told about purchasing the red table.

She decided to buy everything new and keep nothing from our old flat—no furniture, no linens, nothing except her kitchen pots (those I still use today). She, too, must have been fed up with the way we had lived, though she never spoke to me of her inner longings and feelings. But she did, more than once, tell me the story of the table. After she bought the house, she went to Mazor's Department Store, a popular furniture store frequented by all her friends, and in a single afternoon ordered everything for a three-bedroom house, including carpets, house and porch furniture, and lawn chairs. It must have been a huge order, and just as the salesman totaled it up, a garish, neo-baroque card table, with a bright red leather top and four matching red leather chairs, caught her eye. She instructed the salesman to add the table and chairs to the order. He told her that this particular set of table and chairs had already been sold and that, regrettably, most regrettably, there were no other sets—the model had been discontinued. Whereupon my mother told him to cancel the entire order and picked up her purse and prepared to leave.

Perhaps she was serious. Perhaps not. At any rate, her move worked. The salesman caved and the table was hers. Hats off, Mother, for an audacious bluff—I've played a lot of poker, but this was the best bluff I'd ever heard of. Sometimes I've flirted with the idea of writing a story from the point of view of the family that did not get that table. There was some energy in that idea: I would tell the story from both perspectives: my mother's great bluff and triumph and the other family's dejection.

I still have that table despite my wife's lament that it doesn't match anything in our home. Though its aesthetic shortcomings are apparent even to me, that table holds memories of my Sunday chess games with my father and uncles and later with my children and grandchildren. In high school I played on the chess team, and proudly wore an athletic sweater displaying a large chess piece. The team, consisting of five boards, competed with all the Washington, DC, high schools. I played first board, and, after being undefeated in my senior year, I considered myself the Washington, DC, junior champion. But I never improved enough to play at a higher level, in part because of my uncle Abe, who scoffed at the idea of booking up, especially for chess openings. I recall him pointing to my head and pronouncing me "klug" (clever) and urging me to use my good Yalom "kopf" (head) and play in an unorthodox fashion to confound my opponents. This turned out to be extremely bad advice. I stopped playing chess during my college pre-med days, but the day following my acceptance to medical school, I tried out for the university chess team. I played second board for the rest of the semester, and then, when I began medical school, I once again gave it up until I began teaching my sons, Victor and Reid, who became excellent players. Only in the past few years have I gotten more serious about my chess. I began chess lessons with a Russian master and watched my Internet rating rise. But far too late, I fear—my diminishing memory is an invincible opponent.

If it had been up to my father, we probably would have lived over the store indefinitely. He seemed almost indifferent to his surroundings. My mother bought all his clothes and told him what to wear, even which necktie, when we went out on Sundays.

My father had a good voice and I loved hearing him sing Yiddish songs along with my aunt Luba on our family gatherings. My mother did not care for any sort of music and I never heard her sing a line—that gene she must have passed along to me. On Sunday mornings, my father and I almost always played chess together on that red baroque table, and he would play some Yiddish songs on the phonograph and sing along with them until my mother screeched, "Genug, Barel, genug!" ("Enough, Ben, Enough!"). And he always obeyed. Those are the times I was most disappointed in him and wished so much that he would have stood his ground and confronted her. But it never happened.

M y mother was a good cook, and I often think of the dishes she made. Often, to this day, I try to replicate them using her heavy aluminum pots. I feel very attached to those pots. Food tastes better when I use them. My children often covet them, but I am still hanging on to them.

When we moved to our new house, my mother cooked dinner every day, and then she drove the twenty minutes to the store, where she spent the rest of the day and evening. I warmed up the food and ate my meals alone while reading a book. (My sister, Jean, had started at the University of Maryland.) My father came home to eat and take a nap, but our mealtimes rarely coincided.

Blagden Terrace, our new street, was lined with tall sycamore trees standing before large, handsome homes, all filled with

THE AUTHOR'S MOTHER AND FATHER IN FRONT OF THE
BLAGDEN TERRACE HOME, WASHINGTON, DC, 1947.

children my age. I remember being welcomed my first day there. The kids on the street playing touch football waved to me—they needed more players and I dived right in. Later that day, directly across the street on the front lawn of their home, I saw thirteen-year-old Billy Nolan playing catch with his elderly grandfather, who, I later learned, had once pitched for the Boston Red Sox. Billy and I were destined to play a lot of baseball together. I remember also my first walk around the block. I spotted a front-yard pond with several floating lily pads—that excited me because I knew the water would hold fine pickings for my microscope: swarms of mosquito larvae floating on the surface and hordes of amoebae that I could scrape from the bottom of the lily pads. But how to collect the specimens? In my old neighborhood I would have snuck into the yard at night and stolen a few expendable creatures from the pond. But I had no idea of how to behave here.

Blagden Terrace and environs offered an idyllic setting. No filth, no danger, no crime, and never an anti-Semitic comment. My cousin Jay, who has been my close lifetime friend, had also moved only four blocks away, and we often saw one another. Rock Creek Park was only two blocks from my home with its creek, trails, baseball fields, and tennis courts. There were neighborhood ball games almost every day after school until darkness.

Goodbye to the rats! Goodbye to the roaches, to crime, to danger, and to anti-Semitic threats. My life would now be changed forever. I occasionally went back to the store to help out when there was a shortage of workers, but for the most part I had left those sordid surroundings behind. And never again did I need to lie about where I lived. If only Judy Steinberg, my girlfriend from summer camp, could have seen my new house!

CHAPTER TEN
MEETING MARILYN

I always encourage student therapists to enter personal therapy. "Your own 'self' is your major instrument. Learn all you can about it. Don't let your blind spots get in the way of understanding your patients or empathizing with them." And, yet, I've been so closely bonded to one woman since I was fifteen years old and thereafter so wrapped in my large family that I often wonder whether I can truly enter the world of a person who goes through life alone.

I often think of my years before Marilyn in harsh black and white: the color seeped in after she entered my life. I remember our first meeting with preternatural clarity. I was in the tenth grade of Roosevelt High School and had been living in my new neighborhood for about six months. One Saturday in the early evening after I had spent a couple of hours gambling at the bowling alley, Louie Rosenthal, one of my bowling chums, told me there was a party nearby at Marilyn Koenick's house and suggested we go. I was shy and not very keen on parties, and I didn't know Marilyn, who was in ninth grade, a half-semester behind me, but, as I had no other plans, I agreed to go.

Her home was a modest brick row house, identical to every other house on Fourth Street between Farragut and Gallatin, with a few steps leading to a small front porch. As we approached it we saw a large bolus of kids our age gathered at the stairs and on the small porch, trying to get into the front door. I, socially avoidant as I was, immediately spun around and began to walk home, but my ever-resourceful chum, Louie, grabbed my arm, pointed to the front window facing the porch, and suggested we raise it and crawl in. I followed him through the window, and we made our way through the throng to the vestibule, where, at the absolute center of the milling crowd, stood a very petite, very cute, vivacious girl with long, light brown hair, holding court. "That's her, the short one, that's Marilyn Koenick," Louie said as he moved into the next room to find himself a drink. Now, as I said, I was generally very shy, but that night I astounded myself and, instead of turning back and retreating through the window, I pushed through the crowd and made my way to the hostess. When I got to her I had no idea what to say and simply blurted out, "Hi, I'm Irv Yalom and I just crawled in through your window." I don't recall what else we said before her attention was diverted by others, but I do know I was a goner: I was drawn to her like a nail to a magnet and had an immediate feeling, no, more than a feeling, a *conviction*, that she was going to play a crucial role in my life.

I nervously phoned her the following day, my first phone call to a girl, and invited her to see a movie. It was to be my first date. What did we talk about? I remember her telling me she had recently stayed up all night reading *Gone with the Wind* and had to miss school the following day. I found that so lovable I could hardly see straight. We were both readers and immediately fell into endless discussions of books. For some reason she seemed very interested in my dedication to biography at the central library. Who on earth would have ever thought my A–Z biography venture would come in so handy? We each suggested books for the other—I was on a John Steinbeck binge at the time and she was reading books I had never considered—*Jane Eyre* and *Wuthering Heights*. I enjoyed James Farrell, she, Jane Austen, and we both loved Thomas Wolfe—sometimes we read the most melodious passages from *Look Homeward, Angel*, out loud to one another. After only a few dates, I bet my cousin Jay thirty dollars that I would marry her. He paid up on my wedding day!

What was it about her? As I write this memoir and reacquaint myself with my younger self and realize what a mess I was and how much I moaned throughout my life about not having had a mentor, it is suddenly dawning upon me: I *did* have a mentor! It was Marilyn. My unconscious grasped that she was uniquely suited for the task of civilizing and elevating me. Her family history was similar enough to mine for me to feel at home with her, but differed in just the right ways. Her parents were also immigrants from Eastern Europe, but were a quarter- or a half-generation ahead of mine and had had some secular education. Her father had arrived as a teenager, but not in such dire economic straits as mine. He had an education, he was a romantic, he loved the opera, and he traveled throughout the country like his hero, Walt Whitman, working at a variety of menial tasks to support himself. After marrying Celia, Marilyn's mother, a beautiful, sweet woman who had grown up in Krakow and possessed not a trace of my mother's anger and coarseness, he opened a grocery store that we learned, years after we met, was only one block from my father's store! I must have walked or biked by that small DGS (district grocery store) hundreds of times. But her father had had the foresight not to submit his family to living in that turbulent, unsafe, impoverished neighborhood, so Marilyn had grown up in a modest but safe middle-class neighborhood and almost never set foot in her father's store.

Our parents met many times after we started dating, and paradoxically, her parents developed great respect for mine. Her father was aware that my father was a highly successful businessman, and he perceived, correctly, that my mother had a sharp, insightful mind and was really the driving force behind my father's success. Unfortunately, Marilyn's father died when I was twenty-two, and I never had the opportunity to know him well, though he did take me to my first opera (*Die Fledermaus*).

Marilyn was half a year behind me in school, and in those days there were graduation ceremonies both in February and in June. A few months after meeting her I attended her February graduation from McFarland Junior High (which was next door to my high school) and listened in awe as Marilyn, with remarkable poise, delivered the valedictory address. Oh, how I admired and loved that girl!

We were inseparable all through high school and ate lunch together every day, and without fail, we saw one another every weekend. We had such a strong, shared devotion to literature that our other divergent interests seemed of little consequence. She had, very early, fallen in love with the French language, literature, and culture, whereas I preferred the sciences. I managed to accomplish the rather extraordinary feat of mispronouncing every French word I ever saw or heard, while she, for her part, could see only her own eyelashes when she gazed through my microscope. We both loved our English classes and, unlike other students in the school, were oddly entranced by the reading assignments: *The Scarlet Letter*, *Silas Marner*, and *The Return of the Native*.

One day in high school, all afternoon classes were canceled so that the entire school could attend a showing of the 1946 British film *Great Expectations*. We sat next to one another and held hands. The film remains one of our all-time favorites; over the decades, we've probably alluded to it a hundred times. It opened up the world of Dickens for me, and before long I had devoured every book Dickens had written. I've reread them many times since then. Years later, when I lectured and traveled a great deal in the United States and Great Britain, I fell into the habit of visiting used book stores and buying Dickens first editions. It remains the only thing I ever collected.

Marilyn, even then, was so adorable, intelligent, and socially skilled that she won over all her teachers. In those years I was many things, but no one would in their wildest dream have thought of me as adorable. I was a good student and excelled in the sciences and also in English, where Miss Davis regularly increased my unpopularity by praising my compositions and posting them on the bulletin board. Unfortunately, in the twelfth grade I was switched to Miss McCauley, the other English teacher, who was also Marilyn's teacher and prized her greatly. One day in the hall she saw me leaning over Marilyn's locker chatting with her and thenceforth referred to me as a "Locker Cowboy." She never forgave me for courting Marilyn, and I had no chance in my classes with her. She was wont to make scathing and ridiculing comments about my written assignments. She mocked me for my stiff performance as a messenger in the class reading of *King Lear*. Recently two of my children, looking through old papers in our closet, came across a rhapsodic piece I had written about baseball that Miss McCauley had graded C+, and they were outraged that she had mercilessly marked my pages with such comments as "foolish!" or "such enthusiasm about such trivia." And, mind you, I was writing about such giants as Jolting Joe DiMaggio, Phil Rizzuto, King Kong Keller, Smokey Joe Page, and "Old Reliable" Tommy Henrich.

I never lose sight of my great fortune of having had Marilyn in my life since I was fifteen. She elevated my thoughts, prodded my ambition, and offered me a model of grace, generosity, and commitment to a life of the mind. So thank you, Louie, wherever you are. Thank you so much for helping me crawl through that window.

CHAPTER ELEVEN

COLLEGE DAYS

Two years ago I was sitting in a café in Sausalito with my friend Larry Zaroff, looking out over San Francisco Bay. The wind buffeted the seagulls about and we watched the Sausalito ferry lurching toward the city until it disappeared from sight. Larry and I were reminiscing about college: we had been classmates at George Washington University and had taken most of our classes together—grueling courses like organic chemistry, qualitative analysis, and comparative anatomy, in which we dissected every organ and every muscle of a cat. We were hauling in memories of days that were, for me, the most stressful of my life when Larry launched into a story of a wild fraternity party, full of rowdy drinking and packs of friendly coeds.

I bristled. "Fraternity? What fraternity?"

"TEP, of course."

"What are you talking about?"

"Tau Epsilon Pi. What's with you today, Irv?"

"With me? I'm really upset. I saw you every day of college and never heard of a fraternity at GW. Why wasn't I invited to join? Why didn't you invite me?"

"Irv, how can you expect me to remember? This is 2014 and we started GW in 1949."

When I left Larry I phoned my close friend Herb Kotz, in Washington, DC. Herb, Larry, and I were always together in college. We were the top three in every class we took, and we drove to school and ate lunch together nearly every day.

"Herb, I've just been talking to Larry and he told me about belonging to a fraternity, TEP at GW. Did you know about that?"

"Well, yeah. I was a member of TEP, too."

"WHAT? You, too? I can't believe it. Why didn't you ask me to join?"

"Who can remember that long ago? I probably did ask but all we did was have beer parties on Fridays, and you hate beer, and you weren't dating at all then—just staying loyal to Marilyn."

I nursed that grudge a bit until a few months ago, when, during a big housecleaning, Marilyn found a 1949 letter welcoming me to Tau Epsilon Pi and a certificate of membership. I had, indeed, been a member of the fraternity, but I had never attended a meeting and had entirely erased the memory from my mind!

This incident truly depicts how uptight and anxious I was as an undergraduate at George Washington, a fifteen-minute commute from my home. To this day I remain envious of those who remember a joyful undergraduate experience—class spirit, roommates who became lifelong friends, camaraderie surrounding athletic events, fraternity pranks, a close mentoring relationship with a professor, and the secret societies akin to the one depicted in *Dead Poets Society*. It was a part of life I missed out on entirely, yet I also know that I was so anxious and so uncomfortable with myself that it was just as well I didn't attend an Ivy League college: I doubt I would have enjoyed, or even survived, such an undergraduate scene.

In my therapy work I have always been struck by how often my patients recover memories of their own lives at various stages when their children pass through these same stages. It happened to me years ago when my children were in their senior high school year and contemplated college, and it happened once again when my grandson, Desmond, began college. I was astonished and envious at the many resources available to help him and his classmates in choosing a school. Desmond had college advisers, written guides to the best one hundred small liberal arts colleges, and conversations with college recruitment teams. I recall no guidance whatsoever in my day: no high school college advisers, and, of course, my parents and relatives knew nothing of this entire process. Moreover, and this was crucial, I knew no one in my high school or neighborhood who had elected to go away to college: everyone I knew chose one of the two local colleges— the University of Maryland or George Washington University (both, at that time, large, mediocre, and impersonal institutions). My sister's husband, Morton Rose, was an important influence. I respected him greatly: he was an excellent physician who had attended George Washington University both the undergraduate and the medical school, and I was persuaded that if George Washington was good enough for him, it should be good enough for me.

Finally, when my high school awarded me the Emma K. Karr Scholarship—a full-tuition scholarship to GW—the issue was settled: no matter that the annual tuition was only three hundred dollars.

At the time I felt that my whole life, my entire future, was on the line. I had known since my encounter with Dr. Manchester at age fourteen that I wanted to go to medical school, but it was common knowledge that medical schools had a strict 5 percent quota for Jewish students; George Washington Medical School had classes of one hundred and accepted only five Jews each year. The high school Jewish fraternity I belonged to (Upsilon Lambda

Phi) had far more than five intelligent seniors who planned to take a pre-med curriculum and apply to medical school, and that was only one of several such fraternities in Washington. The competition seemed overwhelming, and so, from my first day of college, I settled upon a strategy: I would put everything else aside, work harder than anyone else, and make such good grades that a medical school would be forced to accept me.

It turns out I was not alone in that approach. It seemed that all the young men I knew, all the sons of Jewish immigrants from Europe arriving after World War I, deemed medicine to be the ideal profession. If one could not get into medical school, then there was dental school, law school, veterinary school, or, lastly and least desirable for the idealists among us, going into business with one's father. A popular joke of those days: a Jewish male had two options—either become a doctor or a failure.

My parents were not involved in my decision to attend GW. We were not in close communication in those days: the store was about a thirty-minute drive from the house and I saw little of my parents except on Sundays. Even then we rarely spoke about anything consequential. I had hardly spoken to my mother for years, ever since she had accused me of causing my father's heart attack. I made a decision to protect myself by keeping my distance. I would have liked more closeness with my father, but he and my mother were too tightly attached.

I remember driving my mother to the store as a senior in high school. Just as we reached the area of the Soldiers Home Park only five minutes from the store, she asked about my future plans. I told her I was going to start college next year and that I had decided to try to get into medical school. She nodded her head and seemed extremely pleased, but that was the end of it. We didn't speak of my future plans again. When I think about it now, I wonder whether she and my father might have somehow been intimidated by me, whether they felt they could no longer relate to me, and had already lost me to a culture they didn't understand.

Nonetheless, I took it for granted they would pay my tuition and all other expenses throughout college and medical school. Regardless of the state of our relationships, it would have been unthinkable in my parents' culture for them to act otherwise, and I have followed their example with my own children.

Thus, for me and for my closest friends, undergraduate school was no dreamed-of destination: it was an obstacle to be overcome as quickly as possible. Ordinarily, students entered medical school after four undergraduate years and a bachelor's degree, but, on occasion, medical schools accepted outstanding applicants after only three years of undergraduate work, provided they had taken all the required classes. I, along with my peers, opted for that plan and consequently took almost nothing but required pre-med courses (chemistry, physiology, biology, physics, vertebrate anatomy, and German).

What do I remember of my college days? During my three years of college I took only three electives, all of them literature courses. I lived at home and followed a brutal routine: hard work, memorization, laboratory experiments, staying up all night to prepare for exams, studying seven days a week.

Why such a frenzy? Why such a rush? It would have been absolutely unthinkable for me, or, for that matter, for any of my close friends, to have decided to take what is now called a "gap" year, to join an organization like the Peace Corps (which did not yet exist), or volunteer for humanitarian work in other countries, or choose one of the many other options so commonplace in the world of my children and their peers. For all of us there was the ever-present pressure of the medical admission process. It never occurred to any of us to take any longer than necessary to reach medical school. But I felt an additional pressure: I needed to lock in my relationship with Marilyn. I needed to succeed, to show her I would have a solid career and would become a person of such consequence that she would be persuaded to marry me. She was half a year behind me, and her French teacher urged her to apply to Wellesley College, which immediately accepted her. In her senior year of high school, her sorority big sister advised her that she was too young to be permanently pinned down and she should, at least occasionally, go out with other guys. This did not sit well with me and I still remember the names of the two boys she dated. As soon as she left for Wellesley, I grew extremely anxious about losing her: I felt I couldn't compete with the Ivy League guys she would be meeting. I wrote her constantly expressing my worry that I could not possibly be interesting enough for her, that she was meeting other men, that I might lose her. My whole life at that time was lived in the pre-med sciences, in which Marilyn took no interest whatsoever. I saved Marilyn's letters, and a few years ago, *Wellesley*, the college magazine, published a number of them.

D uring those years, I was so weighed down with anxiety and had such great difficulty sleeping that I should have seen a therapist, but it didn't seem like an option then. However, if I *were* to have seen a therapist like me then, I imagine the dialogue would have gone something like this:

> Dr. Yalom: You said on the phone your anxiety was almost unbearable. Tell me more about that.
>
> Irvin: Look at my fingernails, bitten to the quick. I'm ashamed of them and I try to hide my nails when I'm with anyone: look at them. A vise-like pressure in my chest. My sleep is screwed up completely. I use Dexedrine and coffee to pull all-nighters to study for exams and now I can't sleep without sleeping pills.
>
> Dr. Yalom: What are you taking?
>
> Irvin: Seconal, every night.
>
> Dr. Yalom: Who prescribes it for you?
>
> Irvin: I just snitch it from my folks. For as long as I can remember they've both popped a Seconal every single night. I've wondered if perhaps insomnia is genetic.

DR. YALOM: You mentioned a lot of academic pressure this year. How was your sleep in previous years—for example, in high school?

IRVIN: Sometimes I had too much sexual pressure and I had to masturbate to fall asleep. But in general I've slept fine until this year.

DR. YALOM: That provides the answer to your question about insomnia being genetic. You think your classmates are all having the degree of anxiety and sleep problems you're experiencing?

IRVIN: I doubt it—certainly not the gentile pre-med students I know. They seem more relaxed. One of them pitches for the GW baseball team, others date a lot, or they're busy with fraternity events.

DR. YALOM: So that suggests that it is neither genetic nor environmental but instead a function of the particular way, or maybe we should even say, the unique way, you're responding to your environment.

IRVIN: I know, I know—I'm a fanatic. I've over-studied for every course, for every exam I've taken. Whenever a graph of the class grades for any exam is posted, I see the class curve and then I see my score, an outlier, far, far ahead of the score I would have needed for an A grade. But I need certainty: I'm frantic.

DR. YALOM: Why so frantic? What do you think is behind it?

IRVIN: Well, for one thing, there's the 5 percent quota on Jews accepted to medical school: that's pressure enough!

DR. YALOM: But you say you over-studied. That an A wasn't enough—it had to be a "Super A." Are your close Jewish friends in the same situation as frantic as you?

IRVIN: They work hard as hell too. We often study together. But they're not quite as frantic as I am. Maybe a more pleasant home life. They have other things in their lives, do some dating, play basketball—I think they're better balanced.

DR. YALOM: And *your* balance? What's that like?

IRVIN: About 85 percent studying and 15 percent worrying.

DR. YALOM: Is the 15 percent worrying about admission to medical school?

IRVIN: That and something else—my relationship with Marilyn. I absolutely, desperately, want to spend my life with her. We went steady all through high school.

DR. YALOM: Do you see her now?

IRVIN: She's at Wellesley in Massachusetts for the next four years but we write almost every other day. I phone sometimes, but long distance is way too expensive. My mother is giving me a very hard time about that. Marilyn loves Wellesley and is having a normal healthy undergraduate life that includes meeting other guys, and every time she alludes to some Harvard guy she went out with I go bananas.

DR. YALOM: You're afraid of? . . .

IRVIN: The obvious—that she will meet some boy who has more to offer—better looking, upper class, sophisticated family, better future ahead of him—all that stuff.

DR. YALOM: And you can offer? . . .

IRVIN: That's exactly why medical school admission means everything to me. I don't feel I have much else going for me.

DR. YALOM: Are you dating other women?

IRVIN: No, don't have time.

DR. YALOM: So you're living a monastic life? But that must be hard, especially when she is not.

IRVIN: Right! In other words, I'm going steady but she's not.

DR. YALOM: Usually these are the years of pressing sexual urges.

IRVIN: Yep, I feel half-crazed, sometimes three-quarters crazed by sex much of the time. But what can I do? I can't meet a girl and say, "I'm in love with someone else who is very far away and all I want from you is sex." So do I lie? I'm not good at that. I'm not what you call smooth and, for the time being, I'm sentenced to frustration. I daydream all the time of meeting a beautiful, really horny next-door neighbor who pines for sex when her husband's out of town. That would be perfect. Especially the next-door bit—no travel time involved.

DR. YALOM: Irvin, I'm persuaded you're far more uncomfortable than you need to be. I think you could profit with some therapy—you're carrying around a ton of anxiety and you've got a lot of work to do: to understand why your life is so out of balance, why you need to over-study, why you believe you have so little to offer, why you may be so smothering to this woman that you run the risk of driving her away. I believe I can help you and I suggest that we start meeting now twice a week.

IRVIN: Twice a week! And it takes me almost half an hour to get here—and half an hour to get back. That's four hours a week. And I have an exam almost every week.

DR. YALOM: I suspected you might respond in this manner. So I want to make another point. You haven't said this, but I have a strong hunch that as you go along in your medical studies you may find psychiatry of particular interest, and, if so, then the hours we spend together will serve a dual function: not only will these hours help you, but they will enhance your understanding of the field.

IRVIN: I can see the merit in that, but that future seems so . . . so . . . futuristic. Anxiety is the looming enemy right now, and I worry that taking four hours out of my week of study might just create more anxiety than we could assuage here in our talks. Let me think on it!

L ooking back, I wish I *had* started therapy as an undergraduate, but in the 1950s I knew no one who had had psychotherapy. Somehow I got through those three horrible years. It helped enormously that Marilyn and I spent summers together as counselors. Those days at camp were free of academic stress, and I basked in my love for her and took care of my young campers and played and taught tennis and made friends with guys who were interested in something other than medicine. One year my fellow counselor was Paul Horn, who became a well-known flutist, and we remained friends until his death.

Aside from these summer interludes, my undergraduate years were relentlessly grim, involving huge classes and minimal contact with professors. However, despite the tension and the unimaginative lectures, I found the content of all my science courses fascinating. That was especially true for organic chemistry—I found the benzene ring, with its beauty and simplicity, coupled to endless complexity, fascinating, and for two summers I earned pocket money tutoring other students in the subject. My favorite courses, though, were my three electives—all literature courses: Modern American Poetry, World Drama, and The Rise of the Novel. I felt alive in these courses and relished reading the books and writing the papers, the only papers I wrote in college.

My course on world drama stands out in my mind. It was the smallest class I attended—only forty students—and the content was enthralling. In that class I had my only memorable personal contact with a teacher, an attractive middle-aged woman who wore her blonde hair in a tight bun and once asked me to come to her office. She critiqued my paper on *Prometheus Bound* by Aeschylus in the most positive manner, informing me that my writing was superb and my thinking original, and asked if I had considered a career in the humanities. To this day I remember her shining face—she was the only professor who ever knew my name.

Aside from a B+ in one German course, I had a straight A+ record in college, but, even so, applying to medical school was

a nerve-wracking process. I applied to nineteen schools and received eighteen rejections and one acceptance (to GW Medical
School, which could not reject a GW undergraduate with a near
4.0 average). Somehow the anti-Semitism in the medical school
quota didn't outrage me—it was ubiquitous, I had never known
anything else, and, following my parents' example, simply took it
for granted. I never took an activist posture or even seethed at the
vast unfairness of the system. Looking back now, I believe my lack
of outrage was due to my lack of self-esteem—I had bought into
the worldview of my oppressors.

I can still feel the shivers of exhilaration I experienced when
I received my letter of admission from GW: it was the greatest
thrill of my life. I rushed to the phone to call Marilyn. She tried
to be enthusiastic but had never really doubted I would be accepted. My life changed after that—suddenly, I had free time. I
picked up a Dostoevsky novel and began reading again. I tried out
for the college tennis team and managed to play one varsity doubles match, and joined the university chess team, where I played
second board for several intercollegiate matches.

I consider the first year of medical school the worst year of my
life, not only because of the academic demands but because
Marilyn was off to France for her junior year abroad. I dug in and
memorized what I was asked to learn and worked perhaps even
harder than I had as a pre-med student. My only pleasure in medical school sprang from my relationship with Herb Kotz and Larry
Zaroff, my lifelong friends. They were my anatomy lab partners as
we dissected our cadaver, whom we christened Agamemnon.

Unwilling to bear separation from Marilyn any longer, I decided, toward the end of my first year, to transfer to Boston and,
mirabile dictu, I was accepted as a transfer student by Boston
University Medical School, and when Marilyn returned from her
year in France, we got engaged. In Boston, I rented a room in a

THE AUTHOR'S ROOM IN BOSTON DURING
MEDICAL SCHOOL DAYS, 1953.

large four-story Back Bay boardinghouse on Marlborough Street. It was my first year away from home, and my life, inner and outer, began to change for the better. Some other medical students lived in the same house and I soon made friends. Soon three or four of us were commuting together daily to school. One of them, Bob Berger, was to become a close lifelong friend. More on Bob later.

But the pièce de résistance of being in Boston for my second year of medical school was my weekends with Marilyn. Wellesley College had a very strict code about unchaperoned students spending time off campus at night, and so each week, Marilyn had to invent some legitimate-sounding excuse to be away and obtain an invitation from a broad-minded friend. We studied part of the weekend, took drives along the New England coast, visited museums in Boston, and ate dinner at Durgin-Park.

My inner life was also changing. I was no longer frantic, only minimally anxious, and I was finally sleeping soundly. I knew, even during my first year of medical school, that I would go into psychiatry, though I had only had a few psychiatry lectures, and had never spoken to a psychiatrist. I think I had decided upon psychiatry before even entering medical school: it flowed from my passion for literature and from a belief that psychiatry offered me proximity to all the great writers I loved. My deepest pleasure was to lose myself in the world of a novel, and over and over again I told myself that the very best thing a person could do in life was to write a fine novel. I've always had a hunger for stories, and since I first read *Treasure Island* as a young adolescent I have dived deeply into the narratives that great writers offer us. Even as I write these words at the age of eighty-five, I can hardly wait to return tonight to Joseph Roth's *The Radetzky March*. I ration it and fight the urge to devour it all at once. When the story, as in that book, is more than a life narrative, and is an exploration of human desire, dread, and search for meaning, then I am enthralled, and enthralled that the drama is doubly meaningful—pertaining not only to a particular existence but to a parallel process taking place in an entire culture, i.e., the pre–World War I Austrian-Hungarian Empire.

Despite my love for literature, medicine was never a default decision, because I had always been fascinated by science, too, especially biology, embryology, and biochemistry. And also there was that strong desire to be of help, and to pass along to others what Dr. Manchester had offered me at my time of crisis.

CHAPTER TWELVE
MARRYING MARILYN

In 1954 when we married, Marilyn was already a confirmed Francophile. Having spent her junior year in France, she dreamed of a honeymoon in Europe, whereas I, a provincial lad who had never left the northeastern United States, had zero interest in going abroad. But she was canny: "How about a honeymoon in France on a motorcycle?" She knew I was fascinated with motorcycles and motorbikes, and knew, also, that one could not rent such vehicles in the United States. "Here, look at this," she said, and handed me an advertisement about renting a Vespa in Paris.

So off we went to Paris, where I excitedly selected a large Vespa at a rental station a block from the Arc de Triomphe. Although I had never even touched, let alone driven, a Vespa, I needed to reassure the suspicious manager of the station that I was an experienced driver. I mounted the Vespa and, as nonchalantly as possible, asked him for the location of the starter and gas pedal. He looked seriously concerned as he showed me the small button starter and told me that turning the handlebars controlled the gas flow. "Oh," I said, "it's different in the US," and, without another word, took off for a practice ride while Marilyn wisely waited for me at a nearby café. Alas, I was on a one-way street that immediately fed directly into the hectic ten-lane thoroughfare circling the Arc de Triomphe. That ninety-minute drive was one of the most harrowing experiences of my life: autos and taxis zoomed past on both sides of me, horns blaring, windows unrolled, shouts hurled, fists shaken. I understood no French, but had a strong feeling that the cacophonies of the phrases shouted at me were not words of welcome to France. I stalled perhaps thirty times in my heroic circumnavigation of the Arc de Triomphe, but an hour and a half later, when I ended up back at the café next to the rental stand to collect my wife, I knew how to drive a Vespa.

Three weeks earlier in Maryland, on June 27, 1954, we had been married, and our wedding luncheon was held at the Indian Spring Country Club owned by Marilyn's wealthy uncle, Samuel Eig. Immediately afterward I set about raising money for our European vacation—my parents were supporting me and paying my medical school tuition, and there was no way I could ask them to pay for this trip. For the past couple of years, my cousin Jay and I had sold fireworks for the Fourth of July at a stand we had built (Jay was the one who had bet me thirty dollars that I would not marry Marilyn). The previous year had been disastrous for the firework-stand business because of heavy rains on July 3 and 4, and we had the brainstorm of buying the entire leftover inventory from the other stands at a very low price and storing it over the following year in huge steel oil barrels. We had tested such storage the year before and the year-old fireworks had performed perfectly. We were blessed with splendid weather in early July 1954, and I earned more than enough money for a European honeymoon with my bride.

Immediately after renting the Vespa, Marilyn and I took off with small packs on our back for the French countryside. For three weeks, we motored through the Loire Valley, Normandy, and

WEDDING, 1954.

JULY FOURTH FIREWORKS STAND, MANNED BY JAY
KAPLAN AND THE AUTHOR, WASHINGTON, DC, 1954.

Brittany exploring beautiful chateaux and churches, mesmerized by the miraculous blues of the stained-glass windows of Chartres. In Tours, we visited the lovely family that had hosted Marilyn for the initial two months of her year abroad. Every day on the road we lunched in beautiful pastures on heavenly French bread and wine and cheese. Marilyn enjoyed ham as well. Her parents were more secular and adhered to no religious dietary laws, whereas I am one of the vast army of irrational Jews who have entirely jettisoned all religious beliefs but still eat no pork (except, of course, pork buns in Chinese restaurants). After three weeks we returned to Paris, took a train to Nice, then rented a tiny Fiat Topolino to drive through Italy for a month. One vivid memory that remains of our excursion through Italy was our stay on our first night at a small inn facing the Mediterranean. For the dessert of the prix fixe dinner, a large bowl of assorted fruit was placed on the table. We were delighted: money was growing short and we stuffed our pockets with fruit for our next day's lunch. When we paid our bill the next morning we felt like dolts, as we learned that the fruit had been carefully counted and we were charged heavily for each piece snitched.

Though it was a divine trip, I remember often being impatient and jittery, perhaps from culture shock, perhaps from not knowing how to live without grinding and studying. This sense of not feeling comfortable in my skin plagued me during my early adulthood. From the outside I was doing splendidly: I had married the woman I loved, I had gained admission into medical school and was performing well in every way, but deep inside, I was never at ease, never confident, and never grasping the source of my anxiety. I had some unclear sense that I had been scarred deeply by my early childhood and felt that I didn't belong, that I was not as worthy or deserving as others. How I would love to repeat that trip now with the serenity of my current self!

Today, over sixty years later, memories of our honeymoon always bring a smile to my face. However, the details of our wedding day have faded—except for one scene: toward the end of the large wedding luncheon, Marilyn's uncle, Sam Eig, the family's stern and unapproachable patriarch, who had built a considerable part of Silver Spring, Maryland, and hobnobbed with the governor, named streets after his children, and never before deigned to speak to me, walked over to me, put his arm around my shoulder, and whispered in my ear as he pointed his other arm toward the entire assembly of guests, "Congratulations, my boy. You're getting the best of the lot."

Uncle Sam's words of support still ring true: rarely does a day pass that I do not feel gratitude for having been able to spend my life with Marilyn.

CHAPTER THIRTEEN

MY FIRST
PSYCHIATRIC
PATIENT

M y first practicum in psychiatry in the spring of 1955, during my third year of medical school, was in the Boston City Hospital outpatient department. Each medical student was required to see a patient weekly for twelve weeks, and we each had to present the patient at a formal case conference attended by the other clerkship students and a dozen faculty members, many of them intimidating denizens of the Boston Psychoanalytic Association. I had attended other students' presentations and had cringed at the faculty's brutal reactions as they competed to demonstrate expertise and erudition without a scrap of gentleness or empathy.

My turn to present came after I had seen my patient for approximately eight sessions, and I quavered as I began. I had decided not to follow the example of other presenters, who used the formal traditional structure of presenting the patient's chief complaint, past history, family history, education, and formal psychiatric examination. Instead, I fell back on what felt natural to me: I told a story. In straightforward language I described my eight encounters with Muriel, a young, slim, attractive woman with vibrant red hair, downcast eyes, and tremulous voice. I described our first meeting, at which I began by saying that I was a medical student just beginning my training and that I would be seeing her over the next twelve weeks. I asked her why she had sought help from our clinic, and she responded, in a soft voice, "I'm a lesbian."

At that moment, I hesitated, swallowed hard, and replied, "I don't know what that means. Would you mind educating me?"

And so she did—she told me what "lesbian" meant and what her life was like. I asked questions to help her talk and told her that I admired her courage in speaking so openly. I said that I would do all I could to be helpful to her during the next three months.

At the start of my next session with Muriel I acknowledged how embarrassed I had been to admit my ignorance. She told me that our conversation had been a "first" for her: I was the first male to whom she had revealed her true story, and that it was exactly my honesty that made it possible for her to continue to be open.

I told the staff that Muriel and I had become close, that I looked forward to our meetings, that we talked about her problems with her lover in the same manner as we would discuss any human relationship, that she now met my glance often, that she was returning to life again, and that she said she regretted that we had only four more sessions. At the end of my presentation I sat down, lowered my head, and braced myself for the onslaught.

But nothing happened. No one spoke. After a long silence, Dr. Malamud, the department chairman, and Dr. Bandler, an eminent analyst, concurred that my presentation spoke for itself and they had no additional comments. One by one each faculty member around the table made similar comments. I left the meeting stunned: all I had done was to tell a story that seemed so natural and easy for me. Throughout my college and medical education I had always felt invisible, but at that moment everything changed. I walked out thinking I might have something special to offer the field.

M arried life was both wonderful and stressful during my last two years of medical school. Money was tight and, for the most part, my parents supported us. Marilyn earned some money by working part-time in a dentist's office while studying for a master of arts in teaching degree at Harvard, while I continued to earn money by selling blood to the hospital. I had applied to be a sperm donor, but the urologist told me that my sperm count was too low and advised me not to delay any attempt to have children.

How wrong he was! Marilyn conceived instantaneously on our honeymoon. Our daughter Eve's middle name is "Frances" to indicate "made in France," and a year and a half later, during my fourth year of medical school, Marilyn became pregnant again.

My clinical clerkships in my last two years of med school demanded long hours, but somehow my anxiety had calmed, replaced perhaps by honest exhaustion and the gratification of feeling that I was being helpful to my patients. I grew more committed to psychiatry and began reading extensively in the field. Certain horrific scenes from my psychiatry clerkships stay in my mind: a room of human statues at the Boston State Hospital—an entire ward of catatonic patients spending their lives in absolute stillness. The patients were mute and spent hours standing in one position, some by their beds, some by a window, some sitting, sometimes muttering but usually silent. All the staff could do was to feed them, keep them alive, and speak to them kindly.

Such scenes were to be found in every large hospital in the mid-1950s before the advent of the first tranquilizer, Thorazine, and, soon thereafter, Stelazine, followed by a continuous stream of new, more effective major tranquilizers.

Another scene at the Boston State Hospital stays with me: At some point in my clerkship I was able to observe Dr. Max Day, a Harvard psychiatrist, leading a group of about twelve psychiatric residents who had been asked to study their own group process. As a medical student I was permitted to attend a single meeting but not to participate, not one word. Although more than half a century has passed, I can still see that room in my mind's eye. The residents and Dr. Day sat in a circle in the center of a large room. I sat in a corner outside of the circle and recall being fascinated by the idea of a group of people discussing their feelings toward each other. What an extraordinary concept! But it fell flat. There were long silences and everyone seemed uncomfortable, while the leader, Dr. Day, just sat there. Why? I could not understand. Why didn't he break the ice or in some way help the members open up? Later I attended one of Dr. Day's clinical conferences and was greatly impressed by his acumen and articulateness. But that made it even *more* baffling. Why wouldn't he help the floundering group? Little did I know that I would be wrestling with this question for many years of my professional life.

CHAPTER FOURTEEN

INTERNSHIP:
THE MYSTERIOUS
DR. BLACKWOOD

After graduation, we former medical students, now Doctors of Medicine, entered a one-year internship where we had hands-on experience diagnosing and caring for patients in the hospital. In the first month of my internship at Mount Sinai Hospital in New York, I was assigned to the obstetrical service and was struck by how frequently one particular doctor, Dr. Blackwood, was paged on the hospital loudspeakers. While assisting in a delivery I asked the chief resident, "Who is this Dr. Blackwood? I hear his name all the time, but I never see him."

Dr. Gold smiled, and the other nearby staff members chuckled. "I'll introduce him to you later," Dr. Gold said. "As soon as we're finished here." Later that evening, Dr. Gold escorted me into the doctors' on-call room, where a spirited poker game was in process. I couldn't believe my eyes: I felt like a kid in a candy store.

"And which one is Dr. Blackwood?" I asked. "And why is he always being paged?"

Another loud guffaw from everyone. I seemed to be amusing the entire obstetrical staff. Finally the chief resident clued me in:

"Do you play bridge?" he asked.

I nodded.

"You know the Blackwood convention in bridge bidding?"

I nodded again.

"Well, there you have it. That's your Dr. Blackwood. He exists only as a Mount Sinai poker symbol: whenever there is a hand short in this poker game, they page Dr. Blackwood."

The players were mostly obstetricians in private practice whose patients were in labor. House staff and interns were allowed into the game only when they were hard up for a player. Thereafter, for the rest of the year, when I had finished my rounds and was on call and had to spend the night at the hospital, I listened for the "Dr. Blackwood" page, and whenever I was free I charged over to the obstetrics department. The stakes were high, and interns were paid only twenty-five dollars a month (plus a free all-you-can-eat dinner, from which we made lunch sandwiches the next day—we took care of breakfast by ordering extra-large breakfasts for some of our patients).

I lost my entire salary at the poker games for the next three or four months before I got a read on the game. After that I took Marilyn to quite a few Broadway shows compliments of Dr. Blackwood.

I rotated through several services during the year at Mount Sinai: internal medicine, obstetrics, surgery, orthopedic surgery, emergency room, urology, and pediatrics. I learned how to deliver babies, how to tape sprained ankles, how to treat congestive heart failure, how to draw blood from an infant's femoral artery, how to diagnose neurological conditions from observing the gait of a patient. In my surgery rotation I was permitted only to hold retractors for the surgeon. On a couple of occasions when I was permitted to suture the skin at the end of the procedure, the laser-eyed surgeon rapped me sharply on the knuckles with some surgical instrument and barked at me for tying "grocery-store knots." Naturally I had the urge to respond, "Of course I'm tying grocery-store knots—I grew up in a grocery store!" But I never dared: the senior surgeons were formidable and seriously intimidating.

By sheer chance, three of my close friends from George Washington Medical School were also accepted into the Mount Sinai internship, and the four of us stayed in two adjoining rooms—we would be on call and sleep at the hospital every other night for the entire year.

While on my obstetrics rotation at the end of my first month of internship, Marilyn went into labor and Dr. Gutmacher, the department head, delivered by C-section our second child, Reid Samuel Yalom. It had been my turn to assist in the delivery room that day, but Dr. Gutmacher advised me to observe instead. Standing only a few feet away from Marilyn, I had the great pleasure and thrill of seeing Reid draw his first breath.

Public transportation from our apartment to Mount Sinai was very poor, and taxis were far too expensive. For the first couple of months I drove my car to the hospital, but after accumulating a number of parking tickets, I hit upon the idea of a motor scooter. By chance I learned of an art professor at Yale who had bought a beautiful new Lambretta, but because of a severe gastric ulcer, had been advised by his physician to sell it. I phoned him, took a train one Sunday to New Haven, fell in love with the Lambretta, and drove it back to New York the same day. Thereafter the parking problem was solved: I rode the Lambretta to work, took it onto the elevator, and parked it in my room. Several times, Marilyn and I drove down Broadway, parked the Lambretta easily, and attended the theater.

M y internship offered no psychiatry rotation, but I hung around the psychiatry department and attended clinical and research presentations. One project of great interest to me involved a newly discovered compound, lysergic acid diethylamide (LSD), reputed to have psychedelic effects. Two young researchers in the department were examining whether LSD affected subliminal perception (that is, perception that occurs outside of awareness), and they asked for volunteers for a brief experiment. I volunteered. LSD had been synthesized so recently that the only known way of testing its effects was a loony Siamese fighting fish method. When squaring off for battle, the fish always assumed precise formations, and a very few drops of LSD to their water tank profoundly altered their behavior. The number of drops required to disrupt the fighting fish formation became the measure of the potency of the LSD.

We four volunteers were given LSD-laced orange juice, and an hour later sat before a large screen upon which a tachistoscope projected images so quickly that we were unable to view them consciously. The following morning we were asked to recall all the dream images we had had that night and to sketch them. I drew two types of images: several faces featuring very long noses, and a man whose legs were missing. The following day the researchers projected the same images at normal speed for us to see. One was a popular advertisement for Life Saver candy in which a tightrope walker was precariously balancing a package of Life Savers on his nose, and the other a photo of a guard at Buckingham Palace dressed in a scarlet jacket and black trousers, with the trousers blending into the background of the black guardhouse. I was amazed at these results. I had learned firsthand what subliminal perception was: I had "seen" images without knowing that I had.

At the end of my internship many vials of LSD remained, and the researchers gave them to me for personal experimentation. I, Marilyn (only once), and some fellow residents tried them, and I was fascinated by my sensory changes during the LSD trips: sound and vision were remarkably different. I spent an hour watching my wallpaper change colors and heard music in an entirely new way. I had a strange sense of being closer to reality or to nature, as if I were experiencing sensory data raw and direct with no wadding or filter in between me and my surroundings. I felt strongly that the drug's effects were major and that it was no recreational toy. On a couple of occasions I grew frightened to realize that I couldn't willfully turn off the effects, and grew alarmed that they might be irreversible. When I took my last sample on a November night, I went for a long walk outside and felt menaced by the bare November tree branches, which resembled the sinister trees in the Disney film of Snow White. I haven't used it since, but in the following years, several publications appeared suggesting that the effects of LSD mimicked the symptoms of schizophrenia. After I began seeing schizophrenic patients during the beginning of my residency, I wrote an essay on major differences between the LSD experience and the psychotic experience. This piece, appearing in the *Maryland State Medical Journal*, was my first published article.

The internship year was transformative: by the end of twelve months I had assumed the identity of a physician and acquired some degree of comfort dealing with the great majority of medical conditions. But it was also a brutal year with long hours, little sleep, and many all-nighters.

However, as exhausting as my 1956–1957 internship year was, Marilyn's year was even worse. Uncommon as it was at that time for women to pursue doctorate degrees, she and I had always assumed that she would become a university professor. I knew no other married woman with such plans, but I always felt she had an exceptional mind, and her decision to pursue a PhD seemed natural to me. While I completed my last two years of medical school in Boston, she obtained her master of arts in teaching from Harvard, specializing in French and German. As soon as I was accepted for the internship at Mount Sinai in New York, she applied for the PhD program in the Columbia University French Department.

Marilyn's interview with Norman Torrey, the formidable chairman of the Columbia French Department, remains part of our family lore. Professor Torrey glanced at her eight-month pregnant abdomen with wonderment: he had probably never before seen a pregnant applicant. And then he was even more astonished to learn that she also had a one-year-old child. In an apologetic tone, Professor Torrey pointed out that financial aid required the student to teach two courses and take four, suggesting the interview was at an end. But Marilyn instantly replied, "I can do that."

A couple of weeks later, his letter of acceptance arrived: "Materfamilias, We have a place for you." Marilyn found some childcare and plunged into the hardest year of her life. I had the compensatory blessing of comradeship with my fellow interns, but Marilyn was entirely on her own. She took care of our two children, with some help from a housekeeper and almost no help from her husband, who was away every other night and every other weekend. Thereafter, Marilyn always considered this year the hardest one of her life.

CHAPTER FIFTEEN

THE JOHNS HOPKINS YEARS

I'm on my Lambretta, Marilyn is sitting behind, her arms encircling me. I feel the wind in my face as I watch the speedometer. Sixty-five, sixty-eight, seventy-one. I am going to reach eighty. I can do it. Eight O. I know I can do it. Nothing else matters. The handlebars vibrate slightly, then more and more, and I begin to lose control. Marilyn is crying, "Stop, stop, Irv, slow down, I'm scared. Please stop. Please please." She screams and pounds on my back.

I wake up. My heart is racing. I sit up in bed and feel for my pulse—over a hundred. That damn dream! I know that dream too well—I've dreamt it many times. I know exactly what prompted the dream now. Last night in bed I was reading a passage in *On the Move*, a memoir by Oliver Sacks, in which he describes being a member of the "ton club," a group of youthful motorcycle riders who had driven their motorcycles above one hundred miles per hour.

The dream is not only a dream: it is a memory of a real event that I've replayed countless times, both as a daydream and as a nocturnal dream. I know that dream and I hate it! The real event took place after the end of my internship, when I had a week of vacation before starting my three-year psychiatric residency at Johns Hopkins Hospital in Baltimore. Marilyn's mother had agreed to care for our two children for a long weekend, and we took off on the Lambretta for the Eastern Shore of Maryland; it was on this trip that the event accurately depicted in the dream occurred. I didn't think too much of it at the time—perhaps I was actually amused by Marilyn's panic. The road was empty and I just wanted to open the throttle. Like a teenager, I was exhilarated by speed and felt absolutely invulnerable. It was only much later that I realized the extent of my thoughtlessness and stupidity. How could I possibly have involved my wife in this stunt with two young children at home? Aiming for eighty miles per hour, unprotected, bareheaded—those were the days before helmets! I hate thinking about it and even now hate writing about it. I shuddered recently as Eve, my daughter, a physician, described visiting a ward full of paralyzed young men, all with broken necks from accidents on motorcycles or surfboards. They, too, must have once felt invulnerable.

We didn't crash. Eventually, I returned to sanity and slowed down, and for the rest of the time we rode safely through the charming little settlements on Maryland's Eastern Shore. On the way home, when I went for a ride by myself while Marilyn napped after lunch, I hit an oil slick and took a nasty fall, scraping my knee badly. We stopped at an emergency room. The physician cleaned out the wound and gave me a tetanus antitoxin shot, and we returned to Baltimore without further mishap. Two days later, just as I was preparing to report for my first day of residency, I broke out in a rash, which soon developed into massive hives. I had had an allergic reaction to the horse serum in the tetanus shot and was immediately hospitalized at Hopkins for fear that my breathing would become compromised and a tracheotomy required. I was treated with steroids, which proved immediately effective, but I felt fine the next day and was taken off the steroids and discharged. I started my residency the next morning. In those early days of steroid use, physicians did not appreciate the need to taper steroids slowly, however, and I had an acute withdrawal syn-drome with depression, along with such intractable anxiety and insomnia for the next couple of days that I had to load up with Thorazine and barbiturates to get to sleep. Fortunately, it was to be my only personal encounter with depression.

On my third day at Hopkins, we first-year residents had our initial meeting with the very formidable John Whitehorn, the chairman of psychiatry, who would become a major figure in my life. A stern, dignified man who rarely smiled, John Whitehorn had a bald pate ringed by short gray hair. He wore steel-rimmed spectacles and intimidated almost everyone. Later I was to learn that even chiefs of other departments treated him with deference and never referred to him by first name. I did my best to attend to his words, but was so exhausted by my lack of sleep and the sleeping drugs in my body that I could barely move in the morn-ing, and during Dr. Whitehorn's greeting to us I fell asleep in my chair. (Many decades later, Saul Spiro, a fellow resident, and I reminisced about our time together at Hopkins, and he told me he respected me enormously for having had the chutzpah to fall asleep at our first meeting with the boss!)

Aside from some low-grade anxiety and mild depression, I recovered from my allergic reaction in about two weeks, but I was so unnerved by the experience that I decided to seek therapy. I asked the chief resident, Stanley Greben, for advice. In that era it was commonplace, even de rigueur, for psychiatric residents to have a personal analysis, and Dr. Greben recommended that I see his own analyst, Olive Smith, an elderly senior training analyst in the Washington-Baltimore Psychoanalytic Institute, and one with royal lineage: she had been analyzed by Frieda Fromm-Reichman, who, in turn, had been analyzed by Sigmund Freud. I had a great deal of respect for my chief resident, but, before making such a huge decision, I decided to solicit Dr. Whitehorn's opinion about my symptoms following steroid withdrawal and about starting analysis. It appeared to me that he listened with little interest, and then, when I mentioned starting analysis, he slowly shook his head and commented simply, "I believe you will find that a little phenobarbital might be more effective." Remember that these were the pre-Valium days, although a new tranquilizing drug called Equanil (meprobamate) was shortly to be introduced.

Later I learned that other faculty members were highly amused to discover I had the audacity (or stupidity) to pose this question to Dr. Whitehorn, who was known to be extremely skeptical of psychoanalysis. He took an eclectic position, following the psychobiological approach of Adolf Meyer, the long-term previous chair of the Johns Hopkins Psychiatry Department, an empiricist who focused on the patient's psychological, social, and biological makeup. Thereafter, I never spoke of my psychoanalytic experience to Dr. Whitehorn and he never asked.

The Hopkins Psychiatry Department had a split personality: Whitehorn's point of view prevailed in the four-story psychiatric hospital and outpatient department, while a strong orthodox psychoanalytic faction ran the consultation service. I generally dwelled in Whitehorn territory, but I also attended analytic conferences in the consultation department, especially the case conferences led by Lewis Hill and Otto Will, both astute analysts, and also world-class storytellers. I listened enthralled to their clinical case presentations. They were wise, flexible, and thoroughly engaged with their patients. I marveled at the way they described an interaction with a patient: so caring, so concerned, and so generous. They were among my first models for the practice (and narration) of psychotherapy.

But most analysts worked very differently. Olive Smith, whom I was seeing four times a week for analysis, worked in an orthodox Freudian manner: she was a blank screen, revealing nothing of herself through words or facial expression. I rode from the

EN ROUTE TO ANALYST, BALTIMORE, 1958.

hospital to her office in downtown Baltimore only ten minutes away on my Lambretta every day at 11 a.m. Often I could not help taking a quick look at my mail just before leaving, which resulted in my arriving a minute or two late—evidence of resistance to the analysis that we often, and fruitlessly, discussed.

Olive Smith's office was in a suite with four other analysts, all of whom had been analyzed by her. At that time I considered her elderly. She was at least seventy, white-haired, somewhat bent over, and unmarried. Once or twice I saw her in the hospital going to a consultation or an analytic meeting and there she appeared younger and spryer. I lay on the couch, with her chair positioned at the end, near my head, and I had to stretch my neck and look back to see her, sometimes to check that she was still awake. I was asked to free-associate and her responses were entirely limited to interpretations, very few of them helpful. Her occasional lapses from neutrality were the most important part of the treatment. Obviously many found her helpful—including all the analysands in her suite of offices and my chief resident. I have never understood why it worked for them and not for me. In retrospect, I think she was the wrong therapist for me—I simply needed someone more interactive. Many times I have had the unkind thought that the main thing I learned in my analysis was how *not* to do psychotherapy.

Her fee was twenty-five dollars per session. One hundred a week. Five thousand a year. Twice my annual salary as a resident. I paid for my analysis by doing physical exams, at ten dollars each, for the Sun Life Insurance Company of Canada every Saturday, zipping around the back streets of Baltimore on my Lambretta, wearing my hospital whites.

As soon as I decided to take my residency at Johns Hopkins Hospital, Marilyn applied to the Johns Hopkins University PhD program in comparative literature. She was accepted and worked under the guidance of René Girard, one of the most eminent French academics of his time. She chose to write her PhD thesis on the myth of the trial in the works of Franz Kafka and Albert Camus and, with her encouragement, I began to read Kafka and Camus as well, before moving on to Jean-Paul Sartre, Maurice Merleau-Ponty, and other existential writers. For the first time, my work and Marilyn's began to converge. I fell in love with Kafka, whose *Metamorphosis* stunned me as no piece of literature had ever done. And I was also jolted by Camus's *The Stranger* and Sartre's *Nausea*. Through narrative, these writers had plumbed depths of existence in a way that psychiatric writing never seemed to have achieved.

Our family thrived during our three years at Hopkins. Our oldest, Eve, attended nursery school right in the courtyard of the square compound where we lived with the other house staff. Reid, a

lively, playful child, had no trouble adjusting to the care of a housekeeper when Marilyn was pursuing her PhD studies at the Hopkins
campus fifteen minutes away. During our final year in Baltimore,
Victor, our third child, was born in the Johns Hopkins Hospital,
which was just one block up the hill from our home. We were fortunate to have healthy, lovable children, and I looked forward to
seeing and playing with them every evening and on weekends. I
never felt that my family life was an impediment to my professional
life, though I am sure this was not the same for Marilyn.

I loved my three years of residency. From the very beginning,
each resident had the clinical responsibility of running an inpatient ward as well as meeting with a roster of outpatients. The
Hopkins surroundings and staff had a genteel, southern quality
that now feels like a thing of the past. The psychiatry building,
the Phipps Clinic, containing six inpatient wards and an outpatient department, had opened in 1912, when it was overseen by
Adolf Meyer, who was succeeded by John Whitehorn in 1940.
The four-story red brick building was sturdy and dignified; the
elevator operator, a fixture for four decades, was courteous and
friendly. And the nursing staff, young and old alike, sprang to
their feet when any physician entered the nurses' station—ah,
those were the days!

Though hundreds of patients have passed from my memory, I
remember many of my first patients at Hopkins with eerie clarity.
There was Sarah B., the wife of a Texas oil tycoon, who had been
in the hospital for several months with catatonic schizophrenia.
She was mute and often frozen into one position for hours at a
time. My work with her was wholly intuitive: supervisors were of
little help, because no one knew how to treat such patients—they
were considered beyond reach.

I took care to meet with her every day for not less than fifteen
minutes in my small office in the long hallway just outside the
ward. She had been entirely mute for months, and since she never
responded by word or gesture to any question, I did all the talking.

I told her about my day, the newspaper headlines, my thoughts about the group meetings on the ward, issues I was exploring in my own analysis, and the books I was reading. Sometimes her lips moved but no words were uttered; her facial expression never changed, and her large, plaintive blue eyes remained fixed upon my face. And then, one day, as I was babbling along about the weather, she suddenly stood up, walked over to me, and kissed me hard on the lips. I was flabbergasted, didn't know what to say, but kept my composure, and, after musing aloud about possible reasons for the kiss, I escorted her back to the ward and tore over to my supervisor's office to discuss the incident. The one part I didn't acknowledge to my supervisor was that I had rather enjoyed the kiss—she was an attractive woman and her kiss had aroused me, but I never for a moment forgot that my role was to heal her. After that, things continued as before for weeks longer until I decided to try a course of treatment with Pacatal, a major new tranquilizer (now long discarded) that had just come on the market. To everyone's great surprise, Sarah was a changed person within a week, talking often and generally quite coherently. In my office we engaged in long discussions about the stresses in her life preceding her illness, and at some point I commented on my feelings about meeting with her silently for so long and my many doubts that I had offered her anything in those sessions. She replied immediately, "Oh no, Dr. Yalom. You are wrong. Don't feel that way. All through that time *you were my bread and butter.*"

I was her bread and butter. I have never forgotten that utterance and that moment. It returns to my mind often when I'm with a patient, clueless about what is going on, unable to make helpful or coherent remarks. It is then that I think of dear Sarah B. and remind myself that a therapist's presence, inquiries, attention may be nourishing in ways we cannot imagine.

I began attending weekly seminars with Jerome Frank, MD, PhD, the other Hopkins full professor, who, like Dr. Whitehorn, was an empiricist and persuaded only by logic and evidence. He taught me two important things: the basics of research methodology, and the fundamentals of group therapy. At that time, group therapy was in its infancy, and Dr. Frank had written one of the few good books on the topic. Every week, the residents—our eight heads crammed together—observed his outpatient therapy group through one of the first two-way observational mirrors to be used in this context, a hole in the wall that was only about one square foot large. After the group meeting, we met with Dr. Frank for a discussion of the session. I found group observation to be such a valuable didactic format that, years later, I would use it in my own group therapy teaching.

I continued to observe the group every week long after the other residents had finished the course. By the end of the year, Dr. Frank had asked me to lead the group when he was away. From the very beginning I loved leading groups: it seemed obvious that the therapy group offered a rich opportunity for members to give and receive feedback about their social selves. It seemed to me a unique, rich setting for growth, allowing members to explore and express parts of their interpersonal selves and to have their behavior reflected back to them by their peers. Where else could individuals offer and obtain such honest and constructive feedback from a set of trusted equals? The outpatient therapy group had only a few basic rules: in addition to total confidentiality, the members were committed to show up for the next meeting, to keep communicating openly, and not to meet with each other outside the group. I recall envying the patients and wishing I could have participated as a member in such a group.

Unlike Dr. Whitehorn, Dr. Frank was warm and approachable—by the end of my first year, he suggested I call him "Jerry." He was a great teacher and a fine man, modeling integrity, clinical competence, and the necessity for research inquiry. We stayed in touch long after I left Hopkins, and we met whenever he visited California. On one memorable occasion, our families spent a week together in Jamaica. In old age, he developed severe memory problems, and I visited him in a residential center whenever I was on the East Coast. The last time I saw him, he told me that he spent his days looking at interesting things outside his window, and that each morning he awoke with a clean slate. He rubbed his hand over his forehead and said, "Whoosh—all the memories of the preceding day are wiped out. Entirely gone." Then he smiled, looked up at me, and gave his student one final gift: "You know, Irv," he said, reassuringly, "it's not so bad. It's not so bad." What a sweet, lovely man. I smile whenever I think of him. Decades later, I felt greatly honored by being invited to give the first Jerome Frank Psychotherapy Lecture at Johns Hopkins.

Jerry Frank's group therapy method fit neatly into the interpersonal approach then au courant in American psychodynamic theory. The interpersonal (or "Neo-Freudian") approach was a modification of the older, orthodox Freudian position; it stressed the importance of interpersonal relations in the individual's development throughout the life cycle, whereas the older approach placed most of its emphasis on the very early years of life. This approach was American in origin and heavily based on the work of psychiatrist Harry Stack Sullivan, as well as on European theorists who had immigrated to the United States, especially Karen Horney and Erich Fromm. I read a great deal of the interpersonal theoretical literature and found it eminently sensible. Karen Horney's *Neurosis and Human Growth* was by far the most heavily underlined book of my residency days. Though Sullivan had a great deal to teach, he was, unfortunately, such an abysmal writer that his ideas never had the impact they deserved. In general, though, his work helped me understand that most of our patients fall into despair because of their inability to establish and maintain nurturing interpersonal relationships. And, to my mind, it followed that group therapy provided the ideal arena in which to explore and to change maladaptive modes of relating to others. I was fascinated by the group process and, throughout my residency, led many groups in both inpatient and outpatient settings.

As my first year progressed, I began feeling overwhelmed by all the data, all the various clinical conditions I encountered, the idiosyncratic approaches of my supervisors, and I longed for some comprehensive explanatory system. Psychoanalytic theory seemed the most likely option, and most psychiatric training programs at that time in the United States were analytically oriented. Though today's chairmen of psychiatry are generally neuroscientists, in the 1950s most of them were psychoanalytically trained. Johns Hopkins, aside from the consultation service, was a leading exception.

So I met dutifully with Olive Smith, four times weekly, read Freud's writings, and attended the analytically oriented conferences in the consultation wing of the department, but as time went by I grew increasingly skeptical of the psychoanalytic approach. My personal analyst's comments seemed irrelevant and off the mark, and I grew to feel that, though she wanted to be helpful, she was too constrained by the edict of neutrality to reveal to me any of her real self. Moreover, I was coming to believe that the emphasis on early life, and primal sexual and aggressive drives, was severely limiting.

The biopsychological approach at that time had little to offer aside from such somatic therapies as insulin coma therapy and electroconvulsive therapy (ECT). Though I personally administered these many times and sometimes saw extraordinary recoveries, these treatments were disparate approaches discovered by accident. For example, clinicians have for centuries observed that convulsions caused by various conditions, such as fever or malaria, had a salutary effect on psychoses or depression. So they searched for methods of inducing hypoglycemic coma and seizures both by chemical (Metrazol) and electrical (ECT) means.

Toward the end of my first year, a newly published book titled *Existence* by the psychologist Rollo May came to my attention. It consisted of two long, excellent essays by May and a number of translated chapters by European therapists and philosophers, such as Ludwig Binswanger, Erwin Straus, and Eugène Minkowski.

This book changed my life. Though many of the chapters were written in deep-sounding language that seemed designed to obfuscate rather than to illuminate, May's essays were exceptionally lucid. He laid out the basic tenets of existential thought and introduced me to the relevant insights of Søren Kierkegaard, Friedrich Nietzsche, and other existential thinkers. As I look at my 1958 copy of Rollo May's *Existence*, I see notations of approval or disagreement on almost every page. The book suggested to me that there was *a third way*, an alternative to psychoanalytic thought and the biological model—a way that drew from the wisdom of philosophers and writers from the past 2,500 years. As I browsed through my old copy while writing this memoir, I noted, with great surprise, that Rollo, around forty years later, had signed it and written, "For Irv, a colleague from whom *I* learn Existential psychotherapy." This brought tears to my eyes.

I attended a series of lectures on the history of psychiatry, stretching from Philippe Pinel (the eighteenth-century physician who introduced a humane treatment of the insane) to Freud. The lectures were interesting, but, to my mind, flawed in the assumption that our field began with Pinel in the eighteenth century. As I listened, I kept thinking of all the thinkers who had written on human behavior and human anguish long before—philosophers, for example, such as Epicurus, Marcus Aurelius, Montaigne, and John Locke. These thoughts, and Rollo May's book, persuaded me that it was time to begin an education in philosophy, so during my second year of residency I enrolled in a year-long course in the history of Western philosophy at the Johns Hopkins University Homewood campus, where Marilyn studied. Our textbook was Bertrand Russell's popular *History of Western Philosophy*, and, after so many years of physiological, medical, surgical, and obstetrical textbooks, these pages were ambrosia to me.

Ever since that survey course, I've been an autodidact in philosophy, reading widely on my own and auditing courses both at Hopkins and, later, Stanford. I had no idea, at the time, how

I would apply this wisdom to my field of psychotherapy, but, at some deep level, I knew I had found my life's work.

Later in my residency I had a three-month clerkship at the nearby Patuxent Institute, a prison housing mentally ill offenders. I saw patients in individual therapy and led a daily therapy group of sexual offenders—one of the most difficult groups I've ever led. The members spent far more energy trying to persuade me they were well adjusted than they did working on their problems. Since they had an indeterminate sentence—that is, they were incarcerated until psychiatrists declared them recovered—their reluctance to reveal a great deal was entirely understandable. I found my experience at Patuxent fascinating, and by the end of the year decided I had sufficient material to write two articles: one on group therapy for sexual deviants, and another on voyeurism.

The voyeurism article was one of the first psychiatric publications on that topic. I made the point that voyeurs did not simply want to view naked women: if voyeurs were to experience great pleasure, it was necessary that the viewing be forbidden and surreptitious. None of the voyeurs I had studied had sought out strip joints or prostitutes or pornography. Second, though voyeurism had always been considered an annoying, quirky, and harmless offense, I found that not to be true. Many inmates I worked with had started with voyeurism and then progressed to more serious offenses, such as breaking and entering and sexual assault.

As I was writing the article, my medical-school case presentation of Muriel came to mind, and just as I had evoked the audience's interest by beginning that presentation with a story, I began my voyeurism article with the tale of the original Peeping Tom. My wife, while working on her doctorate, helped me retrieve early accounts of the legend of Lady Godiva, the eleventh-century noblewoman who had volunteered to ride naked through the street to save her townspeople from the excessive taxation imposed by her husband. All the townspeople, save Tom, showed their gratitude by refusing to look at her nakedness. But poor Tom could not resist a peek at naked royalty and, for his transgression, was struck blind on the spot. The article was immediately accepted for publication in the *Archives of General Psychiatry*.

Shortly afterward, my article on the techniques of leading therapy groups for sexual offenders was published in the *Journal of Nervous and Mental Disease*. Unrelated to my Patuxent work, I also published an article on the diagnosis of senile dementia. Because it was unusual for residents to author publications, the Hopkins faculty responded very positively. Their plaudits were gratifying but also a bit puzzling to me because writing came so easily.

John Whitehorn always dressed in a white shirt, necktie, and brown suit. We residents speculated he had two or three identical suits, since we never saw him wear anything else. The entire resident class was expected to attend his annual cocktail party at the beginning of every academic year, and we all dreaded it: we had to stand for hours dressed in our suits and ties and were served a small glass of sherry and no other food or drink.

During our third year, the five other third-year residents and I spent the entire day every Friday with Dr. Whitehorn. We sat in the large corner conference room adjacent to his office as he interviewed each of his hospitalized patients. Dr. Whitehorn and the patient sat in upholstered chairs, while we eight residents sat a few feet away in wooden chairs. Some interviews lasted only ten or fifteen minutes, others lasted an hour, and sometimes two or three hours.

His publication "Guide to Interviewing and Clinical Personality Study" was used in most psychiatric training programs in the United States at the time and offered the neophyte a systematic approach to the clinical interview, but his own interviewing style was anything but systematic. He rarely inquired about symptoms or areas of distress, but instead followed a plan of "Let the patient teach you." Now, over half a century later, a few examples still remain in mind: one patient was writing his PhD thesis on the

Spanish Armada, another was an expert on Joan of Arc, and another was a wealthy coffee planter from Brazil. In each of these
instances, Dr. Whitehorn interviewed the patient at great length,
at least ninety minutes, focusing on the patient's interests. We
learned a great deal about the historical background of the Spanish
Armada, the conspiracy against Joan of Arc, the accuracy of Persian archers, the curriculum of professional welding schools, and
everything we wanted to know (and more) about the relationship
between the quality of the coffee bean and the altitude at which it
was grown. At times I was bored and tuned out, however, only to
discover, ten or fifteen minutes later, that a hostile, guarded, paranoid patient was now speaking more frankly and personally about
his or her inner life. "You and the patient both win," John Whitehorn said. "The patient's self-esteem is raised by your interest and
your willingness to be taught by him, and you are edified and will
eventually learn all you need to know about his illness."

After the morning interviews, we had a two-hour lunch
served in his large, comfortable office on good bone china in leisurely southern style: a large salad, sandwiches, codfish cakes, and,
my favorite dish until this very day, Chesapeake Bay crab cakes.
The conversation stretched from salad and sandwiches to dessert
and coffee and ranged over many topics. Unless we steered him
in a particular direction, Whitehorn was prone to discuss his new
ideas on the periodic table. He would walk to the blackboard and
pull down the periodic table chart that was always hanging in
his office. Though he had taken psychiatric training at Harvard
and had been chairman of psychiatry at Washington University
in St. Louis before coming to Hopkins, he had originally been a
biochemist, and had done substantial research on the chemistry
of the brain. I remember posing questions about the origins of
paranoid thinking, to which he responded at great length. Once,
when I was passing through a phase of highly deterministic thinking about human behavior, I suggested to him that total knowledge of all the stimuli imposing upon the individual would allow

us to predict with precision his or her reaction, both in thought and action. I compared it to hitting a pool ball—if we knew the force, angle, and spin, we'd know the reaction of the ball being struck. My position prompted him to take the opposite view, a humanistic perspective that was foreign and uncomfortable for him. After a lively discussion, Dr. Whitehorn said to the others, "It is not out of the question that Dr. Yalom is having a bit of fun at my expense." As I think back on it, he was probably right: I do recall feeling a bit amused that I had maneuvered him into the very humanistic point of view I usually espoused.

My only disappointment with him came when I lent him a copy of Kafka's *The Trial*, which I had loved in part for its metaphorical presentation of neuroticism and free-floating guilt. Dr. Whitehorn returned the book a couple of days later, shaking his head. He told me he just didn't get it and that he'd rather talk to real people. By that time, I had been in psychiatry for three years, and I had yet to encounter any clinician who was interested in the insights of philosophers or novelists.

After lunch we returned to observing Dr. Whitehorn's interviews. By four or five o'clock I began getting antsy, eager to get out and play tennis with my regular partner, one of the medical students. The house staff tennis court was only two hundred feet away in an alcove between the departments of psychiatry and pediatrics, and on many Friday evenings I kept my hopes alive until the last rays of sunshine had vanished, then sighed and turned my full attention back to the interview.

My final contact during my training with John Whitehorn came in my last month of residency. He summoned me to his office one afternoon, and when I had closed the door behind me and sat before him, I noticed his face seemed less severe. Was I mistaken, or did I discern friendliness, even a trace of a smile? After a typical Whitehornian pause, he leaned toward me and asked, "What do you plan to do with your future?" When I said that my next step was my upcoming mandatory two years of service in the army, he grimaced and said, "How fortunate you are that we are at peace. My son was killed in World War II in the Battle of the Bulge—a God-damned meat grinder." I stammered that I was sorry, but he closed his eyes and shook his head to indicate that he didn't wish to speak further of his son. He asked about my plans after the army. I told him I was uncertain about the future and had responsibilities to my wife and three children. Perhaps, I told him, I might enter practice in Washington or Baltimore.

He shook his head and pointed to my published papers lying in a neat pile on his desk and said, "Publications like these say something else. They represent the steps of the academic ladder one must ascend. My gut tells me that if you continue thinking and writing in this manner, there might be a bright future for you in a university teaching department—one, for example, such as Johns Hopkins." His final words rang in my ears for many years: "It would be flying in the face of fortune for you not to pursue an academic career." He ended the session by giving me a framed photograph of himself with the inscription, "To Dr. Irvin Yalom, with affection and admiration." It hangs today in my office. As I write, I see it now, resting uncomfortably alongside a picture of Jolting Joe DiMaggio. "With affection and admiration"—as I think of those words now I am astonished: I never recognized those sentiments in him at the time. Only now, as I write this, do I register that he, and Jerome Frank, as well, had indeed served as mentors to me—great mentors! I know it's time to discard my notion that I am entirely self-created.

As I ended my three years of residency, Dr. Whitehorn was ending his long career at Johns Hopkins, and I, along with the other residents and the entire faculty of the medical school, attended his retirement party. I remember well how he began his farewell address. After a lively introduction by Professor Leon Eisenberg, my supervisor in child psychiatry, who would soon assume the chair of the Harvard Department of Psychiatry, Dr. Whitehorn stood up, walked to the microphone, and began, in

his measured, formal voice: "It has been said that a man's character may be judged by the character of his friends. If that is so . . . ,"
he paused and very slowly and deliberately scanned the large audience from left to right, "then I must be a very fine fellow indeed."

I had only two contacts with John Whitehorn after that.
Several years later while I was teaching at Stanford, a close member of his family contacted me saying that John Whitehorn had
referred him to me for psychotherapy, and I was pleased to be able
to offer him help in a few months of therapy. And then, in 1974,
fifteen years after my last face-to-face contact with him, I received
a phone call from John Whitehorn's daughter, whom I had never
met. She told me that her father had had a massive stroke, was
near death, and had very specifically asked for me to visit him.
I was entirely dumbfounded. Why me? What could I offer him?
But of course I did not hesitate, and the following morning I flew
across the country to Washington, where, as always, I stayed with
my sister, Jean, and her husband, Morton. I borrowed their car,
picked up my mother, who always enjoyed a car ride, and drove to
a convalescent hospital just outside of Baltimore. I arranged comfortable seating for my mother in the lobby and took the elevator
to Dr. Whitehorn's room.

He appeared much smaller than I recalled. He was paralyzed
on one side of his body and had expressive aphasia, which greatly
impaired his ability to speak. How shocking it was to see the most
gloriously articulate person I had ever known now drooling saliva
and grubbing for words. After a few false starts, he finally managed to utter, "I'm . . . I'm . . . I'm scared, so damned scared." And
I was scared, too, scared by the sight of a great statue felled and
lying in ruins.

Dr. Whitehorn had trained two generations of psychiatrists,
a great many of whom were now chairmen at leading universities.
I asked myself, "Why me? What could I possibly do for him?"

I ended up not doing much. I behaved like any nervous visitor,
searching desperately for words of comfort. I reminded him of my

days with him at Hopkins and told him how much I had treasured our Fridays together, how much he had taught me about interviewing patients, how I had taken his advice and had become a university professor, how I tried to emulate him in my work by treating patients with dignity and interest, how, following his advice, I let patients teach me. He made sounds but could not formulate words, and finally, after thirty minutes, he fell into a deep sleep. I left shaken and still puzzled about why he had called for me. Later I learned from his daughter that he died two days after my visit.

The question "Why me?" ran through my mind for years. Why call for an agitated, self-doubting son of a poor immigrant grocer? Perhaps I was a stand-in for the son he had lost in World War II. Dr. Whitehorn died such a lonely death. If only I could have given him more. Many times I wished for a second chance. I should have said more about how I treasured my time with him, and told him how often I thought of him when I interviewed patients. I should have tried to express the terror he must have been feeling. Or I should have touched him, or held his hand, or kissed his cheek, but I desisted—I had known him too long as a formal, distant man, and besides, he was so helpless that he might have experienced my tender gestures as an assault.

Some twenty years later, in a casual lunch conversation, David Hamburg, the chairman of psychiatry who brought me to Stanford after I left the army, told me he was doing some housecleaning and found a letter of support for my appointment from John Whitehorn. He showed me the letter and I was stunned by its final sentence: "I believe that Dr. Yalom will become a leader of American Psychiatry." Now, as I reconsider my relationship with John Whitehorn, I think I understand why I was summoned to his deathbed. He must have viewed me as someone who would carry on his work. I've just now turned to look at his picture hanging over my desk and try to catch his gaze. I hope he was comforted by the thought that, partly through me, he would continue to ripple into the future.

CHAPTER SIXTEEN
ASSIGNED TO
PARADISE

In August 1960, one month after finishing my residency at
Johns Hopkins, I was inducted into the army. In those years
the universal draft was in effect, but medical students were
given the option of signing on to a deferment program called the
Berry Plan, which allowed them to finish medical school and residency before entering the army. My first six weeks in the army
were spent in basic training in Fort Sam Houston in San Antonio, and while there I was notified that I would be spending the
next two years at a base in Germany. A few days later, another
memo informed me that I would instead be stationed in France.
And two weeks after that, mirabile dictu, I was told to report for
service at Tripler Hospital in Honolulu, Hawaii. And that was the
assignment that stuck.

I remember my first moment in Hawaii with great clarity. As
soon as I stepped from the plane, Jim Nicholas, an army psychiatrist, destined to be my close buddy for the next two years, placed
a lei of plumeria blossoms around my neck. The scent rose into my
nose, a sweet, heavy fragrance, and right there, I felt something

shift within me. My senses awakened and soon I became intoxicated by the aroma of plumeria that was everywhere: at the airport, in the streets, and in the small Waikiki apartment Jim had selected for us and stocked with groceries and flowers. In 1960 Hawaii was a place of great natural beauty: the plumage, palm trees, hibiscus, red spiked ginger, white spider lilies, birds-of-paradise, and, of course, the ocean with its teal-blue waves gently rolling to rest on sparkling sand. Everyone wore strange and wonderful clothes: Jim greeted me wearing a flowery shirt, shorts, and sandals called *zoris* and took me to a Waikiki shop where I took off my army uniform, for a day at least, and walked out wearing zoris, a violet aloha shirt, and brilliant blue shorts.

M arilyn and our three children arrived two days later, and together we drove to the top of the Pali Lookout with an otherworldly view of the eastern part of the island. As we gazed at the dark green crenellated mountains around us, the waterfalls and rainbows, the blue-green ocean, the endless beaches, Marilyn pointed down toward Kailua and Lanikai and pronounced, "This is paradise: I want to live there."

I was delighted by her delight. It had been a horrendous few weeks for her. During my six-week basic training in San Antonio, life had been hard for both of us, but particularly severe for her. We knew no one in San Antonio, where it was over one hundred degrees every day. I had a demanding daily schedule at the army school and was away all day five or six days a week, leaving Marilyn with our three small children. Things reached their low point when I had to undergo a week of basic training at a site a few hours from San Antonio. There I learned such invaluable things as how to handle weapons (I won a sharpshooter medal for rifle accuracy) and how to crawl low under barbed wire while live machine-gun bullets zoomed overhead (at least we were told they were live bullets—no one ever tested it). In those pre-iPhone days, Marilyn and I had no contact whatsoever during this time. When I returned, I learned that she had developed acute appendicitis the day after I left. She had been taken to the military hospital for an emergency appendectomy, while military personnel took care of our children. Four days after her surgery, the chief surgical resident paid a home visit in the evening to tell Marilyn that the pathology report indicated she had an intestinal cancer that would require major resection of the large bowel; he even drew sketches for her to show me indicating the parts of the bowel to be removed. When I returned home the following day, I was shocked by the news and the surgeon's sketches. I rushed to the army hospital and obtained the pathology slides, which I sent by special delivery to physician friends back east. They all agreed that Marilyn had a benign carcinoid tumor that required no further treatment whatsoever. Even now, fifty years later, as I write about it, I feel great anger toward the army for not notifying me, and for suggesting major and irreversible surgery for a completely benign condition.

All that was behind us now as we looked out over the mountains and the light blue water in this new setting, and I was thrilled and relieved to see the lively, vivacious Marilyn back with me again. I looked again toward Kailua and Lanikai. Living there would be entirely impractical: we had very little money and the army offered inexpensive military housing at the Schofield Barracks. But I was as enchanted as Marilyn and, within a few days, we had rented a small house in Lanikai one block away from one of the world's most lovely beaches. The Lanikai beach has taken up permanent residence in both of our minds: it remains the most beautiful we have ever seen, and ever since, whenever we walk on a beach with powdery but firm sand, we look at each other and say, "Lanikai sand."

Long after we left Hawaii, we returned regularly to that beach, which now, alas, has been greatly eroded. We lived there for one year, until we learned that an admiral had unexpectedly been reassigned to the South Pacific, and his house on the neighboring Kailua beach was for rent. We immediately rented it and were so close to the water that I could be surfing or snorkeling while I was on call: Marilyn would signal that I had a phone call by waving a large white towel from the veranda.

Shortly after we arrived, we received letters of greeting from three generals, based in Hawaii, Germany, and France, each welcoming me to their post. The initial confusion about my posting led to many of our belongings being lost somewhere in transit, so we truly had a new start—we bought all our furniture and bedding from a garage sale in a single day.

My army duty was undemanding. I spent most of my time in an inpatient unit with patients coming from various Pacific bases. In 1960, the Vietnam War was yet to come, but many of our patients had seen unofficial military action in Laos. Most of those with serious mental illness had already been screened out and sent directly to stateside hospitals. Hence, many of our patients were young men who were not psychotic but pretended to be, hoping to get a discharge.

One of my first patients, a sergeant with nineteen years of service who was near retirement, had been arrested for drinking while on duty—a serious charge that might threaten his retirement status and pension. He came to me for an examination and incorrectly answered each question I asked. But every one of his answers was so close to the truth that it seemed that some part of his mind knew the correct answer: six times seven was forty-one, Christmas Day was December 26, a table had five legs. I had never seen such a case before, and through speaking to colleagues and searching the literature I learned it was a classic case of the Ganser syndrome (or, as it is often known, the syndrome of approximate answers), a type of factitious disorder in which the patient mimics an illness when he is not really sick but may be trying to avoid responsibility for some illicit act. I spent much time with him in his four-day stay (patients who needed longer hospitalization were shipped back to the continental United States), but could never make contact with his non-deceiving self. The really strange part, as I learned from my study of the literature on the long-term follow-up, was that a high percentage of Ganser patients did, in fact, develop a true psychotic disorder years later!

Every day we had to make decisions as to whether some soldier was truly mentally ill or faking it in order to get a medical discharge. Almost every patient that came to us wanted out of the army or navy or marines—we treated all branches of the military—and my colleagues and I were troubled by the arbitrariness of our decision-making process: guidelines were unclear, and there were times when we were inconsistent in our recommendations.

The duty requirements were exceedingly light compared to my internship and residency: after four years of being on call evenings and weekends, I felt I was on a two-year holiday. There were three psychiatrists, each on call every third night and weekend; I had to go to the hospital at night only a few times during my entire tour of duty. The three of us related well to one another and to our commanding officer, Colonel Paul Yessler, a genial, well-informed colleague who allowed us full autonomy in our work. Though our psychiatric unit, Little Tripler, was only three hundred feet from the large Tripler Hospital, it had a relaxed, nonmilitary atmosphere. I ate lunch at the large Tripler and occasionally did consultations there for other services, but otherwise rarely set foot in it, and often I went for weeks without receiving or giving salutes.

Given this freedom, I chose to continue my interest in group work and formed a variety of therapy groups: daily inpatient groups, outpatient groups for troubled military wives, and, in my off-time, a process group for nonmilitary psychiatry residents at the Hawaii State Hospital in Kaneohe.

I felt most useful in my groups for military wives. Many of them were dealing with being away from their accustomed surroundings, but some chose to engage in deep work exploring their

loneliness and their inability to make connections with others in
their community. The resident group was far more difficult. The
residents wanted a therapy experience that would be both personally therapeutic and instructive for them as group leaders. They
had heard that I was an experienced group therapist, and asked
me to lead. I was uneasy: I had never led this kind of group and,
moreover, was only a year or two more experienced than they, but
since the residents were motivated enough to request it, I agreed
to do it. It was not long before I realized I had gotten myself into
a difficult situation. A group will not work unless members are
willing to take risks and disclose intimate thoughts and feelings,
and this group was extremely reluctant to take that step. Slowly I
began to understand that, since the therapist's chief professional
tool is his or her own person, self-disclosure of personal shortcomings felt doubly risky: not only might one's character be judged,
but one's professional competence as well. Though I became fully
aware of this conundrum, I could not resolve the impasse, and the
group was only moderately successful. In the future I came to the
realization that to be an effective leader in such circumstances
one must be willing to model self-disclosure by taking personal
risks oneself in the group.

I have no doubt that my two years in Hawaii changed my
life. Before then, my long-range plans were to return to the East
Coast, perhaps, as Dr. Whitehorn had suggested, to seek an academic position, or to rejoin my friends and family in Washington,
DC, and enter private practice. But after a few sunny Hawaiian
months, the cold, gray, formal East Coast grew less and less invit-
ing. For years, Marilyn had wanted to move far away from Washington, and soon we were in full agreement: we both wanted to
remain in Hawaii, or as close as possible. Before Hawaii, my entire life had focused on my work, with far too little time for my
wife and children. Hawaii opened me up to the beauty of my surroundings. The beaches, especially, beckoned, and Marilyn and I
walked on them for hours, holding hands just as we had in high

school. I spent much more time with my children, a good bit of it in the warm ocean, teaching them to swim, snorkel, and body surf. (I never mastered surfing on a surfboard—I didn't have the balance.) I took my children to our neighborhood cinema on Friday evenings to watch samurai films, and they wore their pajamas just like the local kids.

The army would not ship my Lambretta to Hawaii, but was willing to ship a telescope, so, while still in Baltimore, I had traded the Lambretta for a mechanized eight-inch reflecting telescope, something I had coveted since my childhood forays into telescope making. However, aside from a couple of times when I lugged it to the top of a mountain, I could make little use of my telescope in Hawaii because of the persistently hazy Hawaiian night sky.

One of my patients was the flight controller at the army air force base, and through him I enjoyed the perk of hopping weekend flights to the Philippines and Japan. I did some snorkeling in the exquisite waters off a small island in the Philippines, and saw sunsets in Manila that remain forever in my mind's eye. I stayed at the officers' club in Tokyo and explored the city. Whenever I was lost, I hailed a taxi and showed him the club card with the address written in Japanese. I had been warned by the club manager to watch the driver when I showed him the card: if he inhaled sharply, then I should jump out of the cab, as Tokyo taxi drivers would not lose face by admitting they didn't know an address.

Shortly after our arrival, Marilyn obtained a faculty position at the University of Hawaii French Department. She was especially delighted to teach a course on contemporary French literature with so many Vietnamese students fluent in French, even though they had great difficulty grasping Sartre's ideas about alienation, as they were planning to swim after class in the warm blue ocean. Marilyn needed our car to drive to the university, so I bought a peppy Yamaha motorcycle and was thrilled with my thirty-minute morning commute to Tripler over the top of the Pali. During our time there, the Wilson Tunnel through the mountains opened, and I then took that shorter route to work and had the daily experience of entering it in bright sunshine and emerging almost always in the midst of a delicious, warm Hawaiian shower. Close to my home in Kailua there was a small tennis club with grass courts where we played against other clubs on weekends. One of my army friends introduced me to snorkeling and scuba diving, and, for the next forty years, I was to derive great pleasure from gliding along the ocean bottom, admiring the fauna and the life of sea critters in Hawaii, the Caribbean, and many other parts of the world. A few times I went night diving, a special thrill, since all the nocturnal creatures were on the prowl, especially large crustaceans.

J ack Ross, one of my army colleagues who had trained at the Menninger Clinic, introduced me to his classmate, K.Y. Lum, a psychiatrist in practice in Honolulu. He and I organized a case presentation group with several Hawaiian psychiatrists who met monthly. We also started a psychiatrist poker game held every other week and persisted for three decades. K.Y. and I became close friends and remain in touch to this day.

One day, during my first weeks in Hawaii, André Tao Kim Hai, an elderly Vietnamese man who lived around the corner, stopped by my house carrying a chess set and asked, "Do you play chess?" Manna from heaven! André and I were evenly matched and played dozens and dozens of games. He had retired to Hawaii after serving many years as the Vietnamese representative to the United Nations, but a few years later, when the Vietnam War broke out, he left the United States in protest and moved to Paris, and then to the island of Madeira. We continued our friendship and our chess rivalry in later years when I visited him at both of his later homes.

My parents visited us in Hawaii, as did Marilyn's mother and my sister, Jean, and her family. Marilyn made friends at the university and for the first time we developed a social life, forming an eight-person salon with sociologist Reuel Denney, coauthor of *The Lonely Crowd*, and his wife, Ruth; the Indonesian philosopher and poet Takdir Alisjahbana and his German wife; and George Barati, conductor of the Hawaiian Symphony Orchestra, and his lovely wife, another Ruth, a yoga devotee. We spent many happy evenings with them reading translations of Takdir's poetry, discussing one of Reuel's books, listening to music, or, one night, listening to a tape of T. S. Eliot reading *The Waste Land*, which left all of us dejected. To this day I remember our little group having a luau on the beach, enjoying Hawaiian drinks and guava, lychees, mangos, pineapple, and papaya, my favorite. I can still recall the flavor of Takdir's beef skewers dipped in his Indonesian peanut sauce.

With poker, snorkeling, beach walking, motorcycling, playing with my children, and chess, I led a far more playful life than I ever had before. I loved the informality, the sandals, the simple act of sitting on the beach and staring out to sea. I was changing: work wasn't everything. The gray East Coast, with its frigid winters and oppressively hot summers, no longer beckoned. I felt at home in Hawaii and began to fantasize about staying there for the rest of my life.

As we approached the end of our two years in Hawaii, we were faced with the decision of where to live. I had published two more professional articles and was leaning toward an academic career. But, alas, staying in Hawaii was not an option: the medical school offered only the first two nonclinical years and had no full-time psychiatry faculty. I felt very much on my own and sensed the lack of a mentor, someone who might have given me guidance about how to proceed. Not for an instant did it occur to me to contact my Hopkins teachers, John Whitehorn or Jerry Frank. Now, as I look back upon that time, I'm mystified: Why didn't I think of asking them for advice or for a reference? I must have thought that I had passed entirely out of their minds when I had finished my residency.

Instead, I took the least imaginative path possible: the want ads! I checked the ads in the American Psychiatric Association newsletter and found three postings of interest: faculty positions at Stanford University School of Medicine and the University of California at San Francisco (UCSF) Medical School, and a staff position at the Mendota State Hospital in Wisconsin (of interest only because the eminent psychologist Carl Rogers worked at that hospital). I applied for all three positions. They all agreed to interview me, and I caught a military plane to San Francisco.

My first interview, at UCSF, was with a senior faculty member, Jacob Epstein, who at the end of an hour offered me a clinical faculty position and an annual salary of $18,000. Since my third-year salary as a resident had been $3,000, and my military salary $12,000, I was inclined to accept, even though I knew the demands on my time would be very high: I would not only be teaching medical students and psychiatric residents, but also running an extremely large, busy inpatient ward.

The following day, David Hamburg, who was the new chairman of the Stanford Psychiatry Department, interviewed me. The Stanford Medical School and Hospital had just moved from San Francisco to newly constructed buildings on the Stanford campus in Palo Alto, and he was given full charge for creating an entirely new department. I was struck by Dr. Hamburg's lofty vision, his concern about our field, and his wisdom. And by his sentences! Hearing one stately, complex sentence after another roll off his tongue was like listening to a fine concerto. Furthermore, I had the strong sense that, in addition to his mentorship, I would be provided with all the resources and academic freedom I needed.

I say that in retrospect: at that time I don't believe I had any idea what my future might be or what I was capable of. I knew what private practice was like, I knew that it would be a worthy life, and I also knew that private practice would offer me probably triple what I would earn as an academic psychiatrist.

Dr. Hamburg offered me a junior faculty position (a lectureship) and a salary of only $11,000 a year—$1,000 less than my army salary. He also clarified the Stanford policy: full-time faculty members were expected to be scholars and researchers and could not supplement their income with private practice.

The sharp salary discrepancy between Stanford and UCSF shocked me at first, but as I pondered my two offers, it ceased to be a factor. Though we had zero savings and lived from paycheck to paycheck, money was not a major concern. David Hamburg's vision impressed me, and I wanted to be part of the university department he was building. I realized that what I really wanted was a life of teaching and research. Besides, if an emergency arose, I believed I had the security of my parents' financial backing, as well as income from Marilyn's potential career. After consulting with Marilyn on the phone, I accepted the Stanford position, and canceled my flight to the Mendota State Hospital.

CHAPTER SEVENTEEN

COMING ASHORE

In 1964, three years into my career at Stanford, I decided to attend an eight-day National Training Laboratory Institute at Lake Arrowhead in Southern California. The weeklong institute program offered many social psychological activities, but the heart of it, and my reason for going, was the daily three-hour small-group meeting. I arrived a few minutes early the morning of the first meeting, took one of the thirteen chairs placed in a circle, and glanced about at the leader and the other early arrivals. Though I had much experience leading therapy groups, and was heavily involved in group therapy research and teaching, I had never been a member of a group. It was time to remedy that.

No one spoke as the others filed in and took seats. At 8:30, the leader, Dorothy Garwood, a therapist in private practice with two PhDs (biochemistry and psychology), stood up and introduced herself: "Welcome to the 1964 Lake Arrowhead NTL Institute," she said. "This group will be meeting every morning at this time for three hours for the next eight days, and I'd like us to keep everything we say, all of our comments, in the here-and-now."

A long silence followed. I thought, "That's all?" and looked around to see eleven faces radiating perplexity and eleven heads shaking in bewilderment. After a minute, members responded:

"That's a pretty skimpy orientation."

"Is this some kind of joke?"

"We don't even know anyone's name."

No response from the leader. Gradually, the collective uncertainty began to generate its own energy:

"This is pathetic. Is this the kind of leadership we're getting?"

"That's rude. She's doing her job. Don't you get that this is a process group? We have to examine our own process."

"Right, I have a hunch, more than a hunch, she knows exactly what she's doing."

"That is blind faith: I've never liked blind faith. The truth is we're floundering, and where is she? Sure as hell not helping us."

There were a few pauses between comments as members waited for the leader to respond. But she smiled and remained silent.

Other members pitched in.

"And, anyway, how are we supposed to stay in the here-and-now when we have no history together? We've just met today for the first time."

"I'm always uncomfortable with this kind of silence."

"Yeah, me too. We're paying a good bit of money and we're sitting here doing nothing and wasting time."

"Personally, I like the silence. Sitting here quietly with all of you mellows me out."

"Me, too. I just slip into meditation. I feel focused, ready for anything."

As I engaged in this interchange and reflected upon it, I had an epiphany—I learned something that I later incorporated into the very core of my approach to group therapy. I had just witnessed a simple but extraordinarily important phenomenon: all the group members being exposed to a single stimulus (in this instance, a leader asking that all comments remain in the here-and-now), and the members responding in very different ways. A *single shared stimulus and eleven different responses! Why?* There was only one possible solution to this puzzle: *There are eleven different inner worlds! And these eleven different responses may be the royal road into these different worlds.*

Without the leader's assistance, we each then introduced ourselves and said something about what we did professionally and why we were there. I noted that I was the only psychiatrist—there was one psychologist, and the rest were educators or social scientists.

I turned and addressed the leader directly. "I'm curious about your silence. Could you say a bit about your role here?"

This time she answered (briefly): "My role is to be the leader and to hold all the feelings and fantasies that members have about leaders."

We continued meeting for the next seven days and began examining our relationships with one another. The psychologist member of the group was a particularly angry individual and often laced into me for being pompous and overbearing. A few days in, he related a dream he had had about being chased by a giant—which seemed to be me. And ultimately, he and I did a good bit of work—I on my discomfort with his anger and he on the competitive feelings I aroused in him—and we worked through some of the distrust between our respective professions.

Since I was the only physician at this conference, I was called upon to care for and eventually hospitalize a member in another group who developed a psychotic reaction to the stress generated in his group. This outcome made me even more aware of the power of the small group—power not only to heal but also to harm.

I grew to know Dorothy Garwood well, and years later she and her husband and Marilyn and I had a lovely vacation on

Maui. She was by no means a withholding person, but had been trained in a tradition from the Tavistock Clinic—a large psychotherapy training and treatment center in London—in which the leader remained outside the group and confined all her observations to mass group phenomena. Three years later, on a sabbatical at the Tavistock Clinic, I understood more clearly the rationale for her leadership posture.

When our family of five had first arrived in Palo Alto after my discharge from the army nearly three years before, in 1962, Marilyn and I had set about finding a place to live. We could have purchased a home in the faculty housing area of Stanford, but, as in Hawaii, we chose a more diverse neighborhood. We bought a thirty-year-old house (almost ancient by California standards) fifteen minutes from the campus. Economics were so different then: with a small income, we had no difficulty buying a home on an acre of land for $32,000. The price was three times my annual Stanford income; today, the Palo Alto economy has changed so much that an equivalent home would cost thirty to forty times a young professor's salary. My parents gave us the $7,000 down payment on the house, and that was the last time I accepted money from them. Still, even after I completed my training and we were a family of six, my father always insisted on picking up the check at restaurants. I liked his taking care of me and offered only flimsy resistance. And I have passed his generosity on by doing exactly the same for my adult children (who, in turn, also put up flimsy resistance). It's a pathway to being remembered: my father's face often comes to mind as I pay the bill for my children. (And we have also been able to give our children down payments on their first houses.)

When I first reported to my department, I learned that I was assigned to be the medical director of a large ward at the new Stanford Veterans Administration Hospital, ten minutes from the medical school and entirely operated by Stanford faculty. Though I supervised residents, organized a process group for medical students (i.e., a group in which we studied the way we related to one another), and had free time to attend departmental lectures and research symposia, I was not happy at the VA. I felt that too many of the patients, almost all World War II veterans, were unreceptive to my approach to therapy. Quite possibly the secondary gains were simply too great: free medical care, free housing and food, and a comfortable dwelling place. Toward the end of my first year, I told David Hamburg that I foresaw few research opportunities for my particular interests at the VA. When he inquired where I wished to work, I suggested the outpatient department at Stanford, the hub of the training program for residents and a site where I could organize a group therapy program for training and research. Having observed my work and attended a couple of my grand rounds presentations, he had sufficient confidence in me to agree to my request. He was never anything but helpful and supportive, and from that point on, for a great many years, I had no administrative responsibility and almost total freedom to follow my own clinical, teaching, and research interests.

In 1963, Marilyn completed her doctorate (with a dissertation titled *The Motif of the Trial in the Works of Franz Kafka and Albert Camus*) in the program of comparative literature at Johns Hopkins. She flew to Baltimore for the oral exams, passed her orals, and received her doctorate with distinction. She came back hoping for a position at Stanford, but was devastated when the head of the French Department, John Lapp, told her: "We don't hire faculty wives."

A generation later, as my consciousness of women's issues increased, I might have sought a position at another university broad-minded enough to evaluate her solely on her merit, but in 1962 that thought never crossed my mind, nor Marilyn's. I felt for her. I knew she deserved a Stanford position, but we both accepted the situation and simply set about looking for alternatives.

Shortly thereafter, the dean of humanities at the brand new California State College at Hayward contacted Marilyn. Having heard about her from a Stanford colleague, he drove to our home and offered her a position as an assistant professor of foreign languages. Teaching at Hayward entailed a commute of almost an hour each way four days a week, which she negotiated for the next thirteen years. Marilyn's entry salary was $8,000—$3,000 less than my entry salary at Stanford. But our two salaries allowed us to live comfortably in Palo Alto, to pay for a full-time housekeeper, and even to take several memorable trips. Marilyn had a fulfilling career at California State and was soon promoted to tenured associate professor and then to a full professorship.

For the next fifteen years at Stanford I was heavily involved in group therapy, as a clinician, teacher, researcher, and textbook author. I started a therapy group in the outpatient clinic that my students, the twelve first-year psychiatric residents, observed through a two-way mirror—just as I had watched Jerry Frank's group when I was a student. At first I co-led it with another faculty member, but the following year I began the practice of leading it with a psychiatric resident who stayed one year and then was replaced by another resident.

My approach had been evolving steadily toward a more personal, transparent form of leadership and moving away from an aloof professional style. Since the group members, all informal Californians, referred to each other by first name, I felt more and more awkward referring to them by their last name or calling them by their first names and expecting them to refer to me as "Dr. Yalom," so I took the shocking step of asking the group to call me "Irv." For many years, however, I still clung to my professional identity by wearing my white hospital coat like all the other medical professional staff at the Stanford Hospital. Eventually I gave that up as well, coming to believe that what mattered in therapy

was personal honesty and transparency, not professional authority. (I never threw out that white coat—it hangs still in the back
of a closet at home—a souvenir of my identity as a medical doctor.) But despite doffing the accoutrements of my field, I still hold
fast to my respect for medicine and the entire Hippocratic oath,
with its many clauses, such as: "I will practice my profession with
conscience and dignity" and "The health of my patient will be my
first consideration."

After each group therapy session, I dictated extensive summaries for my own understanding and my teaching. (Stanford
generously provided a secretary.) At some point—I don't recall
the precise stimulus—it occurred to me that it might be useful
to patients to read my summary of the session and my post-group
reflections. This led to a bold, highly unusual experiment in therapist transparency: the day following each meeting, I mailed a
copy of the group summary to all the members. Each summary
described the major issues of the session (generally two or three
themes) and each member's contributions and behavior. I added
the reasons behind each of my statements in the group and often
added comments about things I wish I had said or things I regretted having said.

Often the group began a session by critiquing my summary of
the previous meeting. Sometimes members disagreed, and sometimes they pointed out omissions, but almost always the meeting began with more energy and interaction than it had before.
I found this practice to be so useful that I continued these summaries as long as I led groups. When residents co-led the group
with me, they wrote the summary every other week. The summaries require so much time and self-exposure, however, that,
to the best of my knowledge, few, if any, group therapists in the
country followed suit. Though some therapists were critical of my
self-exposure, I cannot recall a single instance in which sharing
my thoughts and my personal feelings was not helpful to the patient. Why did such self-exposure come so easily to me? For one

thing, I had chosen not to enroll in any postgraduate training—no Freudian or Jungian or Lacanian analytic institutes. I was entirely free of governing rules, and was guided only by my results, which I carefully monitored. A number of issues may have been at play: my ingrained iconoclasm (evident in my early responses to religious belief and ritual), my negative personal experience in analysis with an inexpressive and impersonal analyst, and the experimental atmosphere in my young department, overseen by an open-minded chairman.

Weekly department meetings were not my cup of tea: I always attended but rarely spoke. None of the subject matter—funding, obtaining grants, allocation or bickering over space, relationships with other departments, deans' reports—interested me. What *did* interest me was listening to Dave Hamburg speak. I admired his thoughtful reflections, his methods of conflict resolution, and, above all, his amazing rhetorical ability. I love the spoken word in the same way others might love a musical performance, and I am entranced by the words of a truly gifted speaker.

It was obvious that I had no administrative skills, and I never volunteered or was put in charge of anything. Frankly, I just wanted to be left alone to pursue my own research, writing, therapy, and teaching. And almost immediately I began contributing articles to professional journals. This was what I enjoyed and where I felt I had something to offer. I sometimes wonder if I didn't feign administrative ineptness. It's possible, too, that I may have felt powerless to compete with the other young Turks in the department, all of whom were jockeying for power and recognition.

I chose to attend that Lake Arrowhead conference not only to have the experience of being a group member but also to learn as much as possible about the "T-group," an important, nonmedical group phenomenon that emerged in the 1960s and was sweeping the country. (The "T" in T-group stood for "training"—that is, developing skills both in interpersonal relationships and in group dynamics.) The founders of this approach, leaders of the National Education Association, were not clinicians but scholars of group dynamics who wanted to alter attitudes and behavior in organizations and, later, help individuals become more sensitive to others. Their organization, the National Training Laboratories (NTL), held seminars, or social laboratories, of several days' length in Bethel and Plymouth in Maine, and later, the one I attended in California at Lake Arrowhead.

The NTL laboratory consisted of many activities: the small skills training groups, discussion and problem-solving groups, team-building groups, large groups. But it soon became clear that the small T-groups, in which members gave one another instantaneous feedback, were, by far, the most dynamic and compelling exercise.

Gradually, over the years, as the NTL groups moved west and as Carl Rogers entered the field, the T-group shifted its emphasis to individual personal change. "Personal change!" Sounds a lot like therapy, doesn't it? Members were encouraged to give and receive feedback, to be participant observers, to be authentic, to take risks. Eventually, the ethos shifted increasingly toward a type of psychotherapy. The groups sought to change attitudes and behavior and to improve interpersonal relationships—and soon one commonly heard slogans such as "Therapy is too good to be offered only to the sick." The T-group evolved into something new: "group therapy for normals."

It's not surprising that this later development greatly threatened psychiatrists, who viewed themselves as owners of psychotherapy and regarded encounter groups as a wild, illicit form of therapy encroaching on their territory. I felt quite differently. For one thing, I was impressed with the research approach of the founders of the field. One of the early pioneers was the social scientist Kurt Lewin, whose dictum "No research without action, no action without research," generated a vast, sophisticated body of data that I found far more interesting than the medically based group therapy research.

One of the most important things I drew from my Lake Arrowhead group experience was the singular focus on the here-and-now, and I began to implement that forcefully in my own work. As I learned at Lake Arrowhead, it is not enough to tell group members to focus on the here-and-now: we need to supply both a rationale and a roadmap. Over time I developed a short preparation talk that I gave to patients before they entered the group, in which I emphasized that a great many of their interpersonal problems would be re-created in the group, thus offering them a marvelous opportunity to learn more about themselves and to effect change. It followed (and I repeated this more than once) that their task in the group *was to understand everything they could about their relationship with every patient in the group and with the group leaders.* Many new members would generally find some aspects of the preparation puzzling, and often they would raise the objection that their problem was with their boss, or their spouse, or with friends, or with their anger, and it made no sense to focus on their relationships with group members because they would never see these people in the future.

In response to these common questions, I explained that *the group is a social microcosm,* and that the issues raised in the therapy group *would replicate or resemble the types of interpersonal issues that initially brought them into therapy.* This step, I'd learned, was crucial. Later, I conducted and published research demonstrating that patients who were effectively prepared for group therapy fared much better in therapy than those who were not well prepared.

I continued my association with the T-group movement for several years and was part of the faculty of NTL workshops at Lincoln, New Hampshire, as well as in a weeklong workshop for CEOs in Sandusky, Ohio. To this day I am grateful to T-group pioneers for showing me the way to lead and to research interpersonally based groups.

Gradually over the years, I fashioned an intensive group therapy training program for psychiatry residents consisting of
several components: a weekly lecture, observation and post-group
discussion of my weekly therapy group, having the residents lead a
therapy group with weekly supervision, and lastly, participating in
a weekly personal process group that I led with a colleague.

How did overworked first-year residents respond to spending
this much time learning about group therapy? With a good bit of
grousing! Some busy residents particularly resisted the two hours
spent each week observing my group and often showed up late or
skipped sessions entirely. But as the weeks passed, an unexpected
phenomenon occurred: as the group members grew more involved
with one another and took more risks, the students grew more
and more interested in the drama unfolding before them and the
attendance rate sharply increased. Soon they were referring to the
group as "Yalom's Peyton Place" (a takeoff on the name of a TV
soap opera in the 1960s). I think of the effect as similar to being
engrossed in a well-structured story or novel, and I consider it a
propitious sign when therapists are eager to see what will happen
next. Even now, after half a century of practice, I generally look
forward to each new session, whether individual or group, with
anticipation about what new developments will transpire. If that
feeling is absent, if I approach a session with little anticipation,
I imagine the patient may be experiencing a similar feeling and
make an effort to confront and alter that.

What effects did student observation have on the patients?
That gigantic question worried me a great deal as I noticed how
edgy group members were when students were behind the mirror. I tried reassuring patients that student psychiatrists operated
under the same confidentiality rules that professional therapists
followed, but that was of little help. Then I tried an experiment:
I would attempt to turn the annoying presence of observers into
something positive. I asked group members and students to switch
places for twenty minutes at the end of the meeting. Thus the

group members, in the observation room, observed my post-meeting discussion with the students. This step instantly enlivened both the therapy process and the teaching! The therapy group members listened with keen interest to the students' observations about them, and the students felt like they were under so much scrutiny that they paid sharper attention to their observation of the group. Eventually I added yet another step: the group members had so many feelings about the observers' commentary and about the observers themselves (whom they often adjudged to be more uptight than group members) that they wanted additional time to discuss their observations of the observers. So I tacked on an additional twenty minutes in which the students went back to the observation room, and the patients and I returned to the group room and discussed the observers' comments. I realize this is far too time-consuming for everyday practice, but I believe that the format substantially increased the effectiveness of both the therapy group and the teaching.

All this was very new. This was a time when I was grateful not to be a member of some traditional school of therapy. I gave myself free rein to create new approaches and had learned enough about outcome research to test my assumptions. Looking back, I surprise myself. Many veteran therapists would feel queasy about others observing their therapy, and yet I felt perfectly comfortable with observation. This confidence doesn't match with my inner vision of myself—somewhere in there is the anxious, ill-at-ease, self-doubting adolescent and young man that I was. But in the matter of psychotherapy, and especially group therapy, I had come to feel entirely comfortable taking risks and acknowledging mistakes. I had some anxiety about these innovations, but anxiety was old stuff for me and I had learned to tolerate it.

For my eightieth birthday I had a reunion party at my home and invited all my residents from those early years at Stanford. Many of them brought up their group therapy training experience and commented that, in their entire course of training, watching my group *was the only time they ever observed firsthand a senior clinician doing therapy.* Of course, this brought to mind my own training at Hopkins and that tiny-mirrored window through which we watched a therapy group. So, thank you, Jerry Frank.

U niversity faculty members are not promoted for teaching. That old chestnut, *publish or perish*, is no jest: it is a fact of life in academia. The twenty groups in the outpatient program provided an excellent opportunity for research and publication. I examined how therapists can best prepare patients for group therapy, how to compose groups, why some members dropped out of the groups early, and what the most effective therapeutic factors were.

As I continued to teach group therapy, I realized that a comprehensive textbook was sorely needed, and all my experiences—lectures, research, and therapy innovations—could be incorporated in a textbook. A few years into my work at Stanford, I began outlining such a book.

During this period, I also had a strong connection to the Mental Research Institute (MRI), a collective of innovative clinicians and researchers, such as Gregory Bateson, Don Jackson, Paul Watzlawick, Jay Haley, and Virginia Satir. For an entire year, I spent every Friday in an all-day conjoint family therapy course taught by Virginia Satir, and I grew to respect the effectiveness of family therapy—a format in which all members of the household meet together with a therapist. At that time, conjoint family therapy was far more visible than it is today, and I knew at least a dozen therapists in Palo Alto who did family therapy exclusively.

I was treating a patient with ulcerative colitis and asked Don Jackson to be my co-therapist for several family sessions. Together we published a paper about our findings. During my next year I saw several families in therapy, but ultimately I found individual and group therapy more intriguing. I haven't done any family therapy since then, though I often refer patients to family therapists. Another member of the MRI was Gregory Bateson, the famed anthropologist and one of the theorists behind the "double-bind" theory of schizophrenia. Bateson was a memorable raconteur and held open conversations at his home every Tuesday evening, which I often attended and greatly relished.

Another area that interested me during my first years at Stanford was the field of "sexual disorders," to which I had been introduced during my residency when I worked with sexual offenders at the Patuxent Institute. At Stanford, I regularly consulted on weekends with sexual offenders incarcerated at Atascadero State Hospital, and for the next several years I saw a number of patients in my practice who were voyeurs, exhibitionists, or had some other form of disturbing sexual compulsion or obsession. I often treated gay men, who, in retrospect, suffered primarily from society's views of them. I gave a grand rounds presentation at Stanford about some of my work with these patients, and, immediately afterward, a plastic surgeon, Don Laub, in the Stanford Department of Surgery, asked if I would serve as a consultant for a new program he was launching with a series of transsexual patients requesting surgical gender change. (The term "transgender" did not yet exist.) At that time, such surgery was not performed in the United States—patients seeking gender change had their surgery in either Tijuana or Casablanca.

Over the next few weeks the Surgery Department referred about ten patients to me for presurgical evaluation. None of these patients had serious mental disorders, and I was struck by the power and depth of their motivation for sex change. Most of them were poor and had worked for years to save money for the surgery. All were anatomical males who wished to become females: the surgeons were not yet offering the more challenging female-to-male surgery. The Surgery Department enlisted a social worker to lead a presurgical group offering training in feminine mannerisms. I attended one class exercise in which the patients sat at a bar and the instructor rolled coins into their laps and taught them to spread their knees to catch the coins in their skirt, instead of reflexively pressing their knees together as males tend to do.

The project was far ahead of its time but ran into problems after a few months: one of the postsurgical patients became a bottomless nightclub dancer advertising herself widely as a Stanford Hospital creation, and another attempted to sue the hospital for battery after his male genitalia had been removed. The project was closed down, and it was a great many years before Stanford again offered such surgery.

M y family's first five years in Palo Alto, 1962 to 1967, coincided with the beginning of the civil rights, antiwar, hippie, and beatnik movements—all of them radiating from the San Francisco Bay Area. Students inaugurated the Free Speech Movement in Berkeley, and teenage runaways swarmed to Haight-Ashbury in San Francisco. But at Stanford, thirty miles away, things remained relatively calm. Joan Baez was living in the area, and Marilyn once marched in an antiwar demonstration with her. My most vivid memory of this period is attending a huge Bob Dylan concert in San Jose, where Joan Baez unexpectedly came onstage for a few numbers. I became a lifelong Joan Baez fan, and was thrilled, years later, when I had the chance to dance with her after one of her café performances.

Like everyone else, we were devastated by the news of John F. Kennedy's assassination in 1963. It shattered the image that our peaceful lives in Palo Alto would be unaffected by the ills of the outside world, and we bought our first television set to witness the events surrounding Kennedy's death and memorial services. I eschewed all religious belief and practice, but in this instance, Marilyn, feeling the need for community and ritual, took our two older children—Eve, aged eight, and Reid, aged seven—to a religious service at the Stanford Memorial Church. Having not entirely escaped the pull of ceremony, we always held a Passover Seder at

FAMILY PORTRAIT, CA. 1975.

our home with family and friends. Never having learned Hebrew, I always asked a friend to read the ceremonial prayers.

Despite my unpleasant memories of childhood, I continued to favor the type of food I was raised on: Eastern European Jewish cuisine and no pork. Not Marilyn. Whenever I was out of town, the children knew she would serve them pork chops. I clung to some ceremonial rites. I had my sons circumcised, followed by a ceremonial repast with friends and family. Reid, the eldest of my three sons, chose to have a Bar Mitzvah. In addition to these few Jewish traditions, we had a Christmas tree, filled stockings for the children, and laid out a big Christmas Day feast.

I've often been asked whether my lack of religious belief has been a problem in my life or my psychiatric practice. My answer is always no. First, I should say that I am "nonreligious" rather than "antireligious." My stance was by no means unusual: for the overwhelming majority of my Stanford community and my medical and psychiatric colleagues, religion played little or no role in their lives. When I've spent time with my few devout friends (for example, Dagfinn Føllesdal, my Catholic Norwegian philosopher friend), I always feel tremendous respect for the depth of their faith, and I'm inclined to say that my secular views almost never influence my therapy practice. But I have to admit that in all my years of practice, only a handful of committed religious individuals have sought me out. My most frequent contact with devout individuals has come in my work with dying patients, and in every instance I welcome and support any religious comfort they can find.

Though I was deeply immersed in my work in the 1960s and largely apolitical, I couldn't help but notice cultural changes. My medical students and psychiatric residents began to wear sandals instead of "proper" shoes, and year by year their hair got longer and wilder. A couple of students brought me gifts of their home-baked bread. Marijuana infiltrated even faculty parties, and sexual mores were radically changing.

I already felt part of the old guard when these changes occurred and felt shocked the first time I saw a resident wearing red plaid trousers or other outrageous garb. But this was California, and there was no stopping such change. Gradually I loosened up, stopped wearing neckties, and enjoyed marijuana at some faculty parties, where I, too, wore bell-bottomed trousers.

In the 1960s, our three children—our fourth, Benjamin, was not born until 1969—were caught up in their own daily dramas. They attended the local public schools within walking distance of our home, made friends, took piano and guitar lessons, played tennis and baseball, learned to horseback ride, joined the Blue Birds and 4-H, and built a corral for two young goats in our backyard. Their friends from smaller homes often came over to our home to play. Our house was an old Spanish-style stucco with a front door surrounded by bright violet bougainvillea and a patio containing a small pond and fountain. The formal path leading

FAMILY ON WHEELS, PALO ALTO, 1960S.

down to the road was dominated by a majestic magnolia, around which the small children rode their tricycles. There was a neighborhood tennis court half a block from my home, where twice a week I played doubles with my neighbors, or, as they got older, with my three sons.

In June 1964, we visited my family in Washington, DC. We were at my sister's home with our three children when my mother and father drove over. I sat on a sofa with my daughter, Eve, and my son Reid on my lap. My son Victor and his cousin Harvey were playing on the floor nearby. My father, sitting in an adjoining upholstered chair, told me he had a headache, and two minutes later, suddenly and wordlessly, he lost consciousness and slumped over. I could feel no pulse. My brother-in-law, a cardiologist, had a syringe and Adrenalin in his physician's bag and I injected Adrenalin into my father's heart—but to no avail. Only later did I remember that just before he passed out I had seen his eyes fixated to his left, suggesting a stroke in the left side of his brain, not a cardiac arrest. My mother rushed into the room and clung to him. To this moment I can hear her crying, over and over, "Myneh Tierehle, Barel" ("My darling, Ben"). My tears flowed. I was astonished and deeply moved: it was the first time I had ever witnessed such tenderness from my mother, the first time I realized how much they loved one another. When the emergency unit came, I remember my mother still crying but saying to my sister and me, "Take his wallet." My sister and I ignored her pleas, and both of us felt critical of her for focusing on money at such a time. But she was right, of course: his wallet, cards, and money disappeared in the ambulance and were never seen again.

I had seen dead bodies before—my cadaver in the first year of medical school, bodies in pathology courses at the morgue— but this was the first dead body of someone I loved. It would not happen again for many years, until the death of Rollo May. My father's funeral was held at a cemetery in Anacostia, Maryland, and after the service each of the family members ceremoniously threw a shovelful of soil on the coffin. As I did so, I felt lightheaded, and my brother-in-law caught my arm and steadied me, lest I fall into the grave. My father died as he had lived, quietly and unobtrusively. Even to this day I regret not having known him better. When I've returned to the cemetery and walked up and down the rows of tombstones where my father and mother and their entire community from the small shtetl of Cielz lay, my heart has ached for the gulf between me and my parents and all that remained unsaid.

Sometimes when Marilyn describes her tender memories of walks in the park holding hands with her father, I feel bereft and cheated. Where were *my* walks and *my* father's attention? My father worked hard his entire life. His store was open until 10 p.m. five days a week and until midnight on Saturdays: he was free only on Sundays. My only tender memory of time spent with my father revolves around our Sunday chess games. I recall he was always pleased with my play, even when I began to beat him at about the age of ten or eleven. Unlike me, he never, not once, was annoyed by losing games. Perhaps this is the reason for my lifelong engagement with chess. Perhaps the game offers some shreds of contact with my hardworking, gentle father who never got to see me as a more mature adult.

W hen my father died, I was just beginning my life at Stanford. At the time I don't think I fully appreciated my extraordinary good fortune. I had a position at a great university, worked with total independence, and lived in a blessed enclave with perhaps the world's best weather. I never saw snow again (except at ski resorts). My friends, mostly colleagues at Stanford, were easygoing and enlightened. And never once did I ever again hear an anti-Semitic statement. Though we were not wealthy, Marilyn and I had the feeling of being able to do anything we wished. Our favorite getaway was Baja, California, at a colorful if modest location called Mulegé. We took our children there one Christmas, and they fully enjoyed the Mexican atmosphere replete with tortillas and piñatas. My children and I reveled in the snorkeling and spearfishing, which provided several delicious meals.

Marilyn returned to France for a conference in 1964 and wanted very much for the whole family to take a trip to Europe. What turned out was even better: a whole year in London.

CHAPTER EIGHTEEN
A YEAR IN LONDON

I n 1967, I received a career teaching award from the National Institute of Mental Health that permitted me to spend a year at the Tavistock Clinic in London. I planned to study the Tavistock approach to group therapy and begin working in earnest on a group therapy textbook. We found a house on Reddington Road in Hampstead close to the clinic, and our family of five (Ben, our youngest son, was not yet born) began a heavenly and memorable year abroad.

I had swapped offices with John Bowlby, an eminent British psychiatrist from the Tavistock Clinic who was spending the year at Stanford. His London office was in the center of the clinic, allowing me much contact with the faculty. During that year I would walk each morning from our house to the clinic, ten blocks away, passing a fine eighteenth-century church. The small churchyard inside its grounds contained a score of headstones, several of them askew and so worn that the names were unreadable. The larger cemetery across the street was the resting place of a few prominent nineteenth- and twentieth-century figures, such as the writer Daphne du Maurier. Nearby I passed a stately, pillared mansion in which General Charles de Gaulle had lived during the

German occupation of France. It was for sale for 100,000 pounds, and Marilyn and I often wished and fantasized that we had the funds to purchase it. A block farther was the huge mansion that had been used in the Mary Poppins film for the Julie Andrews and Dick Van Dyke rooftop dance scenes. Then, I continued down Finchley Road to Belsize Lane and entered a four-story nondescript building that housed the Tavistock Clinic.

John Sutherland, the head of the Tavistock, was a kind and most genial Scotsman. He greeted me graciously on my first day, introduced me to his staff, and invited me to attend all clinic seminars and to observe the staff-led therapy groups. I was introduced to the psychiatrists involved with group work, and throughout the year I had ongoing contact with Pierre Turquet, Robert Gosling, and Henry Ezriel. Though I found them to be astute and welcoming, their approach to group leadership struck me as bizarrely distant and unengaged. Tavistock group leaders never spoke directly to any particular member, but directed 100 percent of their comments to the ceiling, limiting themselves only to remarks about the "group." I recall a meeting one evening when one of the leaders, Pierre Turquet, said, "If all the members of this group have come in this ghastly rain from the far corners of London and choose to talk about cricket, well then, that's all right with me." The Tavistock group leaders followed the ideas of Wilfred Bion, which focused on the unconscious processes in groups as a whole and had little interest in the interpersonal realm, except as it related to leadership and authority. This was why comments were always made about the group as a whole and therapists never addressed an individual patient.

Though I liked some of the psychiatrists personally, especially Bob Gosling, who invited us to his home in London as well as to his country home, I concluded after a few months that this approach to group therapy was highly ineffective, noting that a great many patients voted with their feet: attendance was exceptionally poor. They had a rule that unless four members attended, the meeting would be canceled and, indeed, that was the case all too often.

Later that year I attended a weeklong Tavistock group conference at Leeds, with one hundred others from the fields of education, psychology, and business. I remember clearly how it began: the attendees were instructed to divide themselves up into five groups using five designated rooms. At the ringing of the starting bell, the attendees charged into the rooms. Some members vied for leadership, some demanded that the doors be closed lest the group get too large, and some insisted on rules for procedure. The workshop continued with ongoing meetings of the small groups, each assigned a faculty adviser who reflected on group process, and large group meetings, attended by all faculty and attendees, so that a study could be made of mass group dynamics.

Although Tavistock groups continue to be used as a training tool to help individuals learn about group dynamics and organizational behavior, the Tavistock approach in group psychotherapy has, to the best of my knowledge, mercifully faded away.

I generally observed one or two small group meetings a week and attended lectures or conferences, but for the most part during that year, I was completely on my own, fully engaged writing my group therapy textbook. The Tavistock faculty found my approach to groups as distasteful as I found theirs. When I presented my research work on "therapeutic factors" based on my interviews with a large number of successful group therapy patients, the British staff scoffed at the typical American fixation on the "satisfied customer." As the only American, I felt isolated and unsupported. A year later, when I met John Bowlby face-to-face, he told me that he had had similar experiences with the Tavistock staff, and at times had fantasized setting off a bomb in the audience. I felt so isolated, unappreciated, and uneasy in my skin that year that I decided to find a therapist for myself, as I've done at various difficult points throughout my life.

There were a great many schools of therapy in the United Kingdom at that time. The well-known British psychiatrist R. D. Laing came immediately to mind. From his writing, he seemed to be an arresting and original thinker. He had recently established Kingsley Hall, a site where psychotic patients and their therapists lived together in a healing community. Moreover, he treated patients in an egalitarian manner, which was very different from the Tavistock approach. When I attended a lecture he gave at Tavistock, I was impressed by his intelligence and rather enjoyed how his iconoclastic views ruffled the feathers of the establishment. But I also found him a bit disorganized, and I could easily understand why many members of the audience suggested that he was on LSD, his then-current drug of choice. Nonetheless, I chose to meet individually with him to discuss entering therapy. I recall asking him about his experience at Esalen in Big Sur, California, and his comments in his lecture about nude marathon groups being conducted there. He responded enigmatically, "I paddle my canoe and others paddle their canoes." I concluded that he was too unfocused for me. (Little did I think I would be attending a nude marathon group at Esalen a few years later.)

Next I consulted with the head of the Kleinian analytic school in London. I recall questioning his intense dredging for information about my first two years of life and asking why Kleinian analysis generally lasted seven to ten years. At the end of our two-hour consultation, he concluded (and I concurred) that my skepticism about his approach was too great. As he put it, "the volume of your background music [i.e., my resistance] will obscure the true chords of the analysis." You have to admire the Brits for their eloquence!

Eventually I chose to work with Charles Rycroft, who had been Laing's analyst. He was a leading London psychiatrist of the "middle school" influenced by the British analysts Fairbairn and Winnicott. For the next ten months, I met with Rycroft two times a week. He was in his mid-fifties, and quite thoughtful and kind, if a bit detached. Each time I entered his Harley Street office, which had a Dickensian air about it and was furnished with a thick Persian carpet, a couch, and two comfortable upholstered armchairs, he hurriedly snuffed out the cigarette he had been smoking between sessions, greeted me with a handshake, and politely invited me to take my chair (not the couch) that faced his. He treated me collegially. I especially recall him recounting his role in the psychoanalytic society's eviction of Masud Khan—an account I later re-created in my novel *Lying on the Couch*.

I profited from our sessions, but wished he would be more active and interactional. His complex interpretations almost never struck me as helpful, but even so, after a few weeks, my anxiety was ameliorated and I felt able to write more effectively. Why? Perhaps because of his reliable acceptance and empathy. It was extremely important for me to know I had someone on my side. In later years when I visited London, I paid him social visits, and we often reviewed our therapy together. When he said he regretted his adherence to the doctrine of offering only interpretations, I much appreciated his candor.

My work time in London was entirely devoted to writing the group therapy textbook. Since this was my first book, I had to invent my method and ended up drawing heavily from three major sources: my lecture notes from the courses I had given to the residents during the previous years, the hundreds of group summaries I had written and mailed to group members, and the group therapy research literature, much of it accessible through the Tavistock Clinic's excellent library. I didn't know how to type (most professionals did not type in those years). Each day I handwrote my three or four pages and gave them to a Tavistock typist, whom I hired privately to type my day's work each evening, to be ready for my revision the following morning.

Where to begin? I started with the very first questions faced by a group therapist: how to select patients and compose a group.

Selection consists of determining whether a particular patient is suitable for a particular type of group therapy. *Composing the group* addresses another question: If the patient is suitable and there are a number of groups with space for a new member, then which group would be best for that patient? Or consider yet another (extremely unlikely) scenario: Imagine a roster of a hundred patients, enough to form twelve groups. How should therapists go about composing these twelve groups so they will be maximally effective? With these questions in mind, I surveyed the research literature and wrote two scholarly, dense, highly detailed, and exceedingly boring chapters.

Just after I had completed the two chapters on patient selection and group composition, my chairman, David Hamburg, visited us in London and gave me the stunning, unexpected news that the tenure board of Stanford had met and granted me early tenure. I was not scheduled to be considered for tenure for another year and was, of course, overjoyed to have been spared the anxiety of waiting for the decision. In later years, as I saw colleagues and patients pass through that tortured ordeal, I grew to appreciate even more my own good fortune.

This news of my tenure dramatically affected my book project. No longer was I writing for the stern, empirically oriented, pinched-faced professors I imagined sitting on my tenure board. I felt joyfully emancipated and now began to write a textbook for an entirely different audience: for student practitioners struggling to learn how to be helpful to their patients. Hence, all subsequent chapters of the book are far livelier and are studded with clinical vignettes, some of them only a few lines, some of them three or four pages. But those first two chapters were like cement; they stuck in my craw and I never could find a way to enliven them. Twenty-five years later I published the fifth edition of *The Theory and Practice of Group Psychotherapy*, and even after four major revisions, each one requiring two years of intense literature review and editing, those two pre-tenure chapters (now chapters eight and nine) written in London seem misfits, written by a different person in stilted, deadly prose. When I write a sixth edition I am determined to renovate these two chapters.

My three children, aged nine, twelve, and thirteen, had been, naturally, reluctant to leave their Palo Alto school friends, but ultimately came to love their year in London. Our daughter, Eve, was dejected when she was turned down by the nearby Parliament Hill School because of poor penmanship, but she came to value the one she did attend, the Hampstead Heath School for Girls, where she made several good friends and ended the year with excellent, if evanescent, penmanship. Our son Reid went to the nearby University College School, where he proudly wore a red-and-black-striped jacket and cap. His poor penmanship, even worse than Eve's, had been duly noted but entirely overlooked because, as the school principal told me on several occasions, he was "a jolly good rugby player." Eight-year-old Victor thrived at the local British school. He was unhappy having to take daily naps there, but took much delight in visiting the penny sweet shop on his way home.

Though we had bought a car in Europe, we rarely used it in London and took the Tube everywhere: to the Royal National Theatre, to local poetry readings, to the British Museum and the Royal Albert Hall. Through Marilyn's contacts at a Franco-American literary magazine called *Adam*, we met Alex Comfort, with whom we remained close friends until his death in 2000. Alex was one of two geniuses I've been close to—the other was Josh Lederberg, a Stanford Nobel Prize–winning molecular biologist. At that time, Alex was splitting his time between a wife and a mistress and had a full wardrobe in each of their homes. With an encyclopedic mind, he could, and did, discourse endlessly on any and every subject—British and French literature, Indian mythology and art, worldwide sexual practices, his professional field of gerontology, seventeenth-century opera. He once told us that he had asked his wife what she wanted for Christmas and she had replied, "Anything but information!"

THE AUTHOR AND FAMILY, LONDON, WINTER 1967–1968.

I always enjoyed speaking to Alex—such a rare, fertile, engaging mind. I knew that he was strongly drawn to Marilyn, but he and I also formed a friendship, not only in London, but also later when he came to our house in Palo Alto.

Alex finally divorced his wife, married his mistress, and wrote *The Joy of Sex*, one of the all-time bestsellers. Then, mainly to escape British taxes, he moved to a Santa Barbara think tank, the Center for the Study of Democratic Institutions, only a few hours away from Palo Alto. Though *The Joy of Sex* was his best-known work, Alex wrote fifty other books, from works in gerontology to poetry and novels. He wrote quickly and with great ease. I was amazed and daunted by his fluency: his first draft was often his last, whereas I have written between ten and twenty drafts of every book I've published. My children knew his name before they ever met him, because several of Alex's poems were included in an anthology of modern poetry that was their textbook in their Palo Alto school. Walking with him down the street in our neighborhood was a treat, as Alex would immediately recognize bird-calls, name the bird, and effortlessly reproduce the sound.

E ven though London entranced us, we were dedicated Californians and greatly missed the sun. A helpful travel agent
sent our entire family off for a week's vacation to Djerba, a large
island off the coast of Tunisia, that, legend has it, was the island
of the Lotus Eaters where Odysseus was stranded. We visited ba-
zaars, Roman ruins, and a 2,000-year-old synagogue. As I entered,
a caretaker dressed in Arab garb asked if I was one of the tribe,
and when I nodded, he took my arm and walked me arm in arm
to the Bimah, the altar in the center of the synagogue. He put an
ancient Bible in my hand but, thankfully, did not test my Hebrew.

CHAPTER NINETEEN
THE BRIEF, TURBULENT LIFE OF ENCOUNTER GROUPS

I n California and in many other parts of the country during the mid-1960s and early 1970s, the encounter group movement exploded. Encounter groups were everywhere—and some of them so closely resembled therapy groups that they interested me enormously. The Free University in Menlo Park, a community adjoining Stanford University, posted advertisements for dozens of personal growth groups. The living rooms of Stanford dorms hosted a variety of encounter groups: twenty-four-hour marathon groups, psychodrama groups, T-groups, human potential groups. Moreover, many Stanford students sought group experiences in nearby growth centers like Esalen, or, like hundreds of thousands across the country, joined EST or Lifespring, which both had large meetings that often broke out into smaller encounter-type groups.

I was as puzzled as anyone. Were these groups, as many feared, a menace, a harbinger of social disintegration? Or were they just the opposite? Was it possible that they effectively enhanced personal growth? The more extravagant the claims, the more raucous the zealots and the more shrill the conservative response. I observed T-groups led by well-trained leaders, and it seemed to me that many members profited. I also attended rather wild drop-in psychodrama groups that concerned me, causing me to wonder whether members might have been psychologically damaged. I attended a twenty-four-hour nude marathon group at Esalen, but had no follow-up on the effects of the experience on the group. It seemed to me that some of the fifteen members of the group profited, but I had no way of knowing the effects on less vocal members. Many praised these new experimental groups; many others damned them. The situation begged for some empirical evaluation.

I heard a talk by Mort Lieberman, a University of Chicago professor, at a group therapy conference in Chicago and was much impressed with his work. We spoke for hours well into the night and agreed to undertake an ambitious inquiry into the effects of encounter groups. Our interests overlapped: not only was he an esteemed social science researcher, but he had also been trained as a T-group leader and as a group therapist. He made plans to spend a full year at Stanford, and we soon enlisted Matt Miles, a professor of education and psychology at Columbia University as well as a researcher and expert statistician, to join our team. The three of us designed an ambitious study of the effectiveness of encounter groups. Encounter groups were much in evidence on the Stanford campus, and many faculty members were concerned that students might suffer harm from the forceful confrontations, the uncensored feedback, and the antiestablishment posture of the groups. In fact, the university administration was so concerned about these groups on campus that they immediately granted us permission to conduct research on them. To ensure a large sample, the university even permitted us to offer college credit for encounter group participation.

Our final research design called for a sample of 210 students who were randomly assigned to a control sample or to one of twenty groups, each group meeting for a total of thirty hours. The students would receive three credits for the course. We selected ten currently popular methodologies and offered two groups from each methodology:

Traditional NTL T-groups
Encounter (or personal growth) groups
Gestalt therapy groups
Esalen (sensory awareness groups)
TA (transactional analytic) groups
Psychodrama groups
Synanon (confrontational "hot seat") groups
Psychoanalytically oriented groups
Marathon groups
Leaderless, tape-led groups

Next we recruited two well-known expert group leaders from each of these modalities. Mort Lieberman developed a large battery of instruments to measure changes in the members and to assess the leaders' behavior, and we enlisted and trained a team of observers to study members and leaders during each meeting. Once the university human research panel approved our research plan, we embarked on this memorable project—it would be the largest and most rigorous study of such groups ever conducted.

At the end of the study we wrote a five-hundred-page monograph published by Basic Books, *Encounter Groups: First Facts*. The overall findings were impressive: *about 40 percent of students taking a one-quarter college course underwent significant positive personal change that endured for at least six months.* However, there were also sixteen "casualties"—students who reported feeling worse six months after their group experience.

I wrote the chapters describing the clinical development and evolution of each group, the behavior of the leaders, and the effects on the "high-learners" and the "casualties." The casualty chapter received enormous attention from opponents of the encounter group movement and was cited in hundreds of newspapers across the country. It provided the conservative right exactly the ammunition they wanted. On the other hand, my chapter on high-learners, the large number of students who reported substantial personal change as a result of twelve group meetings, received no attention whatsoever. This was most unfortunate, for I've always felt keenly that such groups, properly led, have much to offer.

Ten years later, the encounter group movement had faded away—it had been replaced by Bible groups in many of the Stanford dorms. And, with the demise of encounter groups, our book *Encounter Groups: First Facts* lost its readership, aside from scholars, who found many of the research instruments useful. Of all my books, it alone has gone out of print. My wife was never a friend of this project because it demanded so much of my time, and because a crucial staff meeting prevented me from driving her home from the Stanford Hospital after she delivered our fourth child, Benjamin Blake. She recalls that one of the reviewers of the book commented, "These authors must have worked very hard because the prose was so tired."

I continued working on my group textbook (*The Theory and Practice of Group Psychotherapy*) for two more years, and when I finished the final draft I flew to New York to meet publishers whom David Hamburg had contacted on my behalf. I lunched with Arthur Rosenthal, the impressive founder of Basic Books, and chose to publish with him despite offers from other presses. Reviewing my life in these pages reminds me of the extent to which David Hamburg not only supported my research but also facilitated my publishing career.

The Theory and Practice of Group Psychotherapy was immediately successful, and within a year or two it was adopted as a textbook by most of the psychotherapy training programs in the country; later, it was adopted in many other countries as well. Instrumental in the training of group therapists, the textbook has gone through five revised editions and sold over 1 million copies, which, over time, gave Marilyn and me a new degree of financial security. Like most of the young psychiatry faculty, I had augmented my income by consulting on weekends at various psychiatric hospitals, but once the textbook was published, I stopped my weekend consulting and instead accepted invitations to lecture on group therapy.

My entire approach to remuneration was radically altered one day about five years after publication of my textbook, when I addressed a large audience at Fordham University in New York City. As usual, I brought with me a videotape of a group therapy meeting I had held the previous week, which I intended to use in my teaching. However, the Fordham videotape player malfunctioned and the technicians finally threw up their hands, leaving me with the daunting and stressful task of improvising for the entire morning. I gave my two prepared lectures in the afternoon and had a lengthy Q-and-A session with the audience, and by the end of the day I was entirely exhausted. As the audience was filing out, I happened to peruse the printed program and took note that the fee for the workshop was $40 (this was in 1980). I looked around the auditorium and estimated that there were upward of six hundred attendees. A quick calculation indicated that the sponsors of the talk had made over $20,000, and they were paying me $400! From that time on I contracted for a fair share of the funds raised at each conference, and my speaking income soon dwarfed my university salary.

CHAPTER TWENTY
SOJOURN IN VIENNA

Vienna had always loomed large in my consciousness because it was the birthplace of Freud and the cradle of psychotherapy. Having read through many biographies of Freud, I had a great sense of familiarity with the storied city that had housed so many of my favorite writers, including Stefan Zweig, Franz Werfel, Arthur Schnitzler, Robert Musil, and Joseph Roth. Thus, in 1970, I quickly accepted Stanford's offer to teach undergraduate students for a summer quarter at the Stanford campus in Vienna. The move was not without complications: I had four children, then aged fifteen, fourteen, eleven, and one. We brought with us a twenty-year-old neighbor and friend of my daughter's, who would live with us in the students' dorm and help care for Ben, our youngest child. I welcomed the opportunity to work with Stanford undergraduates, and Marilyn, as always, loved the possibility of a European sojourn.

It was wondrous to live in the center of Vienna, where Freud had lived. I plunged into his world, walking the streets he had walked, visiting his cafés, and gawking at a large unmarked five-story apartment building at Berggasse 19, Freud's home for forty-nine years. Years later, the Sigmund Freud Foundation bought this building, turned it into the Freud Museum, prominently marked it with a large red banner, and opened it to visitors, but at the time of my visit, there was no indication whatsoever that he had ever lived and worked there. The city had placed scores of brass plaques marking the homes of prominent and not-so-prominent Viennese, including several for Mozart's residences, but nothing to signal the lifetime dwelling of Sigmund Freud.

Seeing Freud's home and walking through the streets of his Vienna served me well thirty years later when I wrote my novel *When Nietzsche Wept*. I drew on these memories and the photos I took that year to create a credible visual setting for my imagined meetings of Nietzsche and the famed Viennese physician Josef Breuer, who had been Freud's mentor.

My primary teaching assignment in Vienna was a course for Stanford undergraduates on the life and work of Sigmund Freud. The forty lectures I prepared became the basis of a "Freud Appreciation" course that I taught to psychiatric residents for the next fifteen years. I always emphasized to my students that Freud was not just the creator of psychoanalysis (accounting for less than 1 percent of all the therapy offered today), but that he invented the entire field of psychotherapy: it did not exist in any form prior to Freud. Though I have my criticisms of contemporary orthodox Freudian analysis, I have always felt great respect for Freud's creativity and courage. He is very often in my mind when I do therapy. Recently, for example, I met with a new patient who was plagued with obscene obsessions about members of his family, and I immediately thought of Freud's observation that behind such persistent obsessions there is often rage. I regret that Freud has fallen so far out of fashion. As one of my chapter titles in *The Gift of Therapy* declares, "Freud wasn't always wrong."

Just before leaving Stanford for Vienna, I suffered two significant traumatic events. First, I was jolted by the death from adrenal cancer of a close friend, Al Weiss, whom I had met when he was a resident at Stanford. Among other things, Al and I were spearfishing buddies and had taken trips together to Baja.

Then, at a dental appointment the day before my departure, my dentist found a suspicious lesion on my gums. He took a biopsy and told me I would receive the pathology report after my arrival in Vienna. I was reading at the time about Freud's fatal oral cancer, likely caused by heavy cigar smoking, and grew alarmed at my own smoking habits: I smoked a pipe much of the day, choosing a different pipe each day from my collection, and reveling in the aroma of Balkan Sobranie tobacco. As I waited in Vienna for the report, I grew extremely anxious at the thought that I might soon learn I had the same cancer that killed Freud.

I quit smoking cold turkey that first week in Vienna and consequently had difficulty sleeping, and sucked bag after bag of coffee-flavored hard candies to ease my oral cravings. Finally I received a wire from my dentist informing me that my biopsy was negative. Still, however, I was left to mourn my friend as I awaited my family's arrival. I tried to force myself to work—I had come to Vienna a week early to prepare forty lectures—but remained so anxious that I decided to seek help. I attempted to consult with an eminent Viennese therapist, Viktor Frankl, author of the widely read *Man's Search for Meaning*, but was informed by his telephone answering service that he was overseas on a lecture trip.

When my wife and children arrived, I settled down and grew more comfortable, and our three-month stay in Vienna with the Stanford students ended up to be an unforgettably positive experience for all of us. The two older children were especially thrilled by all the daily contact with Stanford students. We took all our meals with the students, including one dinner when our son Ben celebrated his first birthday. A large cake appeared at our table and the entire student body sang "Happy Birthday" while my daughter, Eve, held him up to the audience. Marilyn took each of the children individually to the Sacher Hotel for one of the rightfully famed *Sachertorte*, the best pastry I have ever tasted.

We accompanied the students on two class trips. The first was a boat trip down the Danube, which was lined with millions of dazzling, fully alert sunflowers that turned their faces toward the sun as it moved across the sky. The day ended with a tour of Budapest, gray and austere under Russian occupation, but still charming. Then, at the very end of the quarter, we accompanied the class on a train trip to Zagreb, where we said our final farewells. Having left our children at the Stanford dorm with their nanny, Marilyn and I rented a car for a few days and drove down the unforgettably beautiful Dalmatian coast to Dubrovnik, and from there through the peaceful Serbian countryside.

Though my time in Vienna was heavily focused on coursework and the students, it was impossible to resist the cultural treasures. Marilyn guided me through the Belvedere Museum and introduced me to the work of Gustav Klimt and Egon Schiele, who have since become, along with Vincent van Gogh, my favorite painters. Though I never mentioned Klimt to my German publishers, years later they chose to use his work for the covers of almost all my books in German translation.

The children took walks in the verdant city parks, careful not to step on the grass—lest elderly Viennese woman scold them—and they hiked in the woods around the city, where people greeted each other with a friendly "Grüss Gott." And, of course, we went to the opera for an unforgettable performance of *The Tales of Hoffmann*. Vienna offered us an opulent vista on a legendary world that had only recently recovered from its Nazi past. Not in my wildest dreams could I have imagined that, forty years later, the city would award a prize to one of my books, distribute 100,000 free copies, and honor me with weeklong festivities.

Toward the end of our stay I finally reached Viktor Frankl on the phone and introduced myself as a Stanford professor of psychiatry troubled by some personal issues and in need of help. He said he was extremely busy, but he agreed to see me in the late afternoon of the same day.

Frankl, a short, attractive, white-haired man, greeted me genially at the door and took an immediate interest in my eyeglasses, asking me right away about the manufacturer. I had no idea and took them off and handed them to him. They were cheap frames purchased from a California chain called Four Eyes and, after a brief inspection, he found them of little interest. His own thick steel-gray frames were quite handsome and I told him so. He smiled and guided me to his living room, pointing out, by a wave of his hand, an enormous bookcase filled with translations of his book *Man's Search for Meaning.*

We sat in a sunny corner of the living room and Frankl began by saying he might not be able to meet too long, as he had just arrived home the previous day from a trip to the UK and had answered his fan mail until 4 in the morning. I found that odd: it seemed as if he was attempting to impress me. Moreover, he didn't ask my reasons for contacting him, but instead expressed great interest in the psychiatric community at Stanford. He asked many questions, and then immediately segued into a description of the rigidity of the Viennese psychiatric community, which had refused to recognize his contributions. I began to feel I was at the Mad Hatter's tea party: I had sought him out for a therapy consultation, but he was seeking consolation from me about the disrespectful treatment he had received from the Viennese professional community. His complaints continued for the rest of our session, during which he asked me nothing at all about my reasons for coming. In our next meeting, the following day, he raised the question of whether he might be invited to address the Stanford psychiatric staff and students in California. I promised I would try to arrange it.

Man's Search for Meaning, a moving and inspiring book written in 1946, has been read by millions of people worldwide and even today remains a bestseller in psychology. In it Frankl tells the story of his experience during the Holocaust and how his determination to share his story with the entire world was responsible for his survival. I have heard his primary lecture on meaning in life several times: he was an excellent speaker and never failed to deliver an inspiring talk.

His visit to Stanford a few months later, however, was highly problematic. It was clear during his visit to our home with his wife that he was not comfortable with the informal California culture. On one occasion my au pair, a young woman from Switzerland, who lived with us and helped care for our children, came to us in tears because of the scolding she had received from him: he had requested tea, and she had served it in a ceramic rather than a porcelain cup.

A clinical demonstration he offered to Stanford residents took a catastrophic turn. His logotherapy demonstration consisted, for the most part, of his determining, in a ten- to fifteen-minute inquiry, what the patient's life meaning should be, and prescribing it to the patient in authoritarian fashion. At one point during a demonstration interview, one of the more obstreperous, long-haired, sandal-wearing psychiatric residents stood up in protest and stalked out of the room, muttering, "This is inhuman!" It was a terrible moment for all, and no amount of apology would soothe Viktor, who repeatedly demanded that the resident be dismissed from the program.

There were times I tried to offer him feedback, but he almost always interpreted it as hurtful criticism. We corresponded a good bit after he left California, and a year later he sent me a manuscript, seeking my critique. One passage described, in great detail, a lecture he had given at Harvard, during which the audience had stood and applauded loudly five times. I was in a quandary: he had asked for my commentary, though, so, after agonizing over my response, I decided to be genuine. I replied, as gently as possible, that such heavy focus on the applause deterred from his presentation and might lead some readers to conclude that he was over-invested in the applause. He wrote back immediately, saying, "Irv, you just won't understand—you weren't there: they DID rise and applaud five times." Even the best of us are sometimes blinded by our wounds and our need for praise.

Very recently, I read an autobiographical account of student days at the Medical University of Vienna in the 1960s written by

Professor Hans Steiner, a Stanford colleague and friend, who offered another perspective. As a student in Vienna, Hans had had an extremely positive experience with Viktor Frankl: he described him as an excellent teacher, whose creative approach felt like a breath of fresh air in contrast to the rigidity of the other psychiatric faculty in Vienna.

Years later Viktor Frankl and I both spoke at a large psychotherapy conference and I attended his lecture on *Man's Search for Meaning*. As always, he enthralled the audience and received a thunderous ovation. We met afterward and I got a warm hug from him and his wife, Eleanor. Years later, when writing *Existential Psychotherapy*, I reviewed his work thoroughly and realized, more than ever, the importance of his innovative and fundamental contributions to our field. More recently, I visited a psychotherapy graduate school institute in Moscow that offered a PhD in logotherapy, and I was captivated by a life-sized photograph of Viktor. While gazing at it, I suddenly became aware of the magnitude of his courage as well as the depth of his pain. I knew from his book how the horrors of his stay in Auschwitz had traumatized him, but in those early encounters with him in Vienna and Stanford I was not ready to empathize fully with him or offer the support I might have given. Later, in my relationship with other leading figures in the field, such as Rollo May, I would not repeat that error.

CHAPTER TWENTY-ONE
EVERY DAY GETS A LITTLE CLOSER

W riting this memoir has caused me to look back over the arc of my life's work as a writer. At some point, I made a transition from writing research-oriented articles and books for other academics to writing about therapy for a more general public, and I trace the first stirrings of this metamorphosis to a strange book with a bizarre title, *Every Day Gets a Little Closer*, published in 1974. In this book I moved away from quantitative research language and sought to emulate the storytellers I had been reading all my life. I had no idea at that time that I would go on to teach about psychotherapy through four novels and three collections of stories.

My metamorphosis began when, in the late 1960s, I introduced into my therapy group Ginny Elkins (pseudonym), a Stegner Fellow in creative writing at Stanford. Her therapy was problematic because of her extreme shyness and reluctance to request or accept attention from the group. After a few months she completed her fellowship and took an evening teaching job that conflicted with the meeting time of the group.

Though Ginny wanted to continue individual therapy with me, she couldn't afford the Stanford fee, so I suggested an unusual arrangement. I agreed to waive the fee if she would write a summary after each session describing all the feelings and thoughts she had *not* verbalized during our time together. I, for my part, would do exactly the same, and we would hand them in sealed envelopes to my secretary. Then, after several weeks of therapy, we would read each other's summaries.

Why this unusual, strange proposal? For one thing, Ginny viewed me unrealistically—in psychotherapy lingo, she had soaring positive transference: she idealized me, was persistently deferential, and infantilized herself in my presence. It seemed to me that it might be useful reality-testing for her to read my raw, uncensored thoughts after each of our sessions, and, in particular, to learn of my doubts and uncertainty about how to help her. So I intended to be more self-disclosing in therapy with the hope of encouraging her to do the same.

But there was another, more personal, reason: I longed to be a writer—a real writer. I had felt stifled by the labor of writing a scholarly five-hundred-page textbook, followed by collaborating in a five-hundred-page research monograph on encounter groups. I imagined this plan with Ginny might afford me an unusual exercise, an opportunity to break my professional shackles, to find my voice by expressing anything that came to mind immediately after each hour. Moreover, Ginny was a masterful wordsmith, and I thought she might feel more comfortable communicating through the written rather than the spoken word.

Our exchange of notes every few months was highly instructive. Whenever participants study their own relationship, they are plunged more deeply into their encounter. Each time we read each other's summaries, our therapy was enriched. Moreover, the notes provided a Rashomon-like experience: though we had lived through the same hour, we *experienced* the hour very differently and valued different parts of the session. My elegant and brilliant

interpretations? Alas, she never even heard them! Instead she valued the small personal acts I barely noticed: my complimenting
her clothing or appearance, my awkward apologies for arriving
a couple of minutes late, my chuckling at her satire, my teaching
her how to relax.

For years afterward, I used our summaries in my psychotherapy classes with psychiatry residents, and I was struck by the students' intense interest in our different voices and points of view.
When I showed the summaries to Marilyn, she thought they read
like an epistolary novel, suggested they be published as a book, and
immediately volunteered to edit them. Shortly afterward, she and
our son Victor went on a skiing trip, and while Victor had skiing
classes each morning, she pruned and clarified our summaries.

Ginny was enthusiastic about the publishing project: it would
be her first book and we agreed that we would share the royalties equally, and Marilyn would receive 20 percent. In 1974, Basic
Books published the book under the title *Every Day Gets a Little
Closer*. In retrospect, Marilyn's subtitle suggestion, *A Twice-Told
Therapy* (adapted from Hawthorne), would have been far better,
but Ginny loved the old Buddy Holly song "Everyday" and had always wanted that to be her wedding song. A few years later, when
the Buddy Holly film came out, I listened very carefully to the
lyrics and was startled to discover that Ginny had gotten the line
wrong. The lyrics were actually "Every day it's a-gettin' closer."

Ginny and I each wrote a foreword and afterword, and I have
an indelible memory of writing mine. Though I had done much
professional writing in my office in the psychiatry outpatient department, I found it too busy and noisy for writerly inspiration.
Psychiatry at that time occupied the south wing of the Stanford
Hospital, with offices for the chairman and faculty and many therapy rooms. Just adjacent was the wing occupied by Carl Pribram,
a faculty member conducting research on monkeys, one of which
would from time to time escape and romp through the clinic and
waiting room, wreaking havoc. And just beyond Pribram's lab was

the file room, where patients' records were stored. It was a dusky, windowless spot, but quiet and entirely private, and large enough for me to pace about, construct complex sentences, and read them aloud to myself. I liked that ghastly room: it brought to mind my study in the basement where, for countless hours as an adolescent, I had written poetry meant only for my own ears (though occasionally I read some to Marilyn).

I luxuriated in the hours I spent in that dusky room, searching for the right tone. It was a critical turning point—no data, no facts, no statistics, no teaching—just letting my thoughts rove. I can't sing, but I was singing to myself. I'm certain, too, that the mountain of charts around me, thousands of patient stories, seeped into my consciousness as I began my foreword:

> *It always wrenches me to find old appointment books filled with the half-forgotten names of patients with whom I have had the most tender experiences. So many people, so many fine moments. What has happened to them? My many-tiered file cabinets, my mounds of tape recordings often remind me of some vast cemetery: lives pressed into clinical folders, voices trapped on electromagnetic bands mutely and eternally playing out their drama. Living with these monuments imbues me with a keen sense of transiency. Even as I find myself immersed in the present, I sense the specter of decay watching and waiting—a decay that will ultimately vanquish lived experience and yet, by its very inexorability, bestows a poignancy and beauty. The desire to relate my experience with Ginny is a very compelling one; I am intrigued by the opportunity to stave off decay, to prolong the span of our brief life together. How much better to know that it will exist in the mind of the reader rather than in the abandoned warehouse of unread clinical notes and unheard electromagnetic tapes.*

Writing that foreword was a vital moment of transition. I searched for a more lyrical voice and at the same time turned my attention to the phenomenon of transiency, my entry point into an existential worldview.

About the same time that I was seeing Ginny in therapy, I had another literary encounter. One of Marilyn's colleagues presented us with a rare behind-the-scenes glance at Ernest Hemingway, who had committed suicide in 1961. In a university library her colleague had seen a cache of unpublished letters Hemingway had written to his friend Buck Lanham, the commanding general of one of the Normandy invasion armies. Though he was not permitted to copy them, Marilyn's colleague furtively dictated the letters into a small recorder, transcribed them, and lent us his copy for a few days, permitting us to paraphrase but not quote from them.

The letters shed considerable light on Hemingway's psyche. I collected some more information by traveling to Washington, DC, to visit Buck Lanham, at that time an executive at Xerox, who was kind enough to speak to me of his friendship with Hemingway. After rereading many of Hemingway's works, Marilyn and I hired babysitters and took off for a long, secluded weekend at the Villa Montalvo Arts Center in Saratoga, California, to collaborate on an article.

Our article, "Hemingway: A Psychiatric View," was published in 1971 in the *Journal of the American Psychiatric Association* and was instantaneously picked up by hundreds of newspapers around the world. Nothing that either of us has written, before or since, has ever attracted such attention.

In the article we examined the sense of inadequacy underlying Hemingway's blustering exterior. Though he had toughened and relentlessly driven himself in difficult masculine endeavors, such as boxing, deep-sea fishing, and big-game hunting, he was vulnerable and childlike in his letters to General Lanham. He venerated the real thing—the strong and courageous military leader—and spoke of himself as a "chickenshit writer." Though I appreciate him greatly as a writer, I did not admire his public persona—it was too abrasive, too hypermasculine, too lacking in empathy, too besotted with alcohol. Reading his letters revealed a softer, more self-critical child bedazzled by the truly tough, coura-geous grown-ups in the world.

We laid out our intentions early in the article:

> While we appreciate the existential considerations generated by Hemingway's encounters with danger and death, we do not find the same measure of universality and timelessness as with a Tolstoy, or a Conrad, or a Camus. Why, we ask ourselves, is this so? Why is the Hemingway worldview so restricted? We suspect that the limitations of Hemingway's visions are related to his per-sonal psychological restrictions. . . . Just as there is no doubt he was an extremely gifted writer, there is also no doubt he was an extremely troubled man, relentlessly driven all his life, who in a paranoid depressive psychosis killed himself at the age of 62.

Though Marilyn and I always collaborate closely—each of us reading drafts of each other's writing—this is the only piece we've ever written together. We still remember this experience with pleasure and feel that perhaps, even at our advanced age, we will find another joint project.

CHAPTER TWENTY-TWO

OXFORD AND THE ENCHANTED COINS OF MR. SFICA

My many years at Stanford often blur together in my memory, but my sabbaticals stand out clearly etched in my mind. During the early 1970s I continued to teach medical students and residents and enlisted many of them as collaborators in psychotherapy research. I published journal articles on group therapy for alcoholics and group therapy for bereaved spouses. At some point my publisher asked me to undertake a second edition of my group therapy textbook. Knowing this project would require my full attention, I applied for a six-month sabbatical, and, in 1974, Marilyn and I and our five-year-old son, Ben, left for Oxford, where I would have an office in the psychiatry department of the Warneford Hospital. Our daughter, Eve, had begun college at Wesleyan, and my other two sons remained behind to finish the school year in Palo Alto under the care of old friends, who would stay with them in our home.

We had rented a house in the center of Oxford, but shortly before we arrived, a British airliner crashed, killing all passengers, including the father of the rental family. So, at the last minute, we scrambled to find another Oxford residence. When we found that none were available, we rented a charming old thatched-roof cottage in the small one-pub village of Black Bourton, about thirty minutes away from Oxford.

Black Bourton was small, very British, and very secluded: perfect conditions for writing! Revising a textbook is demanding and dull work, but necessary if the book is to remain relevant. I analyzed some research I had just completed, seeking to understand more about what really helped patients during therapy. I had given a large sample of successful group therapy patients a questionnaire of fifty-five statements (related to catharsis, understanding, support, guidance, universality, group cohesiveness, etc.), and just on a whim at the last minute, I threw in a cluster of five unorthodox statements I labeled as "existential factors"— statements such as "recognizing that no matter how close I get to others, I must still face life alone," or "recognizing there is no escape from some of life's pain and from death." I had asked patients to sort these into piles (a "Q sort") from least to most helpful, and was amazed to find that this whole throw-in category of existential factors ranked far higher than I had expected. Clearly, existential factors were playing a greater role in effective group therapy than we had realized, and I set about making this explicit in a new chapter.

As I was starting to address this idea I received a call from the United States informing me that I had just been awarded the prestigious Strecker Award in psychiatry. I was very pleased, of course, but not for long. Two days later, an official letter arrived providing details: I was required to give an address to a large audience in Pennsylvania a year hence. No problem with that. But next I learned I had to submit a monograph on a topic of my choice within four months to be published by the University of

Pennsylvania in a limited edition. Writing that monograph was the last thing in the world I wanted to do: once I start a writing project I get very single-minded and put everything else on hold. I considered declining the prize, but several colleagues dissuaded me, and eventually I arrived at a compromise: I would write my monograph on existential factors in group therapy, and it would serve double duty—both as the Strecker monograph and as a chapter in my textbook revision. As I look back on that moment, I believe this was the beginning of the work that would culminate in my textbook *Existential Psychotherapy*.

Black Bourton lies in the Cotswolds, a bucolic region in southern England renowned for its vivid green fields ablaze with blossoms in spring and summer. The local preschool where we placed Ben was excellent, and overall the living was superb, but for one thing—the weather. We had been spoiled by sunny California and, in mid-June, Marilyn bought a heavy sheepskin coat. By late July we were so damp and so sun-starved that one rainy morning we found ourselves at a travel agency in Oxford requesting a flight to the nearest sunny and inexpensive spot. The agent smiled knowingly—she had dealt with whining California tourists before—and booked us a trip to Greece. "You and Greece," she assured us, "will become the best of friends."

We enrolled Ben in a congenial summer camp in Winchester, and our son Victor, who had joined us in June at the end of his school term, went on a youth bicycle tour in Ireland. Then Marilyn and I boarded a plane for Athens. From there, the following day, we would begin a five-day bus tour of the promised eternally sunny Peloponnesus.

We landed in Athens feeling lighthearted and ready to explore, but our luggage had failed to arrive. We had only a carry-on containing mostly books, and we found a small general store still open in the late evening near our hotel in Athens, where we purchased travel essentials: a razor, shaving cream, toothbrushes, toothpaste, underwear, and a black-and-red-striped sundress for

Marilyn. For the next five days we wore the same clothes, and when Marilyn wished to swim, she wore her one T-shirt and my underpants. Our dismay over our lost luggage soon evaporated and we grew accustomed to traveling light. In fact, as the days passed, we found ourselves grinning as we watched our fellow tourists grunting as they loaded their big suitcases on the bus, while we hopped on free as birds. Disencumbered, we felt ourselves more deeply connected to the places we visited: Mount Olympus, where the first Olympic Games had taken place over 2,500 years ago; the ancient theater of Epidaurus; and the mountain site of the Delphic oracles, which Marilyn loved most of all, comparing it to Vézelay, France, for its beauty and spiritual loftiness. At the end of the tour we returned to the airport, and there, to our utter astonishment, saw our two bags circling on the empty carousel. With some ambivalence, we collected them and embarked for our next stop, Crete.

At the Crete airport we rented a small car and spent the next week leisurely circling the island. Only shards of memory persist after forty years, but both Marilyn and I remember that first night on Crete sitting in a taverna, looking at the light of the moon reflected in the flowing water of the canal passing only a few feet from our table, marveling at appetizers we'd never seen before: platters of baba ghanoush, tzatziki, taramasalata, dolmades, spanakopita, tiropita, keftedes. I loved these so much I never ordered a main course in Crete.

"I want nothing. I fear nothing. I am free." Nikos Kazantzakis's words brought a shiver to my skin as I read them the following day on his tombstone just outside the ancient Venetian walls surrounding the city of Heraklion, the capital of Crete. Having been excommunicated by the Greek Orthodox Church for writing the very book I had just read on the flight to Greece, *The Last Temptation of Christ*, Kazantzakis was forbidden a burial within the city. I knelt by his tomb to pay homage to this great spirit and spent much of the remainder of our trip reading his *Odyssey: A Modern Sequel*.

At the immense palace of Knossos, we were entranced by the frescoes of powerful bare-breasted women carrying offerings for sacrifices presided over by priestesses. As she has ever since I've known her, Marilyn gave me an informed tour and was particularly attentive to the predominance of these feminine figures. She would discuss them twenty years later in her 1997 book *The History of the Breast*.

We drove up into the mountains and made our way to an austere Cretan monastery. Although we were invited for lunch, we were permitted to visit only a very small part of the monastery, lest we disturb the meditation of the monks. Besides, no females were allowed to enter the main monastery—not even female animals, including hens!

While in Heraklion we set out looking for ancient Greek coins as a high school graduation present for our oldest son, Reid. In the very first shop we were told it was illegal to sell ancient coins to tourists, but every coin merchant ignored that dictum and readily—if furtively—showed us a private cache. Of all the coin shops, we were most impressed by Sfica's, directly across from the National Museum, with a large golden painting of a bumblebee on the front window. After a lengthy discussion with the genial and knowing Mr. Sfica, we bought a Greek silver coin for Reid and two others that Marilyn and I would wear as pendants. He assured us we could return them at any time if we were dissatisfied. The following day we visited a small basement shop owned by a wizened Jewish antique dealer. There we bought some inexpensive silver Roman coins and, in the course of our transaction, showed him the coins we had just purchased from Sfica. He examined them briefly and pronounced, with great authority, "Fakes—good fakes. But fakes all the same."

We returned to Sfica's and requested a refund. As though he were expecting us, he strode, without a word, to his cash register and with great dignity extracted an envelope containing our money. He handed it to us saying, "I return your money as I had promised but with one condition: you will no longer be welcome in this store."

As we continued on our trip around the island, we stopped at other coin shops and more than once described our encounter at Sfica's. "What?" they all said. "You insulted Sfica? Sfica, the official appraiser for the National Museum?" They put their hands to their temples and rocked side-to-side saying, "You owe him an apology."

We never found a suitable replacement gift and began to question our decision to return the coins. On the last night of our stay in Crete we decided to make use of a vacation gift from a colleague at Oxford: a skinny marijuana joint. Unaccustomed to smoking, we lit up and went to dinner at one of the outdoor restaurants in the market area, where for hours we relished the magical food, music, and dancing. After dinner, we wandered through the streets of Heraklion and grew disoriented, then a bit paranoid, thinking we were being followed by the police. Unable to find a taxi, we rushed through the maze of streets trying to find our hotel, and somehow, late at night, ended up on an empty street in front of a store with a large bumblebee painted on the window—Sfica's Coin Store! As we stood gawking at the bumblebee, an empty taxi miraculously appeared. We hailed it and were soon back in the safety of our hotel.

Our flight back to London didn't leave until early afternoon, and as Marilyn and I lingered over our breakfast of Cretan cheesecake, we discussed the previous night. Skeptic though I am, I could not help wondering if we had been sent some type of mysterious message by winding up in front of Sfica's store. The more we discussed it, the more persuaded we grew that we had made a horrific mistake, a mistake that could be rectified only by our apologizing abjectly to Mr. Sfica and repurchasing those coins. We went back to the shop and, defying Sfica's ban, stepped inside. When we encountered Sfica, we started to mutter some words of apology, but he cut them short by placing his fingers over his lips and, without a word, retrieved the three coins. We paid the same price as before. A few hours later, on the airplane back to London, I said to Marilyn, "If he and all the dealers on Crete are in cahoots, and if he had the balls to sell me the same phony coins twice, then I say, 'Hats off to you, Mr. Sfica!'"

On returning to Oxford, we took the coins to the Ashmolean Museum for an official appraisal. One week later we received the verdict: all the coins were fake except for the small Roman coins we had bought from the old Jewish dealer in the small basement shop! Thus began a lifetime of adventures in Greece.

CHAPTER TWENTY-THREE

EXISTENTIAL
THERAPY

E ver since reading Rollo May's *Existence* early in my psychiatric residency and taking my first philosophy courses at Hopkins, I had been wondering how I could begin to incorporate the wisdom of the past into my field of psychotherapy. The more philosophy I read, the more I realized how many profound ideas psychiatry had ignored. I much regretted that I had only a rickety foundation in philosophy and the humanities in general, and was determined to begin to address these gaps in my education.

I started auditing a number of Stanford undergraduate courses in phenomenology and existentialism, many of them taught by a remarkably lucid thinker and lecturer, Professor Dagfinn Føllesdal. I found the material fascinating, if dense and difficult, and struggled particularly with Edmund Husserl and Martin Heidegger. I found Heidegger's *Being and Time* opaque, but also intriguing, so much so that I sat through Dagfinn's Heidegger course twice. He and I were to develop a lifelong friendship. The other Stanford professor teaching courses in my area of interest was Van Harvey, who, despite his staunch agnosticism, was the long-term chair of the Stanford Department of Religious Studies. Sitting in the front row of his classroom, I listened, mesmerized, to his lectures on Kierkegaard and Nietzsche, two of the most unforgettable courses I've ever taken. Van Harvey, too, became a close friend, and to this day we meet for regular luncheons to talk about philosophy.

My whole professional life was changing: less and less did I seek collaboration with scientific projects conducted by members of my department. When psychology professor David Rosenhan went on sabbatical, I stepped in to teach his large undergraduate course on abnormal psychology, but that would be my finale—the last such course I taught.

I gradually drifted away from my original affiliation with medical science and began grounding myself in the humanities. This was an exciting time, but also a time of self-doubt: I often felt like an outsider, losing touch with new developments in psychiatry and, at the same time, becoming just a dabbler in philosophy and literature. Gradually I would pick and choose among thinkers who seemed most relevant to my field. I embraced Nietzsche, Sartre, Camus, Schopenhauer, and Epicurus/Lucretius, and bypassed Kant, Leibniz, Husserl, and Kierkegaard because the clinical application of their ideas was less apparent to me.

I also had the good fortune of attending classes given by English professor Albert Guerard, a remarkable literary critic and novelist, and then the honor of co-teaching with him. He and his wife, Maclin—also a writer—became dear friends. In the early 1970s Professor Guerard started a new PhD program in Modern Thought and Literature, and Marilyn and I both served on his board. I began teaching more in the humanities and less in the medical school. Some of the earliest offerings in Modern Thought and Literature included "Psychiatry and Biography," which I co-taught with Tom Moser, the chair of the Stanford English Department, who also became a good friend. Marilyn and I co-taught "Death in Fiction," and I also co-taught "Philosophy and Psychiatry" with Dagfinn Føllesdal.

My reading had now shifted strongly to existential thinkers in fiction as well as philosophy: such authors as Dostoevsky,
Tolstoy, Beckett, Kundera, Hesse, Mutis, and Hamsun were not
dealing primarily with matters of social class, courtship, sexual pursuit, mystery, or revenge: their subjects were far deeper,
touching on the parameters of existence. They struggled to find
meaning in a meaningless world, openly confronting inevitable
death and unbridgeable isolation. I related to these mortal quan-
daries. I felt they were telling my story: and not only *my* story,
but also the story of every patient who had ever consulted me.
More and more I grasped that many of the issues my patients
struggled with—aging, loss, death, major life choices such as
what profession to pursue or whom to marry—were often more
cogently addressed by novelists and philosophers than by members of my own field.

I began to believe that I could write a book that might bring
some of the ideas of existential literature into psychotherapy,
but at the same time worried about my hubris in taking such a
step. Would not real philosophers see through my thin veneer of
knowledge? Pushing these qualms aside, I started work, but I never
eliminated the pretender-anxiety buzzing in the background. I also
knew that this would be a formidable long-term project. I arranged
to spend four hours every morning reading and taking notes in my
small studio over the garage, and then, at noon, I biked twenty
minutes to Stanford to spend the rest of the day with students and
patients.

In addition to reviewing the academic literature, I turned to
reams of clinical notes on patients. Over and again I attempted
to clear my mind of everyday concerns and meditate on the irre-
ducible experience of being. Thoughts of death often floated into
my waking mind and haunted me in my dreams. During my early
work on the book, I had a powerful dream that remains as fresh as
if I had dreamt it last night.

My mother and her friends and relatives, all dead now, are seated very quietly on a flight of stairs. I hear my mother's voice calling—shrieking—my name. I take particular notice of Aunt Minnie, sitting on the top stair, who is very still. Then she begins to move, slowly at first, then more and more quickly, until she is vibrating faster than a bumblebee. At that point, everyone on the stairs, all the big people of my childhood, all dead, begin to vibrate faster and faster. Uncle Abe reaches out to pinch my cheek, clucking, "Darling Sonny," as he used to do. Then others reach out for my cheeks. At first affectionate, the pinching grows fierce and painful. I awake in terror, cheeks throbbing, at 3 a.m.

The dream was an encounter with death. First, my dead mother calls me, and I see all the dead of my family sitting in eerie stillness on the stairs. Next they all begin to move. I especially note my aunt Minnie, who had died after existing for a year in a locked-in syndrome. A cataclysmic stroke had left her paralyzed for several months, unable to move a muscle in her body aside from her eyes. I had been horrified to think of her in that state. In the dream, Minnie begins to move, but quickly veers into frenzy. I try to alleviate my dread by imagining the dead affectionately pinching my cheeks. But the pinching grows fierce and then malignant: I am being drawn in to join them and death will come for me as well. The image of my aunt vibrating like a bumblebee haunted me for days. I couldn't shake it loose. Her total paralysis, her death in life, was too horrible to bear, and so in the dream I tried to undo it by making her vibrate. I've often been visited by nightmares touched off by films about death or violence, particularly Holocaust films. My chief method of dealing with death terror? Without doubt, avoidance.

I had always believed I would die at age sixty-nine, my father's age at death. Since early childhood I remember my extended family saying two things about Yalom males: they were always gentle and always died young. My father's two brothers died from coronaries in their fifties, and my father's coronary almost killed him when he was forty-seven. When, in medical school, I learned more about physiology and about the impact of diet on coronary arterial plaques, I abruptly and permanently changed my eating habits, sharply reducing my intake of animal fats. I avoided red meat and gradually moved to a diet that was primarily vegetarian. I've taken statins for decades, watched my weight carefully, and exercised regularly, and have surprised myself by living long past sixty-nine.

After months of study and contemplation I reached the conclusion that the confrontation with death would have to be the major focus of an existential approach to therapy. I believed this was because of the intensity and universality of our dread of death, but now, as I look back on that decision, I can't dismiss the possibility that my view may have been unbalanced because of my own personal angst about death. For months I read all I could find about death, beginning with Plato and ending with Leo Tolstoy's *Death of Ivan Ilyich*, Jacques Choron's *Death and Western Thought*, and Ernest Becker's *Denial of Death*.

The scholarly literature on death was so vast, so sprawling, and often so esoteric and removed from psychiatry that I realized my unique contribution could come from my work with patients. At that time, very little had been written about death in the clinical literature, and I knew I would have to find my own way. Yet, no matter how much I tried to discuss concerns about death with my psychotherapy patients, I could not engage them in a sustained discussion. We would address the topic for a few moments and then soon drift elsewhere. Looking back on that era, I now think I must have unconsciously communicated to my patients that I was not ready to talk about it.

Hence I made an important decision that determined my next ten years of clinical practice: I would work with patients who *had* to talk about death because they were imminently confronted with it. I began consulting with patients in Stanford's oncology service who had been diagnosed with untreatable cancer. At that time I attended a lecture by Elisabeth Kübler-Ross, a pioneer in working with the dying, and was struck by her first question to a seriously ill patient: "How sick are you?" I found that question to be of great value: it conveys so much—namely, that I am open and willing to go wherever the patient wishes, even into the darkest places.

I was particularly struck by the great isolation that comes with facing a terminal illness. The isolation is bidirectional: first, patients refrain from discussing their morbid, frightening thoughts, for fear of depressing their family and friends, and, second, those close to the patient stay clear of the subject to avoid upsetting the patient even more. The more patients with cancer I saw, the more persuaded I became that a therapy group could help alleviate this isolation. The oncologists to whom I spoke of my plans were at first wary and unsupportive. This was still the early 1970s, and such a group felt rash and potentially noxious. Moreover, it was unprecedented: there was not a single report of a group for cancer patients in the scientific literature.

But as I gained experience, I became even more persuaded that such a group could offer a great deal, and I began to spread the word in the Stanford medical community. Before long, Paula West, a patient with metastatic breast cancer, showed up at my office. She was to become important to me in my work with cancer patients. Though Paula was dealing with painful metastases in her spinal column, she faced her condition with extraordinary grace. Later I described my relationship with her in the story "Travels with Paula," published in *Momma and the Meaning of Life*. The story begins:

> *When she first entered my office, I was instantaneously captivated by her appearance: by the dignity in her bearing, by her radiant smile which gathered me in, by her shock of short,*

*exuberantly boyish, glowing white hair, and by something I can
only call luminosity, that seemed to emanate from her wise and
intensely blue eyes.*

*"My name is Paula West," she said. "I have terminal can-
cer. But I am not a cancer patient." And, indeed, in my travels
with her through many years I never regarded her as a patient.
She went on to describe in clipped, precise fashion her medical
history: cancer of the breast diagnosed five years earlier, surgical
removal of that breast, then cancer of the other breast, that breast
also removed. Then came chemotherapy with its familiar awful
entourage: nausea, vomiting, total loss of hair. And then radia-
tion therapy, the maximum permitted. But nothing would slow
the spread of her cancer—to her skull, spine, and the orbits of her
eyes. Paula's cancer demanded to be fed and, though the surgeons
tossed it sacrificial offerings—her breasts, lymph nodes, ovaries,
adrenal glands—it remained voracious.*

*When I imagined Paula's nude body I saw a chest criss-
crossed with scars, without breasts, flesh, or muscle, like the
rib-planks of some shipwrecked galleon, and below her chest, a
surgically scarred abdomen, and all supported by thick, ungainly,
steroid-thickened hips. In short, a fifty-five-year-old woman sans
breasts, adrenals, ovaries, uterus, and, I'm sure, libido.*

*I have always relished women with firm graceful bodies, full
breasts, and a readily apparent sensuality. Yet the most curious
thing happened to me the first time I met Paula: I found her quite
beautiful and fell in love with her.*

Paula agreed to join a small group with three other dying
patients. The five of us met for ninety minutes in a comfortable
group room in the psychiatry building. I began by saying simply
that all the members were dealing with cancer and that I believed
we could help one another by sharing our thoughts and feelings.

One of the members was Sal, a thirty-year-old man in a wheelchair who, like Paula, was larger than life. Though he had advanced

multiple myeloma (a painful invasive bone cancer causing many fractured bones) and was encased in a full body cast from neck to thigh, his spirit was indomitable. The imminence of death had flooded his life with a new sense of meaning and so transformed him that he now thought of his illness as a ministry. He agreed to join the group hoping to help the others find similar deliverance.

Although Sal entered our group six months too early—when it was still too small to give him the audience he sought—he found other platforms, primarily high schools, where he addressed troubled teenagers. I heard him deliver his message to them in a thundering voice.

> You want to corrupt your body with drugs? Want to kill it with booze, with grass, with cocaine? You want to smash your body in autos? Kill it? Throw it off the Golden Gate Bridge? You don't want it? Well, then, give me your body! Let me have it. I need it. I'll take it—I want to live!

I trembled when I heard him speak. The force of his delivery was augmented by the particular power we always give to the words of the dying. The high school students listened in silence, sensing, as I did, that he was speaking truly, that he no longer had time for game playing or pretense.

Another patient, Evelyn, gravely ill with leukemia, provided Sal with another opportunity for ministry. Evelyn, wheeled into the group with a blood transfusion in process, told the group, "I know I'm dying: I can accept that. It no longer matters. But what *does* matter is my daughter. She is poisoning my final days!" Evelyn described her daughter as "a vindictive, unloving woman." Months earlier, they had had a bitter and foolish argument after her daughter, caring for Evelyn's cat, had fed it the wrong food. They hadn't spoken since.

After hearing her out, Sal spoke to her simply and passionately: "Listen to what I have to say, Evelyn. I'm dying, too. Let me ask: What does it matter what your cat eats? What does it matter who gives in first? You know you don't have much time left. Let's stop pretending. Your daughter's love is the most important thing in the world to you. Don't die, please don't die, without telling her that! It will poison her life, she'll never recover, and she'll pass on the poison to *her* daughter! Break the cycle! Break the cycle, Evelyn!"

Sal's appeal worked. Although Evelyn died a few days later, the ward nurses told us that Evelyn, swayed by Sal's words, had had a tearful reconciliation with her daughter. I was very proud of Sal. It was our group's first triumph!

After several months, I felt I had learned enough to begin working with larger numbers of patients. I also thought a homogeneous group might be more effective. The majority of patients I had seen in consultation had metastatic breast cancer, so I decided to form a group consisting entirely of patients with that disease. Paula began to recruit in earnest. We interviewed and accepted seven new patients and officially opened for business.

Paula surprised me by beginning the first session with an old Hasidic tale:

> A rabbi had a conversation with the Lord about Heaven and Hell. "I will show you Hell," said the Lord, and he led the rabbi into a room containing a large round table. The people sitting around the table were famished and desperate. In the middle of the table was an enormous pot of stew that smelled so delicious that the rabbi's mouth watered. Each person around the table held a spoon with a very long handle. Although the long spoons just reached the pot, their handles were longer than the would-be diners' arms: thus, unable to bring food to their lips, no one could eat. The rabbi saw that their suffering was terrible indeed.
>
> "Now I will show you Heaven," said the Lord, and they went into another room, exactly the same as the first. There was the same large round table, the same pot of stew. The people were

*equipped with the same long-handled spoons—but here everyone
was well nourished and plump, laughing and talking. The rabbi
could not understand. "It is simple, but it requires a certain skill,"
said the Lord. "In this room, you see, they have learned to feed
each other."*

Though I've led groups for many decades, I have never experienced such an inspired opening. The group cohered quickly, and when members died, I brought in new members, and continued leading the group for ten years. Later, I invited psychiatry residents to co-lead the group for a year, and then a new psychiatry faculty member, David Spiegel, joined me for a number of years.

Not only did the group provide much comfort to a great many patients, but it offered me a profound education. To take but one of a myriad of examples, I think of a woman who came week after week with such a weary, despondent look in her eyes that we all struggled, in vain, to offer her solace. Then suddenly one day she showed up with a spark in her eyes and wearing a bright-colored dress. "What happened?" we asked. She thanked us and said that the group discussion the prior week had helped her make a pivotal decision: *she had decided she could model to her children how to face death with grace and courage.* I've never encountered a better example of how a sense of meaning in life generates a sense of well-being. It is also a striking example of the concept of "rippling" that helps many attenuate the terror of death. Rippling refers to passing parts of our self on to others, even to others whom we do not know, much as the ripples caused by a pebble in a pond go on and on until they are no longer visible but continue at a nano level.

From the very beginning I invited interested Stanford residents, medical students, and occasionally undergraduates to view the group through the two-way mirror. In contrast to the traditional therapy groups at Stanford, which tolerated observation uneasily, the cancer patients responded in a strikingly different

manner: they *wanted* and welcomed students. Their confrontation with death had taught them much about living, and they
were eager to pass that on to others.

Paula was highly critical of Kübler-Ross's stages of grief. Instead, she placed great emphasis on learning and growing from
the confrontation with death and often spoke of the "Golden
Period" she had inhabited for the past three years. Several other
group members shared that experience. As one of them put it:
"What a pity I had to wait until now, until my body was riddled
with cancer, to learn how to live." That phrase took up permanent residence in my mind and helped shape my practice of existential therapy. I often put it this way: *though the reality of death
may destroy us, the idea of death may save us*. It brings home the
realization that since we have only one chance at life, we should
live it fully and end it with the fewest regrets possible.

My work with the terminally ill led gradually to confronting healthy patients with their mortality in order to help them
change the way they lived. Often this entails simply listening and
reinforcing patients' awareness of their finite life span. On many
occasions I have employed an explicit exercise: I ask the patient
to draw a line on a sheet of paper, and then I say, "Let one end
represent your birth and the other end your death. Now please
place a mark on the line to denote where you are now and meditate on that diagram." This exercise rarely fails to incite deeper
awareness of life's precious transiency.

CHAPTER TWENTY-FOUR

CONFRONTING DEATH WITH ROLLO MAY

O f the fifty men and women who passed through our group for cancer patients, all died of their illness except for one: Paula. She survived cancer only to die later of lupus. I knew from the outset that if I were to write honestly and usefully about the role that death plays in life, I had to be taught by those facing imminent death, but I paid a price for this lesson. Often I was severely anxious after the group sessions: I brooded about my own death, had difficulty sleeping, and was often hounded by nightmares.

My student observers also grew troubled, and it was not uncommon for one of them to burst, sobbing, from the observation room before the session was over. To this day I regret I did not properly prepare those students for the experience or provide therapy for them.

As my own death anxiety increased, I began thinking of all the psychotherapy I had had in the past—that long analysis during my residency, my year of therapy in London, a year of Gestalt therapy with Pat Baumgartner, as well as several sessions of behavior therapy and a short course of bioenergetics. As I looked back on all those therapy hours, I could not recall a single open discussion about death anxiety. *Could this be true? That death, the primal source of anxiety, was never mentioned—not in any of my therapies?*

If I were to continue to work with patients facing death, I decided I had to get back into therapy, this time with someone willing to accompany me into that darkness. I had recently heard that Rollo May, the author of *Existence*, had moved to California from New York and was seeing patients in Tiburon, about eighty minutes from Stanford. I phoned him for an appointment, and a week later we met in his lovely house on Sugarloaf Road overlooking San Francisco Bay.

Rollo was a tall, stately, handsome man in his late sixties. He generally wore a beige or white turtleneck sweater and a light leather jacket. His office was his study, just off the living room. He was a fine artist, and several paintings that he had done as a youth hung on the wall. I especially admired one of the high-spired church at Mont Saint-Michel in France. (After his death, Georgia, his widow, gave me that painting, which I now see daily in my office.) After only a few sessions, it occurred to me that I could make good use of my eighty-minute commute by listening to a tape of our prior session. I suggested this to him, and he agreed quite readily and seemed entirely at ease at my recording our meetings. Beginning each hour with him shortly after I had listened in my car to our previous session greatly increased my focus and, I believe, accelerated our work. Since then, when I have had patients with a long commute to my office, I have suggested this format to them.

How I wish I could listen to those taped sessions now as I write these pages, but alas, that is not possible. I stored all the tapes in a drawer of an old desk in my tree-house office that was badly in need of repair. When my family and I took off for Oxford in 1974, I contracted to have the office rebuilt by an elderly, affable, midwestern jack-of-all-trades named Cecil, who had appeared at our front doorstep years before asking for work. We had plenty for him to do, as I have no skills in the art of house maintenance. Before long, Cecil and his chubby, affable, apple-pie-baking wife, Martha, who looked as though she had just popped out of a Mary Poppins film, moved their small trailer into a hidden corner of our property, where they lived and attended to all our upkeep matters for several years. When I returned from my sabbatical I found that Cecil had done a great job rebuilding my studio, but all the old rickety furniture, including the weathered desk and its drawers crammed with the tapes of my sessions with Rollo, had disappeared in the process. I never found those tapes and occasionally have alarming fantasies that their entire contents will appear somewhere on the Internet.

Now, forty years later, I have great difficulty recalling details of our sessions, but I know I focused very much on my thoughts about death and that Rollo, though uncomfortable, never shied away from discussing my most morbid thoughts. At that time my work with dying patients ignited powerful nightmares that vanished immediately upon awakening. At one point, I suggested to Rollo that I spend the night in a nearby motel in order to see him first thing the following morning. He agreed, and those sessions, held while my dreams were fresher, were particularly charged with energy. I told him of my fear that I would die at sixty-nine, my father's age at death. He said it was odd, given my posture toward rationality, that I clung to such a superstitious belief. When I spoke of my work with dying patients and how they evoked death anxiety, he told me I was courageous to undertake such work and it was hardly surprising that I should feel anxiety.

I recall telling Rollo how stunned I had always been by the passage in *Macbeth* where the title character says, "Life's but a walking shadow, a poor player that struts and frets his hour upon the stage and then is heard no more," and how, as an adolescent, I had applied it to every big person who had populated my life—Franklin Roosevelt, Harry Truman, Richard Nixon, Thomas Wolfe, Mickey Vernon, Charles de Gaulle, Winston Churchill, Adolf Hitler, George Patton, Mickey Mantle, Joe DiMaggio, Marilyn Monroe, Laurence Olivier, Bernard Malamud—all those who had strutted and fretted and made history in my world, and who were now gone, all turned to dust. Nothing left of them. Everything, really everything, passes. We all have only a precious, blessed instant in the sun. I have dwelled on that thought many, many times and still it never fails to shake me.

I never asked, but I am certain that many such sessions made Rollo personally uncomfortable, as he was twenty-two years older than me and closer to death. But he never flinched or failed to accompany me into my darkest inquiries about mortality. I recall no major "aha" moment of insight, but gradually I began to change and feel more comfortable working with dying patients. He had read a good bit of my work, including the final draft of *Existential Psychotherapy*, and was always generous in his posture toward me. I remain deeply grateful to him.

I remember the first time Rollo saw Marilyn. It was years after my therapy with him had ended, and we had just arrived for a dinner party he was giving for the British psychiatrist R. D. Laing (with whom I had consulted while in London). Rollo opened his front door, greeted me, and then held out both hands toward Marilyn. She said, "I didn't think you'd be so warm." Without missing a beat, Rollo replied, "And I didn't think you'd be so pretty."

It is uncommon and often highly problematic for patients and therapists to strike up a social relationship after therapy ends, but in this case it worked well for all parties. We became very good friends and our friendship continued until his death. From time to time, I lunched with him at the Capri, his favorite restaurant in Tiburon, and on several occasions we reviewed my therapy with him. We both knew he had been helpful, but the mechanism of help remained a mystery to us. He said, more than once, "I knew you wanted something from me in therapy, but I didn't know what

it was or how to give it to you." As I look back on it now, I believe
that Rollo offered me presence—he unhesitatingly accompanied
me into dark territory and gave me some good, much-needed
re-fathering. He was an older man who understood and accepted
me. When he read the manuscript of *Existential Psychotherapy*, he
told me it was a fine book and wrote a strong blurb for the cover.
The quote he gave for the cover of a later book, *Love's Executioner*
("Yalom writes like an angel about the devils that besiege us"), is
the highest praise I have ever received.

Around this time, Marilyn and I began to have significant
problems in our marriage. She had resigned her tenured professorship at California State University at Hayward to accept a
position at Stanford directing the newly created Center for Research on Women (CROW), where she built a whole new career
for herself in the fledgling field of women's studies. She nurtured
young students and formed close relationships with the leading
women scholars at Stanford. Her work had center stage in her
mind, and I felt she was seriously neglecting our marriage. She
had an entirely new social circle: I saw less and less of her and
sensed we were truly drifting away from one another. I recall with
great clarity a portentous evening in San Francisco when, during
our dinner at Little City Antipasto, I said to her, "Your new life—
your new position and your involvement in women's issues—is
great for you, but it's not great for me. You're so consumed with it
that I'm no longer getting much from our relationship and maybe
we should think of separ . . . " I never finished that sentence because Marilyn broke out into a loud wail, so loud that three waiters rushed to our table and every face in the restaurant turned in
our direction.

This was the low point of our relationship and it happened at
the time when Marilyn and I were often meeting with Rollo and
Georgia. One evening, Rollo, ever willing to experiment, invited

THE AUTHOR WITH ROLLO MAY, CA. 1980.

us over to try out some high-grade Ecstasy he had received as a gift. Georgia abstained and acted as chaperone for the evening. Neither Marilyn nor I had ever taken ecstasy before, but we both felt safe with Rollo and Georgia, and it turned out to be an extraordinarily mellow and healing evening. After taking the ecstasy, we talked, we dined, we listened to music, and to this very day we both believe that somehow, our marital problems simply dissolved. We changed: we let go of negative feelings and cherished each other more deeply than ever. Moreover, the change proved to be permanent! Neither of us quite understands it and, inexplicably, we never tried the drug again.

In the early 1990s, around the time he turned eighty, Rollo suffered from transient ischemic attacks (TIAs) and felt confused and anxious for hours at a time, sometimes as long as a day or two. Sometimes Georgia would phone me when the incidents were extreme, and I would visit and spend time with Rollo, talking and walking in the hills behind his home. Only now, at the age of eighty-five, do I fully appreciate his anxiety. I have fleeting moments of confusion and momentarily forget where I am or what

I'm doing. That was what Rollo experienced, not for moments, but for hours and days at a time. Yet somehow he continued to work until the very end. Late in his life I attended one of his public talks. His delivery was as strong as ever, his voice sonorous and soothing, but, toward the end, he repeated the same story he had told just a few minutes before. I cringed when I heard that, I cringed for him, and often I remind my friends to be honest with me and tell me when it's time for me to stop.

One evening Georgia phoned to say that Rollo might be near death and asked us to come immediately. The three of us spent that night taking turns sitting next to Rollo, who had lost consciousness and was in advanced pulmonary edema, breathing laboriously, sometimes with deep, long breaths followed by shorter, shallower ones. Ultimately, on my watch, as I was sitting by him and touching his shoulder, he took one last convulsive breath and died. Georgia asked me to help her wash his body to prepare him for the mortician, who, the following morning, would take him to the crematorium.

That night, shaken by Rollo's death and his impending cremation, I had a powerful and unforgettable dream:

> I'm walking with my parents and sister in a mall and then we decide to go upstairs. I find myself on an elevator but I'm alone— my family has disappeared. It's a long ascending elevator ride. When I get off I'm on a tropical beach. But I can't find my family though I keep looking and looking for them. Though it is a lovely setting—tropical beaches are paradise for me—I begin to feel pervasive dread.
>
> Next I put on a nightshirt that bears a cute, smiling face of Smokey the Bear. That face on the shirt then becomes brighter, then brilliant. Soon the face becomes the entire focus of the dream, as though all the energy of the dream is transferred onto that cute grinning little Smokey Bear face.

The dream woke me, not so much from terror, but from the brilliance of the blazing emblem on the nightshirt. It was as though floodlights suddenly turned on in my bedroom.

What lay behind the blazing image of Smokey? I'm certain it was connected to Rollo's cremation. His death confronted me with my own, which the dream portrays through my isolation from my family and that endless elevator ride upstairs. I'm shocked by the gullibility of my unconscious. How embarrassing it is that some part of me has bought into the Hollywood version of immortality as a celestial paradise, complete with tropical beach.

I had gone to sleep that night shaken by the horror of Rollo's death and his pending cremation, and my dream attempted to de-terrify that experience, to soften it, to make it bearable. Death is disguised benignly as an elevator trip upstairs to a tropical beach. The fiery cremation is transformed into a nightshirt, ready for the slumber of death, bearing an adorable image of a cuddly bear. But the terror cannot be contained, and Smokey Bear's image blazes me awake.

CHAPTER TWENTY-FIVE
DEATH, FREEDOM, ISOLATION, AND MEANING

For years in the 1970s my existential psychotherapy textbook was always simmering in my mind, but it seemed so diffuse and overwhelming that I was unable to start writing it until one day when Alex Comfort visited us. I recall the two of us sitting in my rebuilt tree-house studio talking. He listened intently as I told him about my reading and my ideas for the book. After about an hour and a half, Alex stopped me and solemnly proclaimed, "Irv, I've listened, I've heard you out, and, with total confidence, I pronounce that the time has come for you to stop reading and start writing."

Exactly what I needed! I could have flailed about for several more years. Alex knew about books—he had published over fifty of them—and somehow his compelling tone and faith in me allowed me to clear my docket and start writing. The timing was perfect, since I had just been invited to spend a scholarly year at the Stanford Center for Advanced Study in the Behavioral

THE AUTHOR WITH CRITIC ALFRED KAZIN AND
STANFORD LAW PROFESSOR JOHN KAPLAN, CENTER FOR
ADVANCED STUDY IN BEHAVIORAL SCIENCES, 1978.

Sciences. Though I continued to meet with a few patients, I wrote almost full-time for the entire 1977–1978 academic year. Unfortunately, I did not take full advantage of the chance to get to know some of the thirty other distinguished scholars, including the future Supreme Court justice Ruth Bader Ginsburg. But I did form a friendship with sociologist Cynthia Epstein, who has remained in our life to this day.

I made such good progress that I completed the book a year later. I began it with an incident from an Armenian cooking class taught by Efronia Katchadourian, the mother of Herant Katchadourian, a good friend and colleague. Efronia was a great cook, but she spoke little English and taught entirely by demonstration. As she prepared her dishes, I jotted down all the ingredients and all her steps, but, try as hard as I could, my dishes never tasted as good as hers. Surely, I thought, this was not an insoluble problem: I resolved to observe her even more closely, and at the next lesson I watched her every step as she prepared her dish and then handed it to her lifelong attendant, Lucy, to place into the oven. This time, I kept my eye on Lucy and saw something extraordinary: on the way to the oven, Lucy casually threw in handfuls of various spices that struck her fancy! I am absolutely persuaded that those extra throw-ins made all the difference.

I used this introductory anecdote to reassure readers that existential psychotherapy was no new strange esoteric approach but had always been present in the form of valuable, but unspoken, throw-ins offered by most experienced therapists.

In each of the book's four sections—death, freedom, isolation, and meaning—I described my sources, my clinical observations, and the philosophers and writers whose work I drew upon.

Of the four sections of the text, the one on death is the longest. Elsewhere in professional articles I had written a good bit about working with patients facing death, but in this text I focused on the role that death awareness can play in the therapy of a physically healthy patient. Though I think of death as the distant thunder at our picnic of life, I also believe that a genuine confrontation with mortality may change the way we live: it helps us trivialize the trivial and encourages us to live without building up regrets. So many philosophers, in one way or another, echo the lament of my patient dying of cancer: "What a pity I had to wait until now, until my body was riddled with cancer, to learn how to live."

Freedom is the ultimate concern most central to many existential thinkers. In my understanding, it refers to the idea that, since we all live in a universe without inherent design, we must be the authors of our own lives, choices, and actions. Such freedom generates so much anxiety that many of us embrace gods or dictators to remove the burden. If we are, in Sartre's terms, "the uncontested author" of everything that we have experienced, then our most cherished ideas, our most noble truths, the very bedrock of our convictions, are all undermined by the awareness that everything in the universe is contingent.

The third topic, isolation, does not refer to interpersonal isolation (i.e., loneliness), but to a more fundamental isolation: the idea that we are each thrown alone into the world and must depart alone. In the ancient *Everyman* tale, a man is visited by the angel of death, who informs him that his time has come to an end and he must take the journey to face judgment. The man pleads that he be allowed to take someone with him on his journey, and the angel of death responds, "Sure—if you can find someone willing to go." The rest of the story depicts his unsuccessful attempts—his cousin, for example, says he cannot go because he has a cramp in the toe. Finally he finds someone to accompany him, but, in this Christian morality tale, it is not another being, but instead *good deeds*. The only comforting thing that can accompany us while dying is the knowledge that we have lived well.

My discussion of isolation focuses a great deal on the therapist-patient relationship, on our wishes to fuse with another, on our fear of individuation. As death approaches, many are aware that when they perish their whole unique separate world will perish as well—that world of sights and sounds and experiences unknown to anyone else, not even life partners. As I reach my mid-eighties, I experience that form of isolation more and more keenly. I think about the world of my childhood—the Sunday-night gatherings at Aunt Luba's home, the odors wafting from the kitchen, the roast brisket, the *tsimmes*, the *cholent*, the games of Monopoly, my chess games with my father, the odor of my mother's Persian lamb coat—and then I shudder as I realize all of this exists now only in memory.

The discussion of the fourth ultimate concern, meaninglessness, touches on such questions as "Why were we put here? If nothing endures, what sense does life have? What is the point of life?" I've always been moved by Allen Wheelis's account of throwing a stick for his dog, Monty, to retrieve.

If then I bend over and pick up a stick, he is instantly before me. The great thing has now happened. He has a mission. . . . It

*never occurs to him to evaluate the mission. His dedication is
solely to its fulfillment. He runs or swims any distance, over or
through any obstacle, to get that stick.*

*And, having got it, he brings it back: for his mission is not
simply to get it but to return it. Yet, as he approaches me, he
moves more slowly. He wants to give it to me and give closure to
his task, yet he hates to have done with his mission, to again be in
the position of waiting . . .*

*He is lucky to have me to throw his stick. I am waiting for
God to throw mine. Have been waiting a long time. Who knows
when, if ever, he will again turn his attention to me, and allow
me, as I allow Monty, my mood of mission?*

It is reassuring to believe that God has a purpose for us. Secular people find it discomfiting to know they must throw their own sticks. How reassuring it would be to know that somewhere out there exists a genuine, palpable purpose-in-life, rather than only the *sense* of purpose-in-life? Ovid's comment comes to mind: "It's useful that there should be gods, so let's believe there are."

Though I've often thought of my book *Existential Psychotherapy* as a textbook for a course that did not exist, I never intended to create a new field of therapy. My intent was to increase all therapists' awareness of existential issues in their patients' lives. In recent years there have appeared professional organizations of existential therapists and, in 2015, I spoke via videoconference at the large first international congress of existential therapists in London. Though I welcome the increased emphasis on existential issues in therapy, I have some difficulty with the concept of a separate school of therapy. The organizers of the international congress had enormous difficulties establishing a comprehensive definition of the school. After all, there will always be patients whose therapy work primarily involves interpersonal issues, or self-esteem, or sexuality, or addiction, and for these patients existential questions may not be immediately pertinent. This has implications for training. Rarely does a week pass without some student asking me where they can be trained as an existential psychotherapist. I always suggest they first become trained as a general therapist, learn an array of therapy approaches, and then, in postgraduate programs or supervision, familiarize themselves with the specialized material of existential psychotherapy.

CHAPTER TWENTY-SIX

INPATIENT GROUPS AND PARIS

I n 1979, I was asked to serve, on a temporary basis, as medical director of the Stanford psychiatric inpatient unit. At that time psychiatric hospitalization nationwide was in turmoil: insurance companies had cut coverage for psychiatric hospitalization, insisting patients be transferred as quickly as possible to less expensive board and care facilities. With the majority of patients remaining in the hospital only a week or less, the composition of each group was rarely the same for two consecutive sessions, and the meetings became chaotic and ineffective. Largely because of this turmoil, staff morale was at an all-time low.

I hadn't planned to undertake another group therapy project, but I was restless and looking for a challenge. My desk was clear, my existential therapy book was finished, and I was ready for a new project. Given my deep belief in the efficacy of the group approach and the enticing challenge of creating a new way to lead inpatient groups, I agreed to take the position for two years. I recruited a psychiatrist who had graduated from the Stanford program to handle medications on the ward (psychopharmacology was never one of my strengths or interests), then concentrated primarily on designing a new group therapy approach for the changing inpatient wards. I began by visiting group meetings on inpatient wards at leading psychiatric hospitals around the country. I found confusion everywhere: not even the best-known academic hospitals had an effective inpatient group program. With such rapid turnover, group leaders felt compelled to introduce the one or two new members at the start of each session and invite them to describe why they were in the hospital. Almost invariably these accounts—followed by therapists coaxing responses from other group members—filled the entire meeting. No one seemed to be getting much benefit from these groups, and attrition was high. An entirely different strategy was needed.

The Stanford acute unit had twenty patients, and I separated them into a higher- and a lower-functioning group, each with six to eight members (the remaining patients, mostly the acute new admissions, were too disorganized to attend any group in their first couple of days). After some experimentation I developed a workable format. Because of the rapid turnover, I entirely gave up on the idea of continuity from one meeting to the next and developed a new paradigm: *the life of each group would be a single session*, and the leader's task would be to make that single meeting as efficient and effective as possible. I developed a schema for higher-functioning patients that would have four stages:

1. Each patient in turn would formulate an agenda of some interpersonal issue to work on in that meeting. (This task consumed at least a third of the meeting.)
2. The rest of the group meeting was spent filling the agenda of each patient.
3. Then, when the group meeting ended, the observers (medical, psychology, or counseling students, residents, and nurses who had observed the meeting through a one-way

mirror) entered the room and discussed the meeting while the patients observed from an outer circle.

4. Finally, for the last ten minutes, the group members responded to the observers' post-group discussion.

The first step, the formulation of an agenda, was the most difficult task for the patients and therapists. As I defined it, the agenda was *not* about why patients entered the hospital—not, for example, about the frightening voices they might hear, or the side effects of antipsychotic medications, or some traumatic event in their life. Instead, the agenda was to be about some problem in their relationships with others—for example, "I'm lonely. I need friends but no one wants to be with me," or, "Whenever I open up, people will ridicule me," or, "I sense that people consider me repulsive and a nuisance and I need to find out if that's true."

The therapist's next step would be to transform that into a here-and-now agenda. When a members says, "I'm lonely . . . " the therapist might say, "Can you talk about the ways in which you feel lonely here in this group?" or, "Who might you want to be close to in this group?" or, "Let's explore, as we proceed, what role you play in being lonely in this group today."

The therapist must be very active, but when it works well, the members of the group help each other improve their interpersonal behavior, and the results are significantly better than when focusing on why the patient has been hospitalized.

I strove to give the observers—nurses, psychiatry residents, and medical students—an active role in the group, and that resulted in the observers making a significant contribution to the therapy group session. On a survey, the patients rated the last twenty minutes of the meeting (the discussion with the observers) as the most worthwhile part of the meeting! In fact, some patients habitually peeked into the observation room before the group started, and if there were no observers that day, they were less inclined to attend. These reactions were similar to the reactions of my outpatient groups. If members can lay eyes on the observers and get feedback from them, the therapy work is facilitated.

For the daily group of lower-functioning patients, I formulated a model that included a series of safe, structured exercises of self-disclosure, empathy, social skills training, and identification of desired personal changes.

And, finally, to address the diminished staff morale, I set up a weekly process group—that is, a group in which the staff (including the medical director and the head nurse) discussed their relationships with one another. Such a group is hard to lead but ultimately becomes invaluable in ameliorating staff tensions.

After leading inpatient groups daily for two years, I decided to take a sabbatical (faculty members at Stanford are entitled to a six-month sabbatical every six years at full salary, or twelve months at half salary) to write a book on my approach to inpatient group therapy. My initial plan was to go to London again, where the writing vibes had been so salubrious, but Marilyn insisted on Paris. So, in the summer of 1981, we set off for France, taking our twelve-year-old son, Ben, with us. (By then, our daughter, Eve, was in medical school, Reid had completed college at Stanford, and Victor was at Oberlin College.)

W e began our trip by visiting our good friends Stina and Herant Katchadourian, at their home on an island off the coast of Finland. Herant had been a member of the Stanford Psychiatry Department for a few years but had such excellent executive skills that he had been appointed to the role of university ombudsman and Dean of Undergraduate Education. He was a gifted lecturer, and his course on human sexuality became legendary, by far the most heavily attended course in the history of Stanford University. Stina, his wife, who was a journalist, translator, and author, shared interests with Marilyn, and their daughter Nina became lifelong friends with our son Ben.

The island was a fairy-tale retreat of pines and blueberries surrounded by a forbidding ocean, and during our visit, Herant convinced me to make the jolting leap from the sauna into the frigid Baltic Sea, which I did—but only once. From Finland we took the overnight ferry to Copenhagen. I ordinarily get seasick even looking at a picture of a boat, but with the aid of a small dose of marijuana I floated serenely to Copenhagen, and there I gave a day's workshop for Danish therapists. We also did some sightseeing, visiting the graves of Søren Kierkegaard and Hans Christian Andersen, buried close to one another in Assistens Cemetery.

Once we arrived in Paris, we settled into a fifth-floor flat, sans elevator, on the rue Saint-André-des-Arts, three blocks from the Seine in the Fifth Arrondissement. With Marilyn's help I obtained an office two blocks from the rue Mouffetard that had been set aside by the French government for foreign scholars.

It was a wonderful sojourn. Ben climbed up and down the five flights to buy our morning croissants and the *International Herald Tribune* before taking the Paris Métro to the École Internationale Bilingue. Marilyn worked on a new book, *Maternity, Mortality, and the Literature of Madness*, a work of psychological literary criticism. I met many of her French friends and we were invited to numerous dinners, but communication was difficult: few of them spoke English, and though I worked hard with a French teacher, I made little progress. At social gatherings I generally felt like the village idiot.

I had taken German in high school and college, and, perhaps because of German's similarity to the Yiddish my parents spoke, I did well enough. But something about the lilt and cadence of French confounded me. Perhaps it is related to my inability to keep a melody in my mind or reproduce it. The bad-language gene must have come from my mother, who had considerable problems with the English language. But the French food! I especially looked forward to our morning croissants and our 5 p.m. snacks. Our street was a lively pedestrian mall with outdoor stands hawking otherworldly sweet strawberries, and gourmet shops selling slices of chicken liver pâté, and rabbit terrine. At the boulangeries and patisseries, Marilyn and I went for the *tarte aux fraises des bois* and Ben for the *pain au chocolat*.

Though I couldn't understand enough French to go with Marilyn to the theater, I accompanied her to a few concerts—a memorable countertenor in the Sainte-Chapelle and a rousing Offenbach at the Châtelet—but most of all I enjoyed the museums. How could I not appreciate Claude Monet's water lily paintings, especially after Ben, Marilyn, and I traveled by train to Monet's rural home in Giverny and saw the storied Japanese-style bridge spanning the floating garden of water lilies. I wandered through the Louvre, lingering especially in the rooms containing the ancient Egyptian and Persian artifacts and the majestic Susa glazed-brick Frieze of Lions.

During this wonderful Parisian stay, I wrote *Inpatient Group Psychotherapy* in six months, far, far more quickly than any other book I've produced. It is also the only book I dictated. Stanford was generous enough to send my secretary, Bea Mitchell, with us to Paris, and every morning I dictated two or three first-draft pages that she transcribed; during the afternoons, I edited, re-edited, and prepared for the next day's writing. Bea Mitchell and I were good friends, and every day we strolled the two blocks to the rue Mouffetard and had lunch at one of the street's many Greek restaurants.

Inpatient Group Psychotherapy was published by Basic Books in 1983 and subsequently influenced the practice of group therapy on many inpatient wards. Moreover, a number of empirical studies have supported the efficacy of this approach. But I never returned to inpatient work; instead, I shifted back to extending my knowledge of existential thought.

I decided to continue my philosophical education by learning more about Eastern thought, an area in which I was abysmally ignorant and had completely left out of *Existential Psychotherapy*. In the last few months before leaving for Paris, I had begun reading in that area and speaking to scholars at Stanford, including one of my residents, James Tenzel, who had attended retreats with a renowned Buddhist teacher, S. N. Goenka, at his ashram, Dhamma Giri, in Igatpuri, India. All the experts I consulted persuaded me that reading was insufficient and that it was important for me to engage in a personal meditative practice. So, in December, toward the end of our stay in Paris, I said goodbye to Paris and to Marilyn and Ben, who remained a month longer, and took off alone to visit Goenka in India.

CHAPTER TWENTY-SEVEN
PASSAGE TO INDIA

This journey was extraordinarily eventful, and even now, thirty-five years later, a great many details remain in my mind. In fact, as I recently have become more interested in, and more respectful of, meditation practices, the events of this journey have taken on a preternatural vividness.

I land in Bombay, now Mumbai, at the time of the annual Chaturthi festival when huge crowds are celebrating enormous statues of the elephant-headed god, Ganesh. I haven't traveled alone for a long time and am thrilled about this new world and new adventure. The following day I begin a two-hour journey from Mumbai to Igatpuri, sitting in a train compartment with three lovely Indian sisters who are clothed in bright saffron and magenta gowns.

The most beautiful of the three sits next to me and I inhale her intoxicating cinnamon and cardamom fragrance. The two others sit across from me. I glance at my traveling companions surreptitiously from time to time—their beauty takes my breath away—but mostly I look out the window at the astonishing sights. The train follows a riverbank full of hordes of people wading and chanting as they immerse small statues of Ganesh in the water, many of them also holding yellow papier-mâché globes. I point out the window and speak to the woman next to me, "Pardon me, but could you tell me what is happening? What are they chanting?"

She turns and looks directly into my eyes and answers me in exquisite Indian-tinged English, "They say, 'Beloved Canapati, come again next year.'"

"Canapati?" I ask.

The two other women titter.

My companion answers, "Our language and customs are very confusing, I know. But perhaps you know this god's more common name, Ganesh."

"Thank you. And may I ask why they immerse him in the river?"

"The ritual teaches us the cosmic law: the cycle of form to formlessness is eternal. The Ganesh statues are formed of clay, and in the water they dissolve to formlessness. The body perishes but the god residing in it remains constant."

"How interesting. Thank you. And one last question: Why are people holding those yellow paper globes?"

All three women again titter at the question. "Those globes represent the moon. There is an old legend about Ganesh in which he ate too many ladoos . . . "

"Ladoos?"

"A ladoo is one of our pastries, a fried flour ball with cardamom syrup. Ganesh loved them and one night ate so many that he fell over and his stomach burst. The moon, the one witness to this event, found it all quite hilarious and laughed and laughed. Enraged, Ganesh banished the moon from the universe. But very soon everyone, even the gods, missed the moon so much that an assembly of them petitioned the Lord Shiva, Ganesh's father, to persuade Ganesh to relent. Even the moon joined in and apologized to Ganesh, who gave in and reduced the moon's punishment: the moon was to be invisible only one day a month and partially visible the rest of the month."

"Thank you," I said. What a fascinating story. And what a droll god with that elephant head!"

My companion thinks for a moment and adds, "Please don't allow my comments to cause you to underestimate the seriousness of the religion. It's interesting to consider the features of Ganesh—each one means something." She unclasps a Ganesh brooch worn around her neck under her robes, and holds it up for me to see. "Look carefully at Ganesh," she says. "His every feature has an important message. The large head tells us to think big, the large ears to listen well, the small eyes to focus hard. Oh, and one other thing, the small mouth tells us to talk less, and that suddenly causes me to wonder if I am talking too much."

"Oh no. Far from it." She is so beautiful that at times I have difficulty concentrating on her words, but of course I say nothing of that. "Please continue. Tell me, why does he have only one tusk?"

"To remind us to hold on to the good and throw away the bad."

"And what's he holding? It looks like an ax."

"Yes, it means that we should cut off attachments."

"That sounds much like Buddhism," I say.

"We must not forget that the Buddha emerged from the great ocean of Siva."

"And one last question. The mouse under his foot? I've seen it in every statue of Ganesh."

"Oh, that's the most interesting attribute of all," she says. Her eyes entrance me; I feel as though I'm melting into her gaze. "The mouse represents 'desire,' and Ganesh is teaching that we must keep desire under control."

Suddenly we hear a squeal of breaks as the train slows. My companion, whose name I have not learned, says, "Ah, we are approaching Igatpuri and I must gather my things for departure. My sisters and I are attending a Vipassana meditation retreat here."

"Oh, I'm attending the retreat too. I've enjoyed our conversation so much. Perhaps we could continue to speak at the retreat— at tea time or lunch?"

She nods, saying, "Alas, there is to be no more speaking . . . "

"I'm confused. You say no but you nod your head yes."

"Yes, yes, our head nodding is always a problem for Americans. When we nod up and down we mean no and when we shake our head side to side we mean yes. I know it is the reverse of what you are accustomed to."

"So then you mean no. But why? Why no more speaking?"

"At the retreat there can be no speech. *Noble silence* is the rule, the law, at the Vipassana retreat—no speech at all for the next eleven days. And *that*, too, is forbidden," she points at the book on my lap. "There must be no distractions from the task at hand."

"Well, goodbye," I say, and add hopefully, "Perhaps we can talk again on the train after the retreat."

"No, my friend, of that we must not think. Goenka teaches that we must inhabit only the present. Past remembrances and future longings produce only disquiet."

I have often thought of her departing words: "Past remembrances and future longings produce only disquiet." So much truth in those words, but at such great cost. I don't think I'm able or willing to pay so much.

A t Igatpuri I taxied a short distance to the meditation center, where I registered and was asked to donate money for the retreat. When I inquired about the average fee attendees paid, I was told that most of the attendees were poor and paid no fee at all. I donated two hundred dollars, considering that a modest fee for an eleven-day retreat that included room and board. Yet the registration staff seemed astounded by my generosity and all shook their heads in approval as I glanced at them. I looked about me and noted, with some concern, that, of the roughly two hundred participants registering for the retreat, I was the only Westerner!

A staff member placed all my books in a locker in the front office and then guided me to my sleeping area. Perhaps because

I had made a sizable donation, I was placed in a room with only four companions. We greeted one another silently. One of them was blind, and on three or four occasions he grew confused and tried to lie down on my pad and I guided him back to his. There was no speech for the entire ten days. Only Goenka, or occasionally his assistant, spoke.

It was only when I looked at the schedule that I began to grasp the severity of what I had signed up for. The day started at 5 a.m. with a light breakfast and then meditation instruction, chanting, and lectures for the entire day. The only real meal of the day was a midday vegetarian lunch, but very soon I lost my appetite and scarcely cared about food—a common occurrence at the retreat.

After breakfast we assembled in the great hall, where there was a slightly elevated podium for Goenka. The hall had a floor of matting and, of course, no furniture. The two hundred attendees all sat in lotus position waiting in silence for Goenka to appear. After a few minutes of silence, four attendants escorted Goenka to the podium. A formidable, bronze-skinned, handsome man clothed in white robes, he opened the teaching with chants from an ancient Buddhist text in Pali, an extinct Indo-European language that is the liturgical language of Theravada Buddhism. He was to do this every morning of the retreat, singing in an extraordinarily rich baritone voice that transfixed me. Whatever else was to come, I knew that the pleasure of listening to Goenka chant every morning would make the hardships of this journey worthwhile. At the end of the retreat I took care to buy some of his discs, and for years I listened to them every night while soaking in the hot tub.

The first thought that enters my mind, when I wonder why the chanting so affected me, is my father's voice as he accompanied Yiddish singers on a phonograph record. And then, too, I think of how much Goenka's chanting reminds me of the cantors chanting in the synagogue. During my adolescence, all I wanted to do was to escape from the synagogue as quickly as possible, but now, looking back, I recall some delight in listening to the cantor's fine voice. I can only guess there is some deeply buried part of me craving enchantment, and the alleviation of the pain of separateness through ritual and authority. I think there are few without such craving. I've seen the emperor without clothes, heard the secrets of too many individuals in high places, and know there is no one immune to despair and longing for the lap of the divine.

G oenka lectured to us in the first couple of days and taught us how to focus on breathing, how to experience the cool air on inhalation and the warmth of the exhaled air that had been cradled by the lungs. After only a few hours on the very first day, however, I developed a significant problem sitting in a lotus position. I have never been comfortable sitting on the floor and my knees and back began to ache. During the lunch break, I spoke of my problem to one of Goenka's assistants (though we had to maintain silence with one another, we were permitted, if it was truly urgent, to speak to an assistant). He looked at me oddly and wondered aloud what I must have done in my previous life to have such an uncooperative back. Still, he offered me a simple wooden chair, and for the rest of the retreat I sat in a chair amidst two hundred acolytes, all sitting serenely in lotus position. The assistant's comment about past lives was, by the way, the only reference to the supernatural that I heard during the entire retreat. Discipline was present but invisible until an evening when someone passed gas loudly. A couple of people laughed out loud, and soon eight to ten people got into a laughing fit lasting several minutes. Goenka cut the day's teaching short, and the following morning I noticed that the audience was smaller: the attendees who had laughed were no longer present, undoubtedly expelled.

On the third day, Goenka began the formal teaching of Vipassana meditation, instructing us to concentrate on our scalps until we sensed some sensation there, perhaps an itch or twinge, and then to move our attention down to the face, waiting for some sensation there that signaled us to move to the next segment of our body, to the neck, to the shoulders, until we reached the soles of our feet, all the while mindful of our breathing, and ever mindful of impermanence. All the later instruction focused only on learning this Vipassana technique, which, Goenka reminded us repeatedly, was the Buddha's own personal way of meditating.

In addition to instruction and chanting, Goenka gave several motivational lectures, almost all of which I found disappointing. He assured us we were now rich, that we now had a technique allowing us to use our time more meaningfully. For example, while waiting at a bus stop, we could meditate in the Vipassana mode and purify our minds, much as a gardener might remove weeds from a garden. Thus, he emphasized, we would have an advantage over the others who waited at the bus stop merely wasting time. This last idea, that Vipassana permitted one to gain an advantage over others, seemed unworthy and at odds with Goenka's spiritual appeal.

After a few days of Goenka's incessant instruction I had an epiphany that entirely changed the nature of my Vipassana exercise. I began to "sweep." I began to feel as though honey were being poured over my head and that it was slowly seeping down to envelop my entire body. It felt delicious, as though my body were buzzing or vibrating, and suddenly I had a flash of insight: now I fully understood why so many adherents might choose to remain in this state for weeks, even years. No worries, no anxiety, no sense of self or separateness, only the heavenly buzzing and warmth sweeping down and through the body.

Alas, this delicious otherworldly state endured only a day and a half and I could not again reenter it. I'm afraid that, overall, I would give myself a flunking grade in Vipassana meditation. It did not help that my sleep became entirely disrupted—I rarely slept for more than four, occasionally five, hours during the retreat.

This was partly due to the impact of so much meditation, partly because of my blind companion's confusion and his attempts to get into my bed, and partly because of the night guards circling the retreat center blowing police whistles loudly all night long to keep thieves away. The time passed far too slowly and I grew increasingly bored. Aside from washing my clothes, I could find little to do, and I washed them often whether they needed it or not, and even checked them frequently to see how quickly they were drying.

From time to time I saw my beautiful train companion at a distance, but, of course, we could not speak, though I was often certain she was gazing deep into my eyes. Despite her warnings about future thoughts disrupting tranquility, I often imagined us meeting again on the train, without her sisters, after the retreat. I tried my hardest to dispel that luscious fantasy—surely such fantasies obstruct the path to equanimity.

And, worst of all, no books! I rarely go a day without reading a chapter or two of a novel, but I had been required to part with all my reading material upon check-in. I felt squirrelly, like an addict in withdrawal. Spotting a wrinkled page of blank paper in my knapsack, I pounced on it, and with a nub of a pencil amused myself by sketching a story. I considered my train companion's words: "Past remembrances and future longings produce only disquiet." Now, with pencil in hand, I considered the catastrophic consequences of that thought. I imagined Shakespeare embracing that phrase and choosing not to write *King Lear*. Not only Lear, but all the great characters of literature would have been stillborn. Yes, the glorification of tranquility is wonderfully calming, but the cost, the cost!

After the retreat I took the train back to Mumbai and never again saw the Indian sisters. Before leaving India I wanted to visit Varanasi, the spiritual capital of India, but the route led through Calcutta, which confronted me, as never before, with the depths of human misery. The taxi that drove me into the city from the airport passed endless wretched shacks of the poor, each with a charcoal stove spewing dark smoke and fumes into air that stung the throat and darkened the sun by two in the afternoon. Gaunt beggars, the blind, lepers, and staring, emaciated children awaited me every time I left the hotel. The lepers chased me for blocks, threatening to touch me with their sores unless I gave alms. I always went out with my pockets full of coins, but the poverty and the need were inexhaustible. I did my best to use the Vipassana techniques I had just learned, but I failed to achieve tranquility. My novice meditation practice seemed powerless against real agitation.

After three days in Calcutta, I boarded the train and arrived at the holy city of Varanasi late at night, the only tourist at the empty train station. After an hour, a bicycle cart driver arrived at the station and agreed, after some spirited bargaining, to take me to Varanasi and help me find lodgings. But the city was so filled with Buddhist pilgrims that empty beds were scarce. Finally, after two hours of searching, I found a tiny room in a Tibetan monastery that was adequate but noisy. I slept very little that night because of the loud and joyful tantric chanting all night long. In the coming days I attended seminars, yoga classes, and meditation exercises at the various monasteries. Though I was a failure as a meditator, I found the seminars and lecture of great interest—not for a minute did I doubt there was great wisdom in the Buddhist tradition. Nor did I consider enlisting in further meditation training. At that time it seemed solipsistic to me—I had a whole life elsewhere: a wife and family that I loved deeply, my own work, and my own method of ministering to others.

I took boat rides on the Ganges, saw the daily cremations along the riverbank, the hordes of monkeys in the trees and on the roofs, and explored the surrounding area with a guide, a college student with a motorcycle. Next I went to Sarnath, the Buddhist holy city with many revered sites—for example, the deer park where the Buddha first taught the Dharma to his acolytes, as well the Bodhi tree grown from a cutting of the original tree under which the Buddha found enlightenment.

When I went to the station to buy my ticket back to Calcutta, where I was to catch my plane back to the United States after a stop in Thailand, the ticket seller informed me that no seats would be available for several days. I was baffled, since the station appeared relatively deserted. Returning to my hotel, I asked the manager for help, and he informed me, with a smile, that the solution to this riddle was quite simple and that I had yet to learn the ways of India. He escorted me back to the train station, asked me for a five-dollar bill, then slipped the bill to the ticket seller, who courteously and instantaneously produced a ticket. Moreover, when I boarded the train, I observed that I was the sole passenger in the entire second-class car.

From Calcutta I flew to Thailand, where I toured floating markets and Buddhist shrines and had an interesting conversation and tea with a Buddhist scholar I'd arranged to meet through a friend at home. In the evening, a friend of my cousin Jay took me out for a secular tour of the town. At the sprawling seafood restaurant where we went to eat, the waiter did not provide a menu but escorted us to a fishpond circling the restaurant and asked us to select our fish. He caught it in a long-handled net and guided us to a large fresh vegetable bin, where I selected side dishes. I did my best to instruct the waiter with my one Thai phrase, "Phrik rxn" ("No hot chili"), but must have mangled the words, for they elicited such boisterous laughter that other waiters came over to join in the merriment. After dinner my guide took me to my first and only Thai full-body massage parlor. I was escorted to a room by an assistant who asked me to undress and bathe, after which she covered me from head to toe with massage oil, at which point the masseuse, an extraordinarily beautiful naked woman, entered and began to massage me. After only a few minutes I realized that I had misunderstood the term full-body massage—it was not so much that *my* whole body was to be massaged, but that she massaged me with *her* whole body. At the end of the massage she smiled, bowed, and inquired in a most delicate fashion, "Is there anything else you might desire?"

From Bangkok I traveled by bus to Chiang Mai, where I watched elephants at work clearing forests. I met a fellow traveler, an Austrian tourist, and we hired a guide to take us on a canoe trip up the Mae Kok River. We stopped at a native village to join the males as they sat in a circle enjoying their daily opium smoke, while the females, of course, did all the tribal work. My one experience with opium was not dramatic: simply a mildly mellow state of mind lasting for several hours. We continued on to Chiang Rei, passing along the way a host of fairyland crenelated temples that looked as though they might take flight at any moment. At Chiang Rei I walked on a bridge with other tourists connecting Thailand to Burma, where, halfway across, we met stern Burmese military guards. The guards permitted us to touch the barrier for a few moments so we could say we had been to Burma. Next I flew to the island of Phuket for a few days of beach walking and scuba diving, and then headed home to California.

Though I loved this trip, I ultimately paid a price for it. Not long after I returned home, I developed a strange illness that plagued me for several weeks with fatigue, headaches, lightheadedness, and loss of appetite. All the paragons of the Stanford Hospital agreed that I had contracted some tropical disease, but no one ever figured out what it was. A few months later, when I had fully recovered, we celebrated with a brief trip to a Caribbean island where we had rented a cabin for two weeks. One of my first days there I took a nap on the couch, and I awoke covered with insect bites. By the following day I felt worse than I had on arriving home from India. We flew home, and the Stanford Department of Medicine spent weeks working me over for dengue fever and other tropical illnesses. Though they used every diagnostic test available to modern medicine, they never solved the puzzle of my illness.

I remained ill for about sixteen months, barely able to get to Stanford each day and requiring a great deal of rest. One of Marilyn's close friends told her later that many people thought I had suffered a stroke. Eventually, I resolved to rebuild my body: I joined a gym and forced myself to work out daily. No matter how bad I felt, I absolutely ignored any pleas or excuses from my body and maintained my regimen at the gym, and eventually I regained my health. Looking back on this time, I recall how often my twelve-year-old son, Ben, came into my bedroom and sat silently with me. For those two years I missed playing tennis with him, never taught him chess, never took bicycle rides with him (though he recalls our playing backgammon and reading aloud *The Chronicles of Thomas Covenant* by Stephen Donaldson).

Ever since that time, I have felt tremendous empathy for patients suffering from mysterious non-diagnosable illnesses, such as chronic fatigue syndrome or fibromyalgia. It was a dark chapter in my life, and almost all memories of those days have faded—but I know it was my ultimate test of endurance.

Though I did not meditate again for many years, I've come to have a higher regard for the practice, partly because I've known many people to whom it has given relief from suffering and offered a path to a compassionate life. In the past three years I've read more about meditation, spoken to colleagues with a meditation practice, and experimented with different approaches. Often, in the evening when I feel agitated, I listen to one of the countless sleep meditations available on the Internet, and often fall asleep before the end of the meditation.

India was my first in-depth introduction to Asian culture. It was not to be my last.

CHAPTER TWENTY-EIGHT
JAPAN, CHINA, BALI, AND *LOVE'S EXECUTIONER*

As I was checking into my Tokyo hotel in the fall of 1987, I encountered the English-speaking psychologist my Japanese hosts had flown in from New York to serve as translator. He was staying in the adjoining hotel room and would be available at all times for the entire week of my consultation.

"Can you tell me exactly what I'll be doing?" I asked.

"The program director at the Hasegawa Hospital has told me nothing specific about your schedule this week."

"I wonder why. I've inquired but they've not replied: they seem almost to be deliberately secretive."

He simply looked at me, hunching his shoulders.

The following morning when he and I arrived at the Hasegawa Hospital, I was greeted graciously with a huge bouquet of flowers by a large contingent of psychiatrists and administrators waiting inside the entrance. They said my first morning was a special occasion: the entire staff of the hospital would be in attendance to listen to my discussion of an inpatient therapy group meeting. They then guided me into an auditorium seating about four hundred people. Having commented on group meetings countless times, I felt relaxed and sat back anticipating a verbal description or a videotape of a group meeting. Instead I was stunned to see that the staff had elaborately prepared a dramatized re-creation of a group meeting. They had taped a group session held on one of the hospital wards the previous month, transcribed it, assigned roles to various staff members, and obviously spent a great many hours rehearsing the drama. It was a polished performance, but, alas, it portrayed one of the most dreadful group meetings I had ever seen. The leaders circled the group, offering advice and prescribing various exercises in turn to each member. Not once did a member of the group address another member—in my view, a clear example of how *not* to do group therapy. If it were only the taping of a real group session, I would have had no problem halting it and then describing alternative approaches. But how could I possibly stop a carefully choreographed production that must have required countless hours of rehearsal? It would have been a horrific insult, and so I sat and attended to the entire performance (with my translator whispering into my ear). Then, in my discussion, I gently, very gently, suggested some interpersonally based techniques.

I tried my best to be a helpful teacher during my week in Tokyo, but I never felt I was being effective. I realized during that week that something deeply embedded in Japanese culture opposes Western psychotherapy, especially group psychotherapy: mainly, shame at revealing oneself or sharing one's family secrets. I volunteered to lead a process group for therapists, but the idea was rejected, and, to be honest, I was relieved. I think there would have been such powerful silent resistance that we would have made little progress. In all my presentations that week, the audience was respectfully attentive, but no one made a comment or asked a single question.

Marilyn had a similar experience on the same trip. She gave a lecture on twentieth-century American women's literature at a Japanese women's institute before a large crowd in a beautifully appointed auditorium. The event was well orchestrated, with a lovely dance recital preceding the lecture and an attentive, respectful audience. But when she asked for questions or comments, there was silence. Two weeks later, she gave the identical talk at the Beijing Foreign Studies University and at the end was bombarded with questions from the Chinese students.

Every imaginable courtesy was given me in Tokyo. I loved our formal bento box luncheons with seven layers of delicate and splendidly arrayed courses. Lavish parties were given in my honor, and my host generously invited me to use his 360-degree-view condominium in Hawaii whenever I wished.

After my consultation, wherever we traveled in Japan we were always treated generously by hosts and strangers. In Tokyo one evening when we were heading toward the Kabuki Theater but had lost our way, we showed our tickets to a woman washing the steps of a building and asked for directions. She instantly dropped what she was doing and escorted us four blocks to the door of our theater. Another time, in Kyoto, we had disembarked from a bus and were strolling through the city when we heard hurried footsteps behind us. An elderly woman struggling to catch her breath approached with the umbrella we had left on the bus. A short time later at a Buddhist temple we fell into a conversation with a stranger, a college professor, who immediately invited us to his home for dinner. But their culture did not welcome my approach to therapy, and very few of my books have been translated into Japanese.

Japan was the first stop of a year's sabbatical. I had just completed a difficult period revising, once again, my group therapy textbook. Beginners, like me, who write a textbook are generally unaware that, if the textbook is successful, they are signing on for life. Textbooks must be revised every few years, particularly if there is new research and change in the field—and that, indeed, was the case for group therapy. If they are not revised, teachers will search for a more current text to assign to their classes.

In the fall of 1987, we had an empty nest: my youngest child, Ben, had left home for college at Stanford. After sending my textbook revision to the publisher, Marilyn and I celebrated our freedom with a full year of travel abroad, stopping for long writing retreats in Bali and Paris.

For a very long time I had been considering a very different kind of book. All my life I have been a lover of narrative, and I have often smuggled therapy stories, some only a few lines long, some lasting a few pages, into my professional writing. Over the years many readers of my group therapy text had informed me that they were willing to put up with many pages of dry theory because they knew there would be another teaching story coming around the bend. So, at age fifty-six, I resolved to make a major life change. I would continue to teach young psychotherapists through my writing, but I would elevate the story to a privileged position: I would put the story first and allow it to be the primary vehicle for my teaching. I felt the time had come to liberate the storyteller within me.

Before leaving for Japan it was imperative to get the hang of my newfangled gadget: a laptop computer. So we rented a cabin for three weeks in Ashland, Oregon, a town we had visited many times for its extraordinary theater festival. We saw plays in the evenings but during the daytime I assiduously practiced writing on the laptop. When I felt confident about its use, we took off for our first stop: the consultation in Tokyo.

I was a one-finger typist at that point. All my prior books and articles had been written in longhand (or, in one case, dictated). But to use this new computer I had to learn to type, and I succeeded via an unusual method: I spent my long flight to Japan playing one of the early video games in which my spaceship was attacked by alien vessels firing missiles in the shape of letters of the alphabet, which could only be repelled by pressing the corresponding key on the keyboard. It was an extraordinarily effective pedagogical device and by the time the plane landed in Japan I knew how to type.

After our visit to Tokyo we flew to Beijing, where we met four American friends and, with a guide, which was mandatory during those years, set off on a two-week tour of China. We went to the Great Wall, the Forbidden City, and, on a river trip, to Guilin, where we were enthralled by the pencil-like mountains in the distance. On all these journeys I continued to contemplate how I would write a collection of therapy stories.

One day in Shanghai I was feeling a bit under the weather and did not accompany the others on their full-day tour, but spent the morning resting. From my briefcase crammed with dictated session notes, I randomly selected one folder (out of twenty-five) and read over the summaries of the seventy-five therapy sessions I had had with Saul, a sixty-year-old biochemistry researcher.

That afternoon, while meandering alone through the back streets of Shanghai, I came upon a large, handsome, and long-abandoned Catholic church. Entering through the unlocked door, I wandered down the aisles until my eye caught the confessional booth. After making certain I was alone, I did something I had always wanted to do: I slipped in and sat down in the priest's seat! I thought of the generations of priests who had listened to confessions in this box and imagined all that they had heard—so much remorse, so much shame, so much guilt. I envied those men of God; I envied their ability to pronounce to sufferers, "You are forgiven." What therapeutic power! My own abilities felt dwarfed.

After sitting and meditating for about an hour in that ancient seat of authority, an amazing thing happened: I slipped into a reverie during which the entire plot of a story, "Three Un-opened Letters," revealed itself. I suddenly knew everything about that story—its characters, its development, and its moments of suspense. I was desperate to record it before it evaporated, but I had no paper or pencil (this was the pre-iPhone era)—no way to record my thoughts. Scouring the church, I found a one-inch stub of pencil in an empty bookshelf, but not a scrap of paper, so I turned to the only paper available to me—the blank pages of my passport—on which I scribbled the essentials of the story. This was the first of a collection I would ultimately title *Love's Executioner*.

A few days later we said goodbye to our friends and to China and flew to Bali for a two-month stay in an exotic house we had rented. There I began to write in earnest. Marilyn also had a writing project (which eventuated in her book *Blood Sisters: The French Revolution in Women's Memory*). Though we dearly loved our four children, we exalted in our freedom: this was our first prolonged sojourn together without children since our honey-moon in France, thirty-three years earlier.

Our Balinese house was unlike anything we had ever encoun-tered. From the outside we could see only the high wall encircling the large property, which was filled with lush tropical flora. The house had no walls, only hanging shades dividing and enclosing the rooms. The sleeping area was upstairs, and the bathroom was in a separate structure. Our first night there was unforgettable: about midnight, a swarm of flying insects descended upon us, mil-lions of them, so overwhelming that we pulled the sheets over our heads. I eyed my suitcases, planning to get as far away from this place as I could as fast as possible when morning arrived. But by the time the sun rose, all was quiet again, not an insect in sight, and the servants swore to us that this termite mating swarm happened only one night a year. Birds in iridescent colors boldly perched in the intricately twisted trees of the garden and caroled strange melodies. The perfume of unfamiliar blossoms

BALI, 1988.

drugged us, and we found the kitchen stocked with several types of strange-looking fruit. A staff of six living in huts on the property spent their days cleaning, cooking, gardening, playing music, and making flower and fruit arrangements for the frequent religious festivals. A three-minute walk out the back gate down a sandy trail took us to the magnificent Kuta Beach—still pristine and deserted in those days. And all of this for far less than the rent we charged for our Palo Alto house.

After writing "Three Unopened Letters," the story about Saul, from the notes I had sketched in my passport, I spent mornings on the garden bench trolling my case notes for the next story. In the afternoons Marilyn and I wandered for hours along the beach, and, almost imperceptibly, a story would take root and develop such momentum as to compel me to put aside all other notes and devote myself to that particular tale. As I started writing, I had no idea where a story would lead me or what shape it would take. I felt myself almost a bystander as I watched it take root and send up shoots that soon interlaced.

I have often heard writers say a story writes itself, but I hadn't understood it until then. After two months, I had an entirely new and deeper appreciation of an old anecdote Marilyn had told me years before about the nineteenth-century English novelist William Thackeray. One evening, as Thackeray came out of his study, his wife asked how the day's writing had gone. He responded, "Oh, a terrible day! Pendennis [one of his characters] made a fool of himself and I simply couldn't stop him."

Soon I became used to listening to my characters speaking to one another. I eavesdropped all the time—even after finishing the day's writing, when I was strolling arm in arm with Marilyn on one of the endless buttery beaches. Before long I had another writerly experience, one of the peak experiences of my life. At some point while deep into a story, I observed my fickle mind flirting with another story, one taking shape beyond my immediate perception. I took this to be a signal—an uncanny one, to myself from myself—that the story I was writing was coming to an end and a new one readying for birth.

Now that all my words existed only on this unfamiliar computer, I grew more and more uneasy at having no paper copies of my work—such things as flash drives, Time Machine, and Dropbox were yet unborn. Unfortunately, my portable Kodak printer did not enjoy travel and, after only one month in Bali, gave up the ghost. Alarmed at the prospect of my work vanishing permanently deep in the computer's innards, I sought help. There turned out to be only one printer in all of Bali, in a computer school in the capital city of Denpasar. One day I brought my computer to the school, waited until the end of class, and begged or bribed—I forget which, perhaps both—the teacher to print a precious hard copy of the work to date.

Inspiration came quickly in Bali. Without mail, a telephone, or other distractions, I wrote better and more rapidly than ever before. In my two months there I wrote four of the ten stories. In each story I spent a great deal of time disguising the identity of the patients. I altered the patients' appearances, occupations, ages, nationalities, marital status, and often even gender. I wanted to be entirely certain that no one could possibly recognize them, and, of course, I would send the patient the finished story and ask for written permission.

In our downtime, Marilyn and I explored the island. We adored the graceful Balinese and admired their art, dancing, puppetry, carving, and painting, and we marveled at the religious parades. The beach-walking and snorkeling were heavenly. One day our driver took us, along with two bicycles, to one of Bali's highest points, and we coasted several miles downhill through villages, passing stands selling slices of jackfruit and durian. To my surprise, chess was popular in Bali, and I found games everywhere. I often went early to a nearby restaurant to play chess with the waiter.

My agreement with Marilyn was to spend the second half of the sabbatical year in Europe. I love tropical islands, and Marilyn loves France, and throughout our marriage we have compromised. Marilyn had just officially left her administrative position at Stanford (though she has stayed on until this day as a senior scholar), and she still had some professional duties that took her back to Palo Alto on our way to Europe. I stopped in Hawaii for a writing retreat on Oahu at our Japanese host's lovely condo, where I wrote two more stories. Finally, after five weeks, Marilyn rang the bell, informing me it was time to resume our trip.

Next stop, Bellagio, Italy. A year earlier we had each applied and been accepted for residence at the Rockefeller Foundation Center in Bellagio, she to work on her women's memoirs of the French Revolution, and I to work on my book of psychotherapy tales.

A residency at Bellagio must be one of the greatest perks of academia. Only a short walk from Lake Como, the Rockefeller compound has beautiful gardens, a superb chef, who hand-made the pasta and served a different variety every night, and a handsome central villa that houses the thirty scholars and provides a separate study for each. The scholars met together at mealtimes and for evening seminars, where we each presented our work. Marilyn and I wrote each morning and in the afternoons we often took the ferryboat to one of the small, charming villages on Lake Como. I spent a great deal of time with one of the other scholars, Stanley Elkins, a marvelous comic novelist. Stanley had been invalided by polio and used a wheelchair. Every night he regularly trolled for plots and characters by listening to talk radio.

After Bellagio we spent the remaining four months of our sabbatical in Paris, renting an apartment on the Boulevard Port Royal. Marilyn wrote at home and I in an outdoor café near the Panthéon, where I finished the last four stories. Once again, I took my daily French lessons—alas, as always, to no avail—and late afternoons and evenings we strolled through the city and had dinner with her Parisian friends.

Writing in an outdoor café agreed with me and I wrote with unusual efficiency. Later, when I returned home, I found an outdoor café in San Francisco in North Beach (Café Malvino) with good writing vibes, where I continued the practice. Since I meant this to be a collection of teaching tales for young therapists, I set out to write a few paragraphs at the end of each story that elaborated upon the theoretical points illustrated within. That idea proved unwieldy, and instead I spent several weeks writing a sixty-page teaching epilogue to appear at the end of the book. Then I mailed the manuscript to my publisher with a sense of great satisfaction.

Two or three weeks later, Phoebe Hoss, the Basic Books editor assigned to the book, contacted me. Phoebe was an editor from hell (but also from heaven) and we were destined for an epic battle. As I recall, Phoebe did only minor editing of the stories except at one point to insert a phrase, "an avalanche of flesh," into the fat lady story. That phrase sticks in my mind because it is the only gratuitous phrase any editor has ever added (even though I often wished for more). But then, when Phoebe read my long epilogue, she went berserk and insisted I ditch it entirely. She was absolutely sure that no final theoretical explanation was needed and that the stories would speak for themselves. Phoebe and I had a major war, battling for months. I submitted one version of the epilogue after another, and each was returned to me cruelly shortened until, after several months, she had reduced my sixty pages to ten and insisted it be moved to the front of the book. As I reread the book today, beginning with the succinct prologue, I am chagrined by memories of my fierce resistance: Phoebe, a blessed editor, whose like I would never again encounter, was absolutely right.

When the book was to be released Marilyn and I flew to New York for the publisher's publication party—such events, now rare, were common in that era. The party was scheduled for a Monday evening, but a negative review in the Sunday *New York Times* put a damper on everyone's spirits. The format of the book had very few precedents: only some of Freud's case histories and Robert Lindner's *The Fifty-Minute Hour*, about patients in hypnotherapy, came close. The *New York Times* reviewer, a child psychiatrist, was affronted by the format and ended her sour review saying that she would prefer to read her case histories in professional journals.

A few minutes after midnight on Sunday night, however, I was awakened by a phone call from my overjoyed publisher saying that the Wednesday *New York Times* would publish a rave review by Eva Hoffman, a well-known writer and reviewer. To this day I am grateful to Eva Hoffman, whom I had the pleasure of meeting years later. I did readings of the book in New York and at bookstores in a dozen cities. Those national book tours are now largely a thing of the past, along with the profession of book tour guides, who met authors at the airport and transported them to speaking engagements. At almost every bookstore, Oliver Sacks had just preceded me, promoting his recently published book *The Man Who Mistook His Wife for a Hat*. Our paths crossed so much that I felt I knew him, but unfortunately we never met. I much admired his work, and after reading his moving final book, *On the Move*, I wrote him a fan letter shortly before he died.

Within a few weeks after publication, to my total astonishment, *Love's Executioner* found its way to the *New York Times* bestseller list, where it remained for several weeks. I was soon overwhelmed with interviews and speaking requests, and remember complaining about my fatigue and stress in a lunch conversation with Phillip Lopate, a fine essayist who had been one of my instructors at a writing workshop at Bennington College. His advice to me: "Chill out and enjoy the attention—bestsellers are rare and, who knows, you might never have another." And, oh, how right he was.

Twenty-three years later, the publisher decided to reissue *Love's Executioner* with a different cover and asked me to write a new afterword. I reread the book—the first time in a great many years—and had strong reactions: pride coupled with chagrin at my aging and envy of my younger self. I couldn't help feeling *this guy writes a lot better than I can*. It was a pleasure to revisit all my dear old patients, many of them no longer alive. But there was one exception: the story "Fat Lady." I remember writing that story in a Paris café and spending hours constructing the opening paragraph, which introduces the concept of countertransference, the therapist's unbidden emotional reactions to a patient.

> *The day Betty entered my office, the instant I saw her steering her ponderous two-hundred-fifty-pound, five-foot-two-inch frame toward my trim, high-tech office chair, I knew that a great trial of countertransference was in store for me.*

The story is meant to be a teaching tale for therapists, and I, even more than the patient, am the main character. It is a story about those irrational, sometimes abhorrent feelings a therapist may feel toward a patient that may constitute a formidable obstacle in therapy. A therapist may have extremely strong feelings of attraction toward a patient, or may have a powerful negative reaction flowing from unconscious sources, perhaps from encounters with negative figures in the therapist's past. Though I wasn't in touch with all the reasons for my negative feelings toward obese women, I felt certain that my relationship to my mother played some role, and I knew I had to struggle hard to overcome my unruly feelings and relate to the patient in a human, positive fashion. That was the story I meant to tell, and to do it I magnified the extent of my countertransference. Thus the conflict between my negative countertransference toward Betty and my desire to help her provided the central drama.

One incident, in particular, evoked strong empathy in me. Betty had set up a date from the personal ads in a local newspaper (the common practice in those pre-Match.com days) and wore a rose in her hair to be identified. The man never appeared. This was not the first time Betty had experienced something similar, and she surmised that he had taken a look at her from a distance and disappeared. My heart went out to her and I had to hold back my tears as she described herself struggling to keep her composure and drinking in solitude at the crowded bar.

I took pride in the denouement expressed in the final words in the story when she asked for a farewell hug: "When we embraced, I was surprised to find that I could get my arms all the way around her."

I opted to write the story with brutal revelation of my shameful thoughts about obesity. No, it went much further than that: for the sake of literary power, I greatly magnified my repugnance and crafted the story into a duel between my role as a healer and the onslaught of bedeviling thoughts in the background.

It was with some trepidation that I handed Betty the story to read and asked her permission. I had, of course, altered all identifying details, and I asked if there were other changes she desired. I told her how I had exaggerated my feelings in the service of teaching more effectively. Betty said she understood and gave me written permission to publish the story.

The response to this particular story was vigorous and loud. "Fat Lady" generated a flood of negative responses from women who were hurt and outraged. But it also resulted in an even greater outpouring of positive letters from young therapists who felt relieved as they tried to work through their own negative feelings toward some of their patients. My honesty, they said, made it easier for them to live with themselves when they harbored negative feelings and enabled them to speak openly of such feelings to a supervisor or colleague.

When Terry Gross interviewed me on *Fresh Air*, a popular PBS radio program, she questioned me, perhaps "excoriated" is the more accurate term, about this story. Finally, in self-defense, I exclaimed, "Didn't you read the end of the story? Did you not understand that the story was about my journey in therapy with someone toward whom I had negative prejudices and that by the end I had changed and had matured as a therapist? I am the main character in this story, not the patient." I was never invited back to her program.

Though she may not have been able to tell me so, I imagine the story did cause Betty pain. I had put blinders on. I was too ambitious, too reckless, too caught up in liberating my writerly impulses. I regret it to this day. Writing that story now, I would try to transform obesity into some entirely different condition and more radically fictionalize the events of therapy.

I ended my afterword to a new edition of *Love's Executioner* with an observation my younger self would have found surprising: namely, that the view from eighty is better than expected. Yes, I can't deny that life in the later years is just one damn loss after another; but, even so, I've found far greater tranquility and happiness in my seventh, and eighth, and ninth decades than I had ever thought possible. And there's one additional bonus: *reading your own work can be more exciting!* Memory loss has some unexpected advantages. As I turned the pages of "Three Unopened Letters," "The Wrong One Died," and the title story, "Love's Executioner," I felt myself burning with curiosity. I had forgotten how the stories ended!

CHAPTER TWENTY-NINE

WHEN NIETZSCHE WEPT

In 1988, I returned to teaching and clinical work and collaborated with Sophia Vinogradov, a former Stanford psychiatric resident, on *A Concise Guide to Group Psychotherapy* for the American Psychiatric Press. Soon a familiar discomfort descended upon me: I missed having a literary project to work on and felt adrift. Before long I found myself drawn again to some of Nietzsche's works. I had always loved reading Nietzsche and soon felt so intoxicated by his powerful language that I couldn't tug my mind away from this strange nineteenth-century philosopher—a man so brilliant, but so isolated and despairing, and so much in need of help. After spending several months immersed in his early works, it dawned on me that my unconscious had already selected my next project.

I now felt split between two desires: to continue my life of research and teaching at Stanford, or to take a plunge and try to write a novel. I recall little of this internal struggle. I only know the solution that finally knit together these two disparate parts: I would write a teaching novel and attempt to transport my students in the field back in time to the Vienna of the late nineteenth century, where they could observe the birth of psychotherapy.

Why Nietzsche? Though he had lived during the era when Freud brought psychotherapy into existence, he had never been considered relevant to psychiatry. Yet many of Nietzsche's pronouncements, sprinkled throughout his work and written before the dawn of psychotherapy, are highly germane to the education of therapists. Consider these:

> *"Physician help thyself; thus you help your patients too. Let this be his best help—that he, the patient, may behold with his eyes the man who heals himself."*

> *"You shall build over and beyond yourself. But first you must be built yourself, perpendicular in body and soul. You shall not only produce yourself, but produce something higher."*

> *"For that is what I am through and through: reeling in, raising up, raising, a raiser, cultivator, and disciplinarian, who once counseled himself, not for nothing: Become who you are."*

> *"He who has a 'why' in life can put up with any 'how.'"*

> *"Often we are more in love with desire than the desired."*

> *"Some cannot loosen their own chains and can nonetheless redeem their friends."*

I imagined an alternative fictional history in which Nietzsche would play a major role in the evolution of psychotherapy. I imagined him interacting with the familiar cast of characters associated with the birth of psychotherapy: Sigmund Freud, Josef Breuer (Freud's mentor), and Breuer's patient Anna O. (the first person treated with the psychoanalytic method). How might the face of

therapy have been altered, I wondered, if Nietzsche, a philosopher, had played a key role in the birth of our field?

During this period of gestation I happened to read André
Gide's novel *Lafcadio's Adventures*, and my eye fell upon this felic-
itous phrase: "History is fiction that *did* happen; whereas fiction is
history that *might* have happened." Those words jolted me: they
described precisely what I wanted to do—to write fiction that
might have happened. I wanted to write a genesis of psychotherapy
that would have been entirely possible if history were rotated only
slightly on its axis. I wanted the events of my novel to have had a
possible existence.

As I began to write, I could sense my characters stirring as
though they strained to live once again. They needed my full attention, but my duties at Stanford were demanding: I taught residents and medical students, attended departmental meetings, and
met with patients in individual and group therapy. To write this
novel I knew I needed freedom from all distractions, so in 1990 I
arranged for a four-month sabbatical. As always, Marilyn chose
the setting for one half, and I the other. I selected one of the qui-
etest, most isolated island chains in the world—the Seychelles—
and she, as always, chose Paris.

We spent our first month on Mahé, the main island of the
Seychelles, and our second month on a smaller island, Praslin.
Both were pristine, ringed with spectacular beaches, and almost
eerily quiet—no newspapers, no Internet, no phones—the most
conducive site for writing I have ever encountered. We wrote the
first half of the day, I on my novel and Marilyn on *Blood Sisters*,
an English expanded version of her French-language book about
women who were eyewitnesses to the French Revolution. In the
afternoons, we explored the island, walked the beaches, and snor-
keled—and all the while, my characters were slowly coming to
life in my mind. In the evenings we read, played Scrabble, and
had dinner at the one nearby restaurant, and I mulled over plot
development for the next day's writing.

I began cautiously, sticking close to historical facts whenever possible. My first decision was the time period. I wanted the ailing Nietzsche to have an encounter with therapy, and several considerations pointed to 1882, the year he contemplated suicide and most urgently needed help. His letters from that era describe great suffering for over three hundred days a year, including excruciating headaches, weakness, severe visual problems, and gastric distress. As a result of his poor health, he had resigned his teaching position in 1879 from the University of Basel and was rootless for the rest of his life, traveling from one guesthouse to another throughout Europe in search of atmospheric conditions that might temper his anguish.

His correspondence reveals a profound depression. A typical 1882 letter to his one good friend, Franz Overbeck, read: " . . . *at the very base, immovable black melancholy. . . . I no longer see any point at all to living even another half year, everything is full, painful, dégoutant. I forgo and suffer too much. . . . I shall do nothing good anymore, so why do anything!*"

A catastrophic event for Nietzsche occurred in 1882: his passionate (though unconsummated) relationship with Lou Salomé, a lovely young Russian woman destined to infatuate other great men, among them Freud and Rainer Maria Rilke, came to an end. Nietzsche and his friend Paul Rée were both enamored of Lou Salomé, and the three made plans to live together in Paris. But the plan exploded in 1882, when Paul and Lou began a sexual relationship. Nietzsche was devastated and fell into great despair. Thus everything seemed to point to 1882 for my book: it was the nadir of Nietzsche's life—the time when he most needed help. And it was also a heavily documented year for all my major characters: Nietzsche, Breuer, Freud (as a medical student), and Lou Salomé.

As a reader I had lived in novels all my life, but I was a rank amateur at writing one. I pondered how to insert my imagined plot into 1882 without changing historical events. I could think of only one solution: to locate the entire novel in an imagined thirteenth month of that year. Perhaps I was overly cautious: I dared leap into fiction but played it safe by keeping one foot in reality, using historical characters and events rather than inventing fictional ones, even to the point of taking some of Nietzsche's dialogue from his letters. I felt as though I were learning to ride a bicycle by using training wheels.

Ultimately I envisioned a thought experiment that served as a keystone for the writing that would follow: *imagine what might have happened if Friedrich Nietzsche had been placed in a moment of history when he could have invented a psychotherapy, derived from his own published writings, that could have been used to cure himself.*

What a pity, I often mused, that it was not possible to have situated the story ten years later and imagined a therapeutic encounter between two towering geniuses: Nietzsche, the philosopher, and Freud, the psychoanalyst. But history did not cooperate. In 1882, Freud was still a young medical student, and he would not become a renowned practitioner for another decade. By that time Nietzsche had suffered a catastrophic brain disease (most likely tertiary syphilis) that resulted in severe dementia for the rest of his life.

If not Freud, then who else in 1882 might Nietzsche consult for help? My historical search yielded no names of practicing therapists in Vienna, or, for that matter, anywhere else in the world: *the field of psychotherapy had yet to be born.* As I've mentioned earlier, we often regard Freud as the father of psychoanalysis, but he was far more than that: *he was the father of psychotherapy per se.*

Ultimately I decided to have Nietzsche consult with Dr. Josef Breuer, Freud's teacher and mentor. Breuer, an outstanding physician, was often called upon to treat eminent figures, including royalty suffering from arcane medical conditions. Moreover, in 1880 Breuer had developed a unique psychological therapy, the forerunner to psychoanalysis, in order to help a patient known as Anna O., who suffered from hysteria. Breuer told no one about his innovative treatment of Anna O. except his medical student Sigmund Freud, who was also a friend of the family, and possibly some of his other medical students, and he did not publish his account of Anna until twelve years later, in *Studies in Hysteria*, a book he coauthored with Freud.

But how to link Breuer and Nietzsche? I chanced upon a convenient historical fact: in 1882, Lou Salomé's brother was a first-year student in the medical school where Breuer taught. I imagined the following scenario: Lou Salomé, stricken with guilt over the psychological pain she had inflicted upon Nietzsche, speaks of her distress to her brother, who, having attended a class where his teacher, Breuer, had discussed his treatment of Anna O., urges his sister to consult Breuer. A more experienced novelist would have had no difficulty fictionalizing all these events, but I stayed close to my mantra, *"Fiction is history that might have happened."*

Eventually, the first part of the plot fell into place. Through Lou Salomé, Nietzsche comes to consult Breuer for help with his physical ailments. Breuer tries to find a way to address Nietzsche's psychological disturbance, but Nietzsche is too proud and refuses to surrender power. Breuer tries every tactic he knows, but to no avail, and the treatment reaches a complete stalemate. At this point, in my attempt to be faithful to the character of both Nietzsche and Breuer, I had written myself into a corner, and I spent a couple of days struggling with how to proceed. I know that many writers produce a detailed outline first, but I turn the job over to my unconscious and allow the characters and events to evolve organically on the stage of my mind, while I simply record and fine-tune the work. In this case, that evolution had come to an impasse.

Marilyn and I had heard of Silhouette, a lovely, rarely visited island near Mahé, and we took a ferry there for a weekend. Soon after our arrival, a tropical storm descended, with heavy winds and torrential rains, and so I had no choice but to stay inside and write. It was here that I had a bolt of inspiration that resolved the Nietzsche-Breuer problem.

I was so excited about my solution that I ran out into the drenching rain to find Marilyn. I finally spotted her in the small hotel lounge, and right there read aloud the last few lines of the chapter, in which Breuer is walking home after Nietzsche had once again rebuffed his attempts to heal him.

> *He listened to the wind, to his steps, to the bursting of the fragile, icy crust of snow underfoot. And suddenly he knew a way—the only way! All the way home he crunched the snow and, with every step, chanted to himself, "I know a way! I know a way!"*

Marilyn's aroused curiosity about what would happen next was an excellent sign, and I continued reading the denouement. Breuer's inventive idea was to treat his fiercely resistant patient by turning the tables and asking Nietzsche to become *his* therapist. That reversal is the core idea around which all the later action revolves.

Years later, when writing an essay on the novel for a collection titled *The Yalom Reader*, I wondered about the source of that core idea. Perhaps it came from Hermann Hesse's novel *Magister Ludi*, which contains a story about two healers, one young, one old, who live on different ends of a continent. The young healer falls ill, sinks into despair, and sets out on a long journey to seek help from his rival, Dion.

During his journey, one evening at an oasis the young man falls into a conversation with another traveler, an older man, who turns out to be Dion himself, the very man he had been seeking! Dion invites the young man back to his home, where they live and work together for many years, first as student and teacher, then as colleagues. Years later, when Dion falls ill, he calls his younger colleague to him and says, "I have a great secret to tell you. Do you remember that night when we met and you told me you were on your way to see me?"

"Yes, yes. I will never forget that night and my first meeting with you."

"Well," says Dion, "I, too, was in despair at that time and I was on my way to seek help from you!"

An analogous role-switching appears in *Emergency*, a little-known fragment of a play by the psychiatrist Helmut Kaiser that was published in a psychiatric journal in 1962. In the play, a woman visits a therapist and begs him to help her husband, also a therapist, who is so depressed he is likely to kill himself.

The therapist agrees. "Yes, of course I'll see him. Ask him to call for an appointment."

The woman replies, "That is the problem. My husband denies that he is depressed and refuses to seek therapy."

"Then," says the therapist, "I'm sorry but I see no way I can be of help."

The woman replies, "You could see him pretending to be a patient and then find a way to help him."

Alas, we never learn whether the strategy worked, since the rest of the play was never written.

It occurred to me later on that I had witnessed something analogous in my own life. I once saw Don Jackson, an inventive psychiatrist, interviewing a chronic delusional schizophrenic patient who wore purple trousers and a flowing, magenta-colored robe. He spent his days on the ward perched imperiously on an elevated chair, silently regarding staff and patients alike as though they were his supplicants. Dr. Jackson observed the patient's regal demeanor for several minutes, then dropped to his knees, bowing his head to the ground, and with outstretched arms he offered the man the keys to the ward, saying, "Your majesty, it is you, not I, who should have these."

The patient, bewildered, stared at the keys and at the genuflecting psychiatrist and uttered his first words in many days. "Mistah, one of us here is very, very crazy."

Toward the end of our stay in the Seychelles I began to experience diminished vision coupled with a very painful reaction to morning light. A local physician gave me some ointment that lessened the pain, but the photophobia continued, and soon I had to remain in the dark until about noon, when the light would become bearable. The only room without windows was the bathroom, and so each morning until noon I wrote in the bathroom, using only the light of my computer. These were the first symptoms of Fuchs' dystrophy, a disorder of my cornea that was to cause me discomfort and visual problems for decades. In this disorder, there is a diminishment in the number of epithelial cells in the cornea that process the fluid accumulated during the night when the lids are closed. The cornea becomes thickened and swollen, which compromises vision. When the eyes open in the morning, the fluid in the cornea slowly evaporates, and vision improves gradually during the day.

The novel was flowing so well that I would have stayed in the Seychelles longer while Marilyn went on to Paris, but it was essential that I see an ophthalmologist. In Paris I learned that my only recourse was a corneal replacement, a procedure I delayed until our return to Stanford.

We rented an apartment near the Luxembourg Gardens with excellent blinds that permitted me to write in the dark for the next two months until the book was finished. I mailed the manuscript to my agent, Knox Burger, who had represented *Love's Executioner*. He rejected it immediately, saying, "There is no way I can sell this novel: nothing happens in it." He then suggested I learn how to write a plot by reading the manuscript of *Red Square*, a new novel by one of his other writers, Martin Cruz Smith. In search of another agent, I sent the manuscript to Owen Laster at the William Morris Literary Agency, who accepted it immediately and sold it to Basic Books, a publishing house of nonfiction works that had only once in its history published a novel (*The Doctor of Desire* by Allen Wheelis).

Upon publication, a short, dismissive review in the *New York Times* described *When Nietzsche Wept* as a "soporific little novel." That was the low point. After that came a series of highly positive reviews in other newspapers and magazines, and, a few months later, *When Nietzsche Wept* was awarded the gold medal for best fiction of the year by the Commonwealth Club of California. Second prize? *Red Square* by Martin Cruz Smith! Marilyn did not hesitate to send notice of this award both to the *New York Times* reviewer and to my former agent, Knox Burger.

Sales of *When Nietzsche Wept* were good in the United States, but dwarfed by its popularity in other countries. It was eventually translated into twenty-seven languages, with the largest audience in Germany and the largest readership per capita in Greece. In 2009, the mayor of Vienna selected it as the book of the year. Each year the mayor chooses a book, prints 100,000 copies, and distributes them free to the citizens of Vienna, leaving stacks of

THE AUTHOR BESIDE A TOWER OF FREE COPIES OF
WHEN NIETZSCHE WEPT, VIENNA, 2009.

THE AUTHOR WITH HIS WIFE, MARILYN, AND PORTRAIT
AT DINNER, VIENNA STADTHAUS, 2009.

books at pharmacies, bakeries, schools, and the annual book fair.
Marilyn and I flew to Vienna for several days of public presenta-
tions, one of them at the Freud Museum. There, in what was once
Freud's living room, I had an open discussion of the novel with an
Austrian philosopher.

The week culminated in a huge evening gala event for several hundred people at the town hall presided over by the mayor.
After my address to the audience, dinner was served, and the evening ended in a lively Viennese waltz. Since I am a poor dancer,
Marilyn waltzed with our good friend Hans Steiner, a Stanford
psychiatrist of Viennese birth, who flew to Vienna with his wife,
Judith, for the occasion. It was an over-the-top experience for all
of us.

Two years after the book's publication, when I was on a
speaking tour in Munich and Berlin, a German filmmaker approached me with the idea of making a documentary based on
my visits to various sites in Germany where Nietzsche had lived.
Together we visited Nietzsche's birthplace and childhood home in
Röcken and the church where his father had preached. Next to
the church is Nietzsche's burial plot, along with those of his sister

and parents. Rumor has it that Nietzsche's sister, Elisabeth, had his body moved so that she could be placed between their mother and father. At Nietzsche's school in Pforta, an old schoolmaster informed me that even though Nietzsche excelled in classics, he was *not* first in his class. At Elisabeth's house in Weimar, which has been turned into a museum, I saw the official admission document for Nietzsche's hospitalization at Jena, shortly before he died; the diagnosis clearly stated "Paretic syphilis." Hanging on the wall of the museum was a photograph of Hitler offering Elisabeth a bouquet of white roses. A few days later, at the Nietzsche archives in Weimar, I had the great pleasure of holding an early draft of *Thus Spake Zarathustra*, written in Nietzsche's own hand.

Years later, filmmaker Pinchas Perry made a film of *When Nietzsche Wept*. Though it was a low-budget film, it features a remarkable portrayal of Nietzsche by Armand Assante, an actor well-known to film buffs. In a conversation with Assante I learned that, of all his sixty films, he is most proud of his performance as Nietzsche.

One of the great surprises of my life occurred eleven years after publication, when I received a letter from a researcher in the Weimar archives, whom I had met there on my earlier trip to Germany. She informed me that she had just discovered an 1880 letter to Nietzsche from a friend urging him to consult with Dr. Josef Breuer for his medical problems! Nietzsche's sister, Elisabeth, scotched the plan, ostensibly because he had already consulted several other noted physicians. Nietzsche referred to his sister as an "anti-Semitic goose," and it's possible that she rejected the plan because Breuer was Jewish. The letter to Nietzsche suggesting he visit Breuer and two follow-up letters can be heard on the English audiobook version of the novel. This startling confirmation reassured me that I had remained true to Gide's aphorism: *Fiction is history that might have happened.*

CHAPTER THIRTY
LYING ON THE COUCH

After living in the clouds with *When Nietzsche Wept*, I was tugged back to earth by my textbook *The Theory and Practice of Group Psychotherapy*, which was squealing for attention. Now ten years old, it needed an update and a facelift if it was to continue competing with other textbooks. For the next year and a half I felt yoked to the plough as I spent day after day in the medical school library at Stanford reviewing the group research of the past decade, adding relevant new research, and, the most painful part, shaving off older material.

All the while, in the back of my mind, another novel was percolating. On my bicycle rides and during quiet moments before falling asleep, I experimented with plotlines and characters, and I soon began working on a tale I would title *Lying on the Couch*. I was amused by the double entendre: my book would deal with a lot of lying and a lot of psychotherapy on the couch.

Having completed my apprenticeship as a novelist, I discarded my training wheels and no longer fretted with fitting the characters and events into a certain historically accurate time and place. On this new project I was going to have the pleasure of composing an entirely fictional plotline peopled only by made-up characters, and unless the world is loonier than I imagined, this was going to be fiction that could *never* have happened. Yet underlying the surreal events of a comic novel, I intended to explore serious and substantial questions. Should we, as the early psychoanalysts insisted, withhold our real selves and offer only interpretations and a blank screen? Or should we instead be open and genuine and disclose our own feelings and experiences to our patients? And if so, what pitfalls might lie in store?

I have written much in the professional psychiatric literature about the overarching importance of the therapy relationship. The mutative force in therapy is not intellectual insight, not interpretation, not catharsis, but is, instead, a deep, authentic meeting between two people. Contemporary psychoanalytic thinking has also gradually arrived at the conclusion that interpretation is not enough. As I write these words, one of the most widely cited psychoanalytic articles in recent years is titled "Non-Interpretive Mechanisms in Psychoanalytic Therapy: The 'Something More' Than Interpretation." That "something more," referred to as "now moments" or "moments of meeting," is not too different from what is presented in the article my fictional character Ernest is attempting to write in *Lying on the Couch*, titled "On In-Betweenness: The Case for Authenticity in Psychotherapy."

In my own practice I strive continuously for an authentic meeting with my patients, both in group and individual therapy. I tend to be active, personally engaged, and often focus on the here-and-now: rarely does a session pass without my inquiring about our relationship. But how much of his/her own self should the therapist reveal? The vital issue of therapist transparency, hotly debated in the field, is analyzed, dissected, and stretched to its limits in this comic novel.

I have just reread *Lying on the Couch* for the first time in years and am struck by many things I had long forgotten. First, though the plot is entirely fictional, it contains a great many real events from my life. This is not rare: I once heard Saul Bellow say,

"When a novelist is born the family is doomed." It is well-known that the characters of Bellow's early life populate the pages of his fiction. I've followed suit. About a year prior to writing this novel, a friend of a friend attempted to swindle me by selling me shares of a company that, as I learned later, did not exist. My wife and I gave him $50,000 to invest. Though we soon received very official-appearing certificates of deposit from a Swiss bank, still there was something about him that aroused my suspicion. I took the certificates to a US branch of the Swiss bank and learned that the signatures were forged. Then I called the FBI and informed the swindler that I had done so. Just before my meeting with the FBI, he appeared at my door with $50,000 in cash. This event and this swindler were the inspiration for Peter Macondo in my novel, a con man who preys on therapists.

But it was not just the con man: a great many other acquaintances, events, and parts of myself found their way into the novel. Details of my poker game are there (including caricatures of myself and other players). Because of my poor vision, I've stopped playing poker, but to this day when I have lunch with my old poker chums, they refer to one another by the names I had given them in the novel. Also, there is a patient (heavily disguised) who was particularly seductive to me in real life, as well as a sophisticated but arrogant psychiatrist who once supervised me. I also included a friend from my Hopkins days, Saul, who is Paul in the novel. Much of the furniture and art is real, including a glass sculpture Saul made and dedicated to me of a man looking over the edge of a bowl, titled "Sisyphus Enjoying the View." The list is very long: pet peeves, books, clothes, gestures, my earliest memories, my parents' history as immigrants, my games of chess and pinochle with my father and uncles—they're all scattered throughout the novel, including my attempt to kick the grocery-store sawdust from my shoes. I tell a story about the father of a character named Marshal Streider, who is the owner of a small grocery store on Fifth and R Streets in Washington, DC. When a customer enters his store asking for a pair of work gloves, he says they are in the back store-room, but then he goes out the back door and gallops down the block to the market to buy a pair of gloves for ten cents, and sells them to the customer for thirteen cents. That is a true story told to me by my father, who had owned a store at that address just before I was born.

The detailed account of an analyst being banished from the psychoanalytic institute was loosely based on Masud Khan's ejection from the British Psychoanalytic Society in 1988. Charles Ry-croft, my British analyst, witnessed the event and described it to me in detail. Even the "Smokey the Bear" dream is my own, from the night after Rollo May died. Many of the characters' names had personal meaning for me—for example, the protagonist's name, Ernest Lash. While writing about Ernest, who was indeed very earnest, and his seductive patient, I often thought of Odysseus, who had himself lashed to the mast of his ship to escape the lusty calls of the sirens—hence, "Ernest Lash." Another character, a figure in my fictional psychoanalytic institute, is Terry Fuller, a name I derived from a former student, Fuller Torrey, who became an eminent figure in psychiatry. Marshal Streider, patterned after one of my Johns Hopkins supervisors, strides firmly and staunchly upholds the law (except for one egregious lapse of judgment).

Though I personally champion the idea of therapist genuine-ness, I decided to present an enormous challenge to Ernest Lash. For reasons explained in the novel, Ernest boldly undertakes an experiment: he will be entirely transparent with the next new patient entering his door. Alas, by sheer novelistic coincidence, Ernest's next new patient, an attorney, has her own hidden agenda: she, unbeknownst to him, is the revenge-seeking wife of one of Ernest's patients, and believes that Ernest has persuaded her husband to divorce her. To retaliate, she is planning to seduce and, thereby, ruin him. I've never had so much fun writing as when I embarked on this tale about a therapist committed to authenticity encountering a patient committed to entrapment. And writing one of the subplots was even more fun, when I described how the novel's version of the British Psychoanalytic Society drums out an offending analyst for heretical interpretations and elects to send out a public recall notice—like those sent by automobile manufacturers—to all his patients who had been treated with damaging interpretations.

Several filmmakers have wanted to turn *Lying on the Couch* into a film. Harold Ramis, the late actor and film director of *Groundhog Day*, *Ghostbusters*, and *Analyze This*, bought the film option, and we had a good deal of contact with one another when he was filming *Bedazzled*, shot on the streets of San Francisco. Alas, *Bedazzled* failed at the box office and the film studio refused to finance *Lying on the Couch* until he first made a surefire big profit movie, *Analyze That*—a sequel to his highly successful *Analyze This*. Unfortunately, *Analyze That* also bombed. Although Harold Ramis continued to purchase film options on the book for several years, he was never able to obtain sufficient financing for the project. I liked Harold Ramis very much and was saddened by the news of his death in 2014.

Another near-life film experience occurred with Wayne Wang, the director of such fine movies as *The Joy Luck Club*, *Smoke*, and *Maid in Manhattan*. He, too, bought the option, but was also unable to find financial backing. Later he made a film called *Last Holiday* about a woman (Queen Latifah) with a fatal illness and asked me to lead a two-day T-group with the cast in New Orleans to sensitize them to the issues around dealing with a fatal illness. I had a lark working with Queen Latifah, LL Cool J, and Timothy Hutton, all of whom I found refreshingly open, well-informed, serious about their work, and interested in my observations.

Finally, Ted Griffin, a talented screenwriter (*Ocean's Eleven*, *Matchstick Men*), entered the scene, and he has had the film rights for the past several years. Having written a screenplay, he approached actor Anthony Hopkins—one of my screen idols, with whom I enjoyed conversing by phone. Alas, nothing has yet materialized. Moreover, there's a part of me dreading a film version, which might ignore the serious messages of the novel and focus excessively, perhaps exclusively, on the conning and sexual parts. I now feel a bit embarrassed by the protagonist's erotic exuberance. My wife, always my first reader, wrote in caps on the last page of the manuscript: "ISN'T THERE ANYTHING ELSE YOU WANT TO TELL AMERICA ABOUT YOUR SEXUAL FANTASIES?"

CHAPTER THIRTY-ONE

MOMMA AND THE MEANING OF LIFE

Every year at departmental graduation, the psychiatry residents put on a skit lampooning some aspect of their Stanford experience. One year I was the target, and the resident lampooning me always appeared caressing a stack of books with "Yalom" on the spine. But I took no offense: instead, I found myself rather pleased at the sight of all those books I had written.

At that time I was working on a publisher-generated book, *The Yalom Reader*, beautifully edited by my son Ben, that contains excerpts from my prior work and new essays. After finishing the final essay, I had a powerful, unforgettable dream about my mother that I described in the title story of my next book, *Momma and the Meaning of Life*.

Dusk. Perhaps I am dying. Sinister shapes surround my bed: cardiac monitors, oxygen canisters, dripping intravenous bottles, coils of plastic tubing—the entrails of death. Closing my lids, I glide into darkness.

But then, springing from my bed, I dart out of the hospital
room smack into the bright, sunlit Glen Echo Amusement Park
where, in decades past, I spent many summer Sundays. I hear
carousel music. I breathe in the moist, caramelized fragrance of
sticky popcorn and apples. And I walk straight ahead—not hes-
itating at the Polar Bear Frozen Custard stand or the double-dip
roller coaster or the Ferris wheel—to take my place in the ticket
line for the House of Horrors. My fare paid, I wait as the next
cart swivels around the corner and clanks to a halt in front of me.
After stepping in and pulling down the guardrail to lock myself
snugly into place, I take one last look about me—and there, in
the midst of a small group of onlookers, I see her.

I wave with both arms and call, loud enough for everyone
to hear, "Momma! Momma!" Just then the cart lurches for-
ward and strikes the double doors, which swing open to reveal a
black gaping maw. I lean back as far as I can and, before being
swallowed by the darkness, call again, "Momma! How'd I do,
Momma? How'd I do?"

Could the dream's message be—and this possibility staggers
me—that I have been conducting my entire life with this lamen-
table woman as my primary audience? All my life I have sought
to escape, to climb away from my past—the ghetto, the grocery
store—yet can it be that I have escaped neither my past nor my
mother?

My mother had a conflictual relationship with her mother,
who spent the last years of her life in a New York nursing home.
In addition to cleaning and cooking and working in the store, my
mother regularly took a four-hour train ride to bring home-baked
pastries to her mother, who instead of thanking her, raved about
Simon, my mother's brother. He never brought her anything but a
bottle of 7-Up.

My mother told me that story so many times that I stopped
listening—I was tired of her ranting. But now I feel differently.

Obviously my mother felt wholly unappreciated by her only son. I often ask myself: *Why didn't I sympathize with her? Why couldn't I have said, "How unfair! You do all that work and baking and travel to see your mother and all she does is praise Simon for his 7-Up. How grating that must have felt!"* Really, how hard would it have been for me to say that? Oh, how I wish I could have been kind enough to utter those words. That simple act of appreciation would have meant so much to her. And perhaps, if I had said this, she wouldn't still be haunting my dreams.

And, of course, the dream staggers me with the idea that as I move toward my death, that dark house of horrors, I am still looking for validation. But not from my wife, my children, my friends, colleagues, students, or patients, but from my mother! That mother whom I disliked so thoroughly and felt so ashamed of. Yes, in my dream, I turn to her. It was to her that I posed my final question, "How'd I do?" What better proof for the lasting power of early life attachments?

Such regret played a role in the therapy of a young woman I'm currently seeing. She had asked for a few consultation sessions on Skype, and in our second meeting I asked about her relationship with her parents. "My mother is a saint, and I've always had a warm, wonderful relationship with her. But my father . . . well, that's a different story."

"Tell me about your relationship with him."

"The best description I can give is that it is very much like your relationship to your mother in *Momma and the Meaning of Life*. My father worked hard and supported the family but he was a tyrant. I've never heard a complimentary or pleasant word from him to anyone in the family, nor to the people who work in his company. Then, about eight years ago, his older brother and business partner committed suicide; the business went under, and my father went bankrupt. He lost everything. Now he's angry and depressed and does nothing but look out the window all day. I've been supporting him financially since the bankruptcy, but not one word of thanks. Yesterday at breakfast we got into a big fight and he threw his plate on the floor and walked out."

My patient and I have only had three meetings, but since my patient had read my story, I decided to share with her my regrets for never having empathized with my mother. "I wonder," I said to her, "if, someday, you'll have such regrets about your father."

She nodded slowly, saying, "Maybe I will."

"I'm only guessing, but I imagine that your father, who was so entirely invested in his role as provider, and who ran a big company and exercised such power in the world and in the family, might be feeling great humiliation at being supported by his daughter."

She nods. "We've never talked about it."

"Are you up to it?"

"I'm not sure. It's something to think about."

The following week she described an encounter with her father. "I own a large clothing store, and we were having a special event to showcase the new collection. I had extra entry tickets and thought my father might enjoy it. He came, but then, without discussing it with me, went to the staff area and jollied up to them, letting them know he was my father. When I heard about this, I lost it and said, 'How could you have done that? I don't appreciate your not checking with me first. I want to keep my business and personal life separate.' He started yelling at me and I yelled back and finally he went to his room and slammed his door."

"And then?"

"I started to leave, but then I started thinking of what a miserable evening this was going to be for my mother . . . and, yes, for my father, as well, and I thought about what you had said about *your* mother. So I took a breath and knocked on his door and talked to him. 'Look, Dad, I'm sorry. But here's my point. I invited you to see one of my events, but I didn't want you to go and cozy up with my employees—what I wanted was to share the event with you. How often do we ever do that?'"

"What a wonderful thing to say. And then?"

"For once he was silent. Almost dumbfounded. And he came over to me and hugged me and he cried. I've never, ever, seen him cry before. And I cried, too. We cried together."

Yes, this is a true story—almost word-for-word.

M*omma and the Meaning of Life* contains the most effective teaching tale I have ever written, "Seven Advanced Lessons in the Therapy of Grief," that was meant to serve as a primer for therapists using an existential approach.

Irene, an esteemed surgeon, called upon me for assistance. Her husband was dying of cancer at a young age, and Irene's grief was understandably acute. Several years before, I had spent two years leading a group for people who had recently lost a spouse, and as a result of this project, I considered myself expert in working with bereaved patients and agreed to work with Irene. Extraordinarily intelligent, but frosty and severe with herself and others, Irene became my patient for two years. Our work together showed me how much I still had to learn about loss: hence the title of the story, "Seven Advanced Lessons in the Therapy of Grief."

My first lesson occurred in our very first session, when she described the dream she had had the night before.

I'm still a surgeon, but I'm also a grad student in English. My preparation for a course involves two different texts, an ancient and a modern text, each with the same name. I am unprepared for the seminar because I haven't read either text. I especially haven't read the old, first text, which would have prepared me for the second.

I asked her if she remembered anything about the name of the texts. "Oh, yes, I remember it clearly. Each book, the old and the new, was titled *The Death of Innocence*." For a therapist with my interests and background, this was a great gift. Imagine, two texts—an ancient and a new one—and the ancient text (i.e., one's earliest years) was needed to understand the new.

It wasn't only that Irene's dream promised an intellectual treasure hunt of the highest order; it was also a *first dream*. As I explain in "Seven Advanced Lessons," ever since 1911, when Freud first discussed it, a mystique has surrounded the initial dream that a patient reports in therapy. Freud believed that the first dream is unsophisticated and highly revealing because beginning patients still have their guard down. Later in therapy, once they have worked through different dreams with the therapist, the dream-weaver residing in the unconscious grows cautious, taking care thereafter to manufacture more complex and obfuscating dreams.

Following Freud, I often imagined the dream-weaver as a plump, jovial homunculus, living the good life in a forest of dendrites and axons. He sleeps by day, but at night, lying on a cushion of buzzing synapses, he drinks honeyed nectar and lazily spins out dream sequences for his host. On the night before the first therapy visit, the patient falls asleep full of conflicting thoughts about the upcoming therapy, and the homunculus within goes about his nighttime job weaving those fears and hopes into a dream. Then, after the therapy session, the homunculus learns that the therapist has deftly interpreted his dream, and from that time forward he takes care to bury the meaning ever deeper in nocturnal disguise. Of course, this is all just a foolish fairy tale—if only I didn't believe it!

I remember with eerie clarity my own dream, on the night before the first session of my personal analysis over fifty years ago, which I also describe in "Seven Advanced Lessons."

> *I am lying on a doctor's examining table. The sheet is too small to cover me properly. I can see a nurse inserting a needle into my leg—my shin. Suddenly there's an explosive hissing, gurgling sound—WHOOOOOSH.*

The center of the dream—the loud *whoosh*—was immediately clear to me. As a child I had been plagued with chronic sinusitis, and every winter my mother took me to Dr. Davis, an otolaryngologist, for a sinus draining and flushing. I hated his yellow teeth and his fishy eye, which peered at me through the center of the circular mirror attached to the headband otolaryngologists used to wear. As he inserted a cannula into my sinus foramen, I felt a sharp pain and then heard a loud *whooooosh*— *the same whooooosh I heard in the dream*—as the injected saline flushed out my sinus. Looking at the quivering, disgusting mess of pus in the chrome drainage pan, I thought some of my brain had been washed out. In my first dream in analysis, that real-life horror had blended with my fear that shameful and disgusting thoughts would come out of me on the analytic couch.

I rene and I worked hard on *her* first dream. "So you hadn't read either text," I began, "*especially* not the old one."

"Yes, yes, I expected you to ask about that. I hadn't read either text, but I *especially* hadn't read the ancient one."

"Any hunches about the meaning of the two texts in your life?"

"Hardly a hunch," Irene replied. "I know exactly what they mean."

I waited for her to go on but she simply sat in silence, looking out the window. I had not yet gotten used to Irene's irritating trait of not volunteering a conclusion unless I explicitly requested it.

Annoyed, I let the silence last a minute or two. Finally I obliged: "And the meaning of the two texts, Irene, is—"

"My brother's death, when I was twenty, was the ancient text. My husband's death to come is the modern text."

"So the dream is telling us that you may not be able to deal with your husband's death until you deal first with your brother's."

"You got it. Precisely."

The *content* that we dealt with was illuminating, but the *process* (that is, the nature of the relationship between us) was confrontational and highly charged, and ultimately the work on our relationship was to be the true source of healing. In one session, our discussion of a dream about a wall of bodies separating the two of us led to an anguished outburst:

"What I mean is, how can you understand me? Your life's unreal—warm, cozy, innocent. Like this office." She pointed to my packed bookshelves behind her and to the scarlet Japanese maple blazing just outside the window. "The only thing missing are some chintz cushions, a fireplace, and a crackling wood fire. Your family surrounds you—all in the same town. An unbroken family circle. What can you *really* know of loss? Do you think you'd handle it any better? Suppose your wife or one of your children was to die right now? How would you do? Even that smug striped shirt of yours—I hate it. Every time you wear it, I wince. I hate what it says."

"What does it say?"

"It says, 'I've got all my problems solved. Tell me about yours.'"

Many times Irene's comments hit home. A story is told about the Swiss sculptor Alberto Giacometti, whose leg was broken in a traffic accident. While lying in the street, waiting for the ambulance, he was heard to say, "Finally, finally, something has happened to me." I know exactly what he meant. Irene had my number, all right. Teaching at Stanford for over thirty years, I'd lived in the same house, watched my children walk to the same schools, and never had to face dark tragedy: no hard, untimely deaths—my father and mother died old, he at sixty-nine, she in her nineties. My sister, seven years older, was still alive at that time. I had not yet lost close friends, and my four children were all healthy.

For a therapist who has embraced an existential frame of reference, such a shielded life is a liability. Many times I have yearned to venture out of the ivory tower into the travails of the real world. For years I imagined spending a sabbatical as a blue-collar worker, perhaps as an ambulance driver in Detroit or a short-order cook on the Bowery or a sandwich maker in a deli. But I never did. The siren call of writing retreats to Bali or a visit to a colleague's Venetian apartment or a fellowship to Bellagio on Lake Como was irresistible. In many ways, I have been insulated from hardship. I've never even had the growth experience of a marital separation, never faced adult aloneness. My relationship with Marilyn has not always been placid—thank God for the *Sturm und Drang*, since we have both learned from it.

I told Irene she was right, and I admitted that I've sometimes envied those who live more on the edge. At times, I told her, I worry that I may encourage my patients to take a heroic plunge for me.

"But," I told her, "you're not right when you say I have *no* experience of tragedy. I can't help thinking about death. When I am with you, I often imagine how it would be if my wife were fatally ill, and each time I am filled with indescribable sadness. I am aware, fully aware, that I'm on the march and that I've moved into another life stage. All the signs of aging—my torn knee cartilage, my fading vision, my backaches, my senile plaques, my graying beard and hair, dreams of my own death—tell me I'm moving toward the end of my life."

She listened but said nothing.

"And another thing," I added, "I've chosen to work with dying patients, hoping they would draw me closer to the tragic core of my own life. And indeed they did; I went back into therapy for three years as a result."

After such a retort, Irene nodded. I knew that nod—that characteristic nod cluster of hers, one sharp chin jerk followed by two or three soft nods—her somatic Morse code to tell me I had made a satisfactory response. I had grasped the first lesson—that to treat grief, the therapist cannot stay distant, but must encounter mortality at close range. And many more lessons followed around which I chose to structure the story. In this tale, the patient was the real teacher, and I was only the intermediary passing on her lessons.

The piece I most enjoyed writing was without a doubt "The Hungarian Cat Curse." In this story, Ernest Lash (on leave from *Lying on the Couch*) attempts to treat Merges, a vicious, German-speaking cat in his ninth and final life. Merges was a well-traveled character who, in an earlier life, had consorted with Xanthippe, a cat living in Heidegger's home, and was now mercilessly haunting Artemis, Ernest's lover.

On one level the story is a farce, but on another level I think it may be my deepest discourse on death and the amelioration of death terror. I wrote much of the story during a visit with Bob Berger, a close friend since medical school who died during the writing of this memoir. I set the story in Budapest, and Bob, who had grown up in Hungary, gave me Hungarian names for the characters, streets, bridges, and rivers.

I fondly remember a public reading of *Momma and the Meaning of Life* at Book Depot in Mill Valley, where my son Ben, a theater director, and I read the Ernest-Merges conversation aloud. I'm not keen on memorial services, but if my family decides to have one after my death, I'd like that dialogue to be read—it would lighten up the event. So please, Ben, play the cat and choose one of your brothers, or one of your favorite actors, to play Ernest.

CHAPTER THIRTY-TWO
ON BECOMING GREEK

O f all the foreign countries that have translated my work, Greece, one of the smallest, looms largest in my psyche. In 1997, Stavros Petsopoulos, the owner of Agra Publications, bought the Greek-language rights to all my books and engaged a married couple, Yannis Zervas and Evangelia Andritsanou, as translators. Thus began a long and meaningful relationship for our family. Yannis is an American-trained psychiatrist and well-known Greek poet, and Evangelia is a clinical psychologist as well as a translator. Though Greece has never played an important role in the field of psychotherapy and has a literate population of roughly 5 million, it immediately became my largest audience per capita in the world, and I am better known as a writer there than anywhere else. I have never understood why.

Since our first encounter with Greece, when our baggage got lost and Marilyn and I traveled light for five days as tourists, we have had two extraordinary visits together. The first was preceded by a visit to Turkey. In 1993, I gave a workshop for psychiatrists at the Bakirkoy Hospital in Istanbul and then led a two-day personal growth group of eighteen Turkish psychiatrists and psychologists in Bodrum, an ancient town on the Aegean Sea that is described by

Homer as "the land of eternal blue." That group worked hard for two full days, and I was much impressed by the sophistication and openness of many of its members. After the workshop, one of the psychiatrists, Ayça Cermak, with whom I have stayed in touch to this day, acted as a guide, driving Marilyn and me through parts of western Turkey and then back to Istanbul. There we caught a plane to Athens and boarded a ferry for the island of Lesbos. Marilyn had long been interested in the poet Sappho, who had lived on Lesbos in the seventh century BC surrounded by her female disciples.

Just off the ferry, I was delighted to see a small motorcycle rental shop, and off we went to explore Lesbos on an ancient but seemingly cooperative motorcycle. Toward the end of the day, just as the sun vanished into the ocean, the motorcycle took a final gasp and expired outside a deserted village. We had no choice but to spend the night in the ruins of an abandoned guesthouse, where Marilyn got little sleep after spotting a large rodent scuttling through the four-foot-high bathroom. By noon the following day, the motorcycle shop had sent a replacement via a truck, and we continued on our way, passing through welcoming villages, idling in tavernas, chatting with other guests, and watching contented, white-bearded old men drinking *retsina* and playing backgammon.

I had met Yannis in 2002 at an American Psychiatric Association Conference in New Orleans, where I was given the Oskar Pfister Award in Religion and Psychiatry. Astonished by this award, I asked the committee why they had selected me, an openly religious skeptic, and they responded that I, more than most other psychiatrists, had dealt with "religious questions." After my presentation, which was subsequently published as a monograph titled *Religion and Psychiatry* and appeared in Greek and Turkish translations, I had lunch with Yannis, who extended an invitation from Stavros Petsopoulos to speak in Athens.

A year later, we arrived at Athens and immediately took a forty-five-minute flight on a small plane to Syros, a small Greek island on which Yannis and Evangelia had a summer home.

Suffering badly from jet lag, I always require a couple of days' acclimation before speaking appearances. We rested on the island at a little inn in the small town of Hermoupolis, breakfasting every morning on home-baked croissants and jam made from figs growing on a sprawling tree on the front lawn. Two days later we were scheduled to leave the island for a press conference in Athens, but, the night before our departure, the ferryboat personnel went on strike, and Stavros then booked a small four-seat plane.

On the short flight to Athens, the pilot, who had read *When Nietzsche Wept*, talked to me animatedly about the book. Then the taxi driver at the airport recognized me and, during our ride, told me about his favorite parts of *Lying on the Couch*. At the Hilton I walked into a press conference with approximately twenty journalists. Never before, in the United States or in any other country, had I ever had a press conference. It was as close as I've ever come to real celebrity.

The following day, 2,500 people came to hear my address in the hotel ballroom. The lobby was so packed that I could get there only via a circuitous path through the underground kitchen. Only nine hundred headphones had been ordered, and the idea of simultaneous translation had to be scrapped at the last minute. I cut my comments by half so as to permit sequential translation. The translator, who had been prepared to work from a written copy of my presentation, went into a panic, but she got through it and did an excellent job. Listeners interrupted the speech throughout with questions and comments. Someone in the audience heckled me so vociferously for not answering all the questions fully that the police had to remove him.

After my talk, when I signed books, many buyers brought gifts—honey from their own beehives, bottles of home-brewed Greek wine, paintings they had done. One dear elderly woman insisted that I accept a gold coin her parents had sewn into her coat when she escaped from Turkey as a child.

That evening, I felt exhausted, gratified, and beloved, but puzzled by the extent of the acclaim. There was little more I could do but go with the flow and try to keep my equilibrium. Laden with gifts, we returned to our hotel room and saw yet another gift: a boat, two feet long, with fluttering sails entirely made of chocolate. Marilyn and I happily munched away.

The following day I signed books at Hestia Bookstore, a small shop in the center of Athens. I've done dozens of bookstore signings before and since, but this was the granddaddy of all signings. The queue led out of the store and continued for eight blocks, causing considerable traffic disruption. People not only bought new books at the store but also brought with them some previously bought books for me to sign. Writing their names was taxing, as most were foreign to me—for example, Docia, Ianthe, Nereïda, Tatiana—and difficult to spell. Customers were then asked to print their names in large letters on yellow slips of paper to hand to me with their books. Many were taking photographs, but that held up the line and soon they were asked not to take photos. After an hour the book purchasers were told I would be able to sign a maximum of only four, and then, an hour later, three, and eventually only one old book along with new books. Even so, the signing lasted almost four hours, and I signed over eight hundred new books and a great many more older ones. Recently I was saddened to hear that the venerable Hestia Bookstore had closed its doors for good, a victim of the Greek monetary crisis.

The great majority of bookstore customers in that line were women—as is always the case at my book signings—and I had the singular experience of having at least fifty lovely Greek women whisper in my ear, "I love you." Lest it get to my head, Stavros pulled me aside and told me that Greek women use those words frequently, with a more casual meaning than Americans.

The signing at the Hestia Bookstore came to mind ten years later, when an elderly British physician asked to see me in consultation. Dissatisfied with his life as a bachelor and his own unrealized potential, he was highly ambivalent about consulting me: on the one hand, he wanted my help; on the other, he was also deeply envious of my success as a writer, because he was convinced that he, too, had the talent for writing fine books. Toward the end of our consultation, he recounted a key story that had haunted him for fifty years, ever since he had spent two years in Greece teaching English at a girls' school. At the end of the farewell ceremonies, just as he was preparing to leave, a beautiful young Greek student gave him a goodbye hug and whispered in his ear, "I love you." Ever since then, he had thought of that young student, heard her whispered words in his mind, and tortured himself for not having had the courage to embark upon the life that was meant for him. I offered him all I could but I knew that the one thing I could *not* say was, "When Greek women say 'I love you,' it doesn't mean the same to them as in the US or perhaps in the UK. In fact, one afternoon fifty Greek women whispered those same words to me."

The day after the Hestia signing, the Panteion University awarded me my only honorary doctorate. I was awed to stand before a large audience in a grand hall whose walls were covered with paintings of Aristotle, Plato, Socrates, Epicurus, and Aeschylus. The following evening, Marilyn spoke at the University of Athens on feminist issues. Heady stuff for the Yalom family!

My next visit to Greece came four years later, in 2009. Marilyn had been invited by the University of Ioannina to speak about her book A *History of the Breast*. Knowing we were coming to Greece, the Onassis Foundation invited me to give an address about my new book, *The Schopenhauer Cure*, in the Megaron, the largest concert hall in Athens.

When we arrived in Athens, we were given a private tour of the new Acropolis Museum, due to open in a few weeks. Upon entering, we were astounded at the glass floors that allowed us to see, under our feet, layer after layer of ruins of civilizations going back thousands of years. Elsewhere in the museum were the Elgin Marbles, known by the name of the Englishman who carried

LECTURE AT MEGARON IN ATHENS, 2009.

ACROPOLIS MUSEUM, ATHENS, 2009.

about half of them off from the Acropolis to the British Museum.
The missing (some would say stolen) sections were presented in
plaster casts of a different color from the originals. Returning
works of art to their country of origin is a bedeviling problem for
all museums today. When in Greece, however, we empathized
with the Greeks.

From Athens we flew to Ioannina, where Marilyn had been
invited by Professor Marina Vrelli-Zachou to speak at the university, an impressive institution of 20,000 students. As always, when
I heard Marilyn address an audience, I sat back happily and re-
strained my impulse to shout out, "Hey, hey, that's my wife." The
following day our hosts took us on a tour of the countryside and
to Dodona, an ancient site mentioned in Homer. We sat for a long
time in the Greek amphitheater on seats constructed 2,000 years
ago, and then strolled over to the grove of trees where oracles had
once interpreted the language of blackbirds. Something about the
site—its massiveness, its dignity and history—was deeply moving,
and despite my skepticism, I had a taste, a faint taste, of the sacred.

We strolled through the town of Ioannina, which bordered
a beautiful lake, and ended up at a synagogue dating to Roman
times that still functions as a place of worship for the city's small
Jewish community. During World War II, almost all the Jews in
Ioannina were killed, and very few survivors returned. The remaining group is so small that the synagogue now permits women
to count among the *minyan*, the ten Jewish males required by Jewish law to hold a religious service. Walking through the market-
place, watching the old men playing backgammon and sipping
ouzo, we inhaled the wonderful smells associated with this country, but one irresistible aroma—baklava—enticed me, and I followed my nose to the bakery, where I found two dozen different
varieties. I still fantasize about a writing retreat in Ioannina, pref-
erably in the neighborhood of the bakery.

In a bookstore in the town of Ioannina, as we both signed
books, Marilyn asked the owner about my popularity with Greek

readers. "Yalom is the best-known American writer here," he said. Marilyn asked, "What about Philip Roth?" "We like him too," he answered, "but we think of Yalom as Greek."

Journalists have asked me over the years about my popularity in Greece, and I can never really answer. I know that, despite not speaking a word of Greek, I nonetheless feel at home there, and even in the United States I feel warmly disposed toward people of Greek descent. I am enthralled by Greek drama and philosophy, and by Homer, but this doesn't explain it. It may be more of a Middle Eastern phenomenon, since my readership is also disproportionately high in Turkey, Israel, and Iran.

Surprisingly, I regularly get email from Iranian students, therapists, and patients. I do not know how many copies of my books have been sold in Farsi: Iran is the only country that publishes my work without permission and without offering royalties. My professional contacts in Iran tell me they are familiar with books by Freud, Carl Jung, Mortimer Adler, Carl Rogers, and Abraham Maslow and would like more contact with Western psychotherapists. Unfortunately, as I am no longer traveling abroad, I have had to refuse their invitations to speak in Iran.

With so much devastating news in the world today, all of us grow fatigued or numb, but whenever a newscaster mentions Greece, Marilyn and I always pay attention. I will always feel a sense of wonder toward the Greeks and grateful to be considered an honorary Greek.

CHAPTER THIRTY-THREE

THE GIFT OF THERAPY

Rilke's book *Letters to a Young Poet* has occupied a special niche in my mind, and for years I imagined writing such a work for young therapists, but I could never find a shape and structure for that project. That changed one day in 1999 when Marilyn and I visited the Huntington Gardens in San Marino in Southern California. We went there to see the extraordinary grounds, and especially the Japanese garden and its bonsai trees. Toward the end of our visit, I wandered into the Huntington Library and browsed through a new exhibit, "Best Sellers of the English Renaissance." *Best sellers?* That caught my attention. I was struck by the fact that six of the ten bestsellers in the sixteenth century were books of "tips." For example, Thomas Tusser's *A Hundreth Good Pointes of Husbandry*, from 1570, offered a hundred tips about crops, livestock, and good housekeeping to farmers and farmers' wives. It was reprinted eleven times by the end of the century.

Almost always, my books have germinated slowly in my mind, with no single moment of conception. *The Gift of Therapy* is the single exception. By the time I left that Renaissance bestseller exhibition I knew exactly what my next book would be. *I would write a book of tips for young therapists.* A patient's face came to mind, a writer I had seen years before. After abandoning two unfinished novels she had announced to me that she would never again start another unless some idea for a book came along and bit her on the ass. Well, that day at the Huntington, a book bit me on the ass, and I put everything else aside and the next day began to write.

The process was straightforward. Since my early days at Stanford I had kept a file labeled "Thoughts for teaching," into which I dropped ideas and vignettes from my clinical work. I simply raided my "Thoughts for teaching" file. I read my notes over and over until one caught my fancy and I fleshed it out in several paragraphs. The tips were written in no particular order, but, at the end, I surveyed what I had written and grouped them into five clusters:

1. The nature of the therapist-patient relationship
2. Methods of exploring existential concerns
3. Issues arising in the everyday conduct of therapy
4. The use of dreams
5. The hazards and the privileges of being a therapist

I had originally been hoping for a hundred tips, as in *A Hundreth Good Pointes of Husbandry*, but by the time I reached eighty-four, I had entirely eviscerated my file. (I started building it up again as I continued to see patients, and nine years later, in a second edition, I added eleven more tips.)

From the very beginning I had a title in mind: I would modify Rilke's title and call it *Letters to a Young Therapist*. But as I was nearing completion, an amazing coincidence occurred: Basic Books invited me to participate in a mentoring series titled "Letters to a Young . . . " (Therapist, Mathematician, Contrarian, Catholic, Conservative, Chef, etc.). Loyal as I was to Basic Books, I preferred not to be part of the series. However, since they had co-opted Rilke's title, I needed a new one. *One Hundred Tips for Therapists* wasn't possible, and everyone vetoed *84 Tips for Therapists*. Eventually my agent, Sandy Dijkstra, suggested *The Gift of Therapy*. I wasn't wild about the title, but I never came up with a better one and it's grown on me over the years.

I wrote the book in opposition to the brief, manualized, problem-solving, cognitive behavioral approach to psychotherapy spawned by economic pressures. I was fighting, too, against psychiatry's overreliance on medications. This battle continues today, despite overwhelming research evidence that good outcomes depend on the intensity, the warmth, the genuineness, and the empathy of the therapeutic relationship. I hoped *The Gift of Therapy* would help preserve a human and humane approach to psychological suffering.

To that end, I intentionally use provocative language: I go out of my way to tell students exactly the opposite of what many have been taught in behaviorally oriented training programs. "Avoid Diagnosis," "Create a New Therapy for Each Patient," "Let the Patient Matter to You," "Blank Screen? Forget It. Be Real," "Check into the Here-and-Now Each Hour."

Several sections of *The Gift of Therapy* stress the importance of empathy and convey the Roman playwright Terence's ancient sentiment that "I am human and nothing human is alien to me." One section, "Empathy: Looking Out the Patient's Window," relates one of my favorite clinical stories. Throughout adolescence, one of my patients had been locked in a long, bitter struggle with her naysaying father. Yearning for reconciliation and a new beginning to their relationship, she had looked forward to her father driving her to college—a rare occasion when just the two of them would be together for several hours. But the long-anticipated trip proved a disaster: her father behaved true to form by grousing at length about the ugly, garbage-littered creek by the side of the road. She, on the other hand, saw no litter whatsoever in the beautiful, rustic, unspoiled stream. As a result, she gave up on her father and lapsed into silence, and the two of them spent the remainder of the trip (and of their lives) looking away from each other. A great many years later, she happened to make the same drive again and was astonished to note that there were *two* streams—one on each side of the road. "This time I was the driver," she said sadly, "and the stream I saw through the window on the driver's side was just as ugly and polluted as my father had described it." But by the time she had looked out her father's window, it was too late—her father was dead and buried. "So look out the patient's window," I urge therapists. "Try to see the world as the patient sees it."

Rereading *The Gift of Therapy* now makes me feel quite exposed: all my favorite ploys and responses are out there for all to see. Only recently, a patient wept in my office and I said to her, "If those tears could speak what would they say?" When I reread the book and saw these exact words in one of the tips, I felt as if I were plagiarizing myself (and hoped she hadn't read the book).

Some of the tips encourage therapists to be honest by acknowledging errors. *It's not the commission of errors that is important: it's what you do with them.* Several tips encourage student therapists to use the here-and-now, that is, to stay focused on what is happening in the therapist-patient relationship.

The final tip in *The Gift of Therapy,* "Cherish the Occupational Privileges," particularly moves me: I am very often asked why, at the age of eighty-five, I continue to practice. Tip number eighty-five (sheer coincidence that I am now eighty-five years old) begins with a simple declaration: *my work with patients enriches my life in that it provides meaning in life.* Rarely do I hear therapists complain of a lack of meaning. We live lives of service in which we fix our gaze on the needs of others. We take pleasure not only in helping our patients change, but also in hoping their changes will ripple beyond them toward others.

We are also privileged by our role as cradlers of secrets. Every day patients grace us with their secrets, often never before shared.

The secrets provide a backstage view of the human condition without social frills, role-playing, bravado, or stage posturing. Being entrusted with such secrets is a privilege given to very few. Sometimes the secrets scorch me and I go home and hold my wife and count my blessings.

Moreover, our work provides the opportunity to transcend ourselves and to envision the true and tragic knowledge of the human condition. But we are offered even more. We become explorers immersed in the grandest of pursuits—the development and maintenance of the human mind. Hand in hand with patients, we savor the pleasure of discovery—the "aha" experience when disparate ideational fragments suddenly slide smoothly together into a coherent whole. Sometimes I feel like a guide escorting others through the rooms of their own house. What a treat it is to watch them open doors to rooms never before entered, discover unopened wings of their house containing beautiful and creative pieces of identity.

Recently I attended a Christmas service at the Stanford Chapel to hear a sermon by Rev. Jane Shaw that underscored the vital importance of love and compassion. I was moved by her call to put such sentiments into practice whenever we can. Acts of caring and generosity can enrich any environment in which we find ourselves.

Her words motivated me to reconsider the role of love in my own profession. I became aware that I have never, not once, used the word *love* or *compassion* in my discussions of the practice of psychotherapy. It is a huge omission, which I wish now to correct, for I know that I regularly experience love and compassion in my work as a therapist and do all I can to help patients liberate their love and generosity toward others. If I do *not* experience these feelings for a particular patient, then it is unlikely I will be of much help. Hence I try to remain alert to my loving feelings or absence of such feelings for my patients.

Very recently, I began working with Joyce, a depressed, angry young woman recovering from extensive surgery for a life-threatening cancer. As soon as she entered my office, I sensed her terror, and my heart went out to her. Yet in our first sessions, I did not feel close to her. Though she was obviously tormented, she also emanated the message that she had it all under control. And I felt confused by her vacillating complaints: one week she spoke bitterly of the irritating habits of her neighbors and friends, and the next week she bemoaned her isolation. Something was off, and each week as I thought about our next session, I could feel myself wince. I sometimes considered referring her to another therapist. But I nixed that idea because she had read many of my books, and she had emphasized from the very start that she had seen many therapists and I was her last resort.

During our third session, something odd happened: it suddenly dawned on me that she had a remarkable physical resemblance to Aline, a good friend's wife, and on several occasions I had the fleeting, uncanny experience of thinking I was speaking to Aline, not Joyce. Each time that happened, I had to jerk myself back to reality. Though I was now on good terms with Aline, I had, at first, found her smug and off-putting. Had she not been the wife of a good friend, I would have avoided her. Was it possible, I began to wonder, if, in some strange fashion, my unconscious had transmitted some of my Aline irritation to Joyce?

Joyce began our fourth session uncharacteristically. After a brief silence, she said, "I don't know where to start." Knowing that it was imperative for us to focus on our problematic relationship, I responded, "Tell me how you felt at the end of our previous meeting."

She had previously skirted such inquiries, but today she startled me: "Exactly the same way I felt after each of our sessions: I felt awful. Totally confused. I suffered for hours afterwards."

"I'm so sorry to hear that, but say more, Joyce. Suffered how?"

"You know so much. You write all those books. That's why I contacted you. You're wise. And I feel so inferior. And I know you think I'm nothing. I'm sure you know all about my problem but you're not telling me what it is."

"I see how painful this is for you, Joyce, but at the same time I'm glad you're speaking out honestly: this is exactly what we must do."

"Then why don't you tell me what's wrong? What is my problem? How do I solve it?"

"You give me too much credit. I don't know your problem. But I *do* know that we can find it out together. And I do know you're frightened and you're angry. And, considering what you've gone through, I can understand that: I'd feel like that, too. I can help you if we keep working like we are today."

"But *why* do I feel like this? That I'm not worth your time? Why am I getting worse?"

I knew what I had to do and took the plunge. "Let me say something that may be important for you to hear." I hesitated— this was heavy-duty self-disclosure and I felt very unsure of myself. "You look remarkably like the wife of one of my close friends— and at our last session there were a couple of times when, for just a moment or two, I had the strange thought it was *her*, not you, sitting in your chair. Though I'm friendly now with this person, I did not get along with her at first. I found her sharp and off-putting and just didn't enjoy being with her. I'm telling you this because— and I know this sounds strange and I'm embarrassed by it—I may have unconsciously conveyed these feelings that belonged to her toward you. And I think you may be picking that up."

We were silent for a few moments and I added, "But, Joyce, I want to be clear, that is *not* what I feel for you. I'm entirely on your side. I feel only compassion and I'm committed to helping you."

Joyce seemed astonished and tears flowed down her cheeks. "Thank you for that gift. I've seen a lot of shrinks but this is the first time any of them has ever shared something personal with me. I don't want to leave your office today—I want us to talk for the next twelve hours. I feel good."

My patient had received my disclosure in the spirit that I had offered it, and from that time on, everything changed. We worked well and hard and I looked forward to each of our meetings. How to describe my intervention? I believe it was an act of compassion, of love. I can find no other words for it.

CHAPTER THIRTY-FOUR

TWO YEARS WITH SCHOPENHAUER

My philosophical reading has always been concentrated on *Lebensphilosophie*, the school of thinkers who address life's meaning and values. These include many of the ancient Greeks, Kierkegaard, Sartre, and, of course, Nietzsche. Only later did I discover Arthur Schopenhauer, whose ideas about the unconscious influence of the sexual drive foreshadowed Freud's theories. To my mind, Schopenhauer set the stage for the birth of psychotherapy. As Philip, a character in my novel *The Schopenhauer Cure*, says, "Without Schopenhauer there could have been no Freud."

Schopenhauer was abrasive, fearless, and exceedingly isolated. He was the nineteenth-century Don Quixote, attacking all forces, including religion. Schopenhauer was also a tormented man, and his unhappiness, pessimism, and relentless misanthropy provided much of the energy behind his work. Consider his view of human relationships in his well-known Porcupine Parable: The cold air drives porcupines to huddle together for warmth, but their huddling causes them to prick one another with their quills.

Eventually they discover they are best off remaining at some distance from one another. Thus, a man (like Schopenhauer) who has an abundance of inner heat is well advised to stay entirely away from others.

Schopenhauer's profound pessimism bowled me over when I first encountered it. I wondered how, given such despair, he continued to think and to work. Over time I came to realize that he believed that understanding can lighten the burden of even the most wretched character. Though we are ephemeral beings, we take pleasure in understanding even when that knowledge reveals our basest impulses and confronts us with the brevity of life. In "On the Vanity of Existence," he wrote:

> *A man never is happy, but spends his whole life in striving after something which he thinks will make him so; he seldom attains his goal, and when he does, it is only to be disappointed; he is mostly shipwrecked in the end, and comes into harbor with mast and rigging gone. And then, it is all one whether he has been happy or miserable; for his life was never anything more than a present moment always vanishing; and now it is over.*

In addition to such extreme pessimism, Schopenhauer's intense sexual drive tormented him, and his inability to relate to others in nonsexual ways left him chronically bad tempered. Only in childhood, before sexuality arose, and in later life when his appetites mellowed, did he experience happiness. For example, in his major work *The World as Will and Representation*, he wrote:

> *Just because the terrible activity of the genital system still slumbers, while that of the brain already has its full briskness, childhood is the time of innocence and happiness, the paradise of life, the lost Eden on which we look back longingly through the whole remaining course of our life.*

But no affirmation is to be found in Schopenhauer: his pessimism was unrelenting:

At the end of his life, no man, if he be sincere and in possession of his faculties, would ever wish to go through it again. Rather than this he will much prefer to choose complete nonexistence.

The more I learned about Arthur Schopenhauer, the more tragic I found his life: how sad that one of our great geniuses was so relentlessly tormented. He was a man, it seemed to me, desperately in need of therapy. His relationship to his parents resembles a stark Oedipal drama. First he infuriated his father by refusing to enter the family mercantile business. He adored his mother, a popular novelist, and when his father committed suicide, the sixteen-year-old Arthur was so persistent in his attempts to possess and control her that she ultimately broke off their relationship, refusing to see him during the last fifteen years of her life. He was so terrified of being buried when not yet fully dead that he ordered in his will that he not be interred for several days, until the stench of his body pervaded the nearby countryside.

As I considered his sad life, I began to wonder whether Schopenhauer might have been helped by psychotherapy. If he had consulted me, could I have found a way to offer him comfort? I began to imagine scenes of our therapy, and gradually the outline of a novel about Schopenhauer materialized.

Schopenhauer in treatment—imagine that! Oh yes, yes—what a deliciously challenging thought! But who could have served as his therapist in this story? Schopenhauer was born in 1788, more than a century before the first stirrings of psychotherapy. For weeks I considered a compassionate, literate, philosophically trained ex-Jesuit, who could have offered intensive meditational retreats that Schopenhauer would have been willing to attend. This idea had some merit. During Schopenhauer's lifetime, there were hundreds of Jesuits out of work: the pope had disbanded the Jesuit order in 1773 and did not reinstate it for forty-one years. But that plot never cohered and I abandoned the idea.

Instead, I decided to create a Schopenhauer clone, a contemporary philosopher endowed with Schopenhauer's intelligence, interests, and personality characteristics (including misanthropy, sexual compulsivity, and pessimism). And so the character Philip was conceived. I would set Philip down in the twentieth century when psychotherapy was readily available. But what type of therapy might be most effective for Philip? Such acute interpersonal problems cried out for an intensive therapy group. And the group therapist? I needed an experienced, skillful group therapist, and I created Julius, a wise, elderly practitioner with an approach to group therapy similar to my own.

Next, I created the other characters (the members of the therapy group), introduced Philip into the group, and then set the characters free to interact with one another. I had no pre-formulations: I simply recorded the action as it ensued in my imagination.

Think of it! A Schopenhauer clone enters a therapy group, creates turmoil, challenges the leader, and infuriates the other members, but ultimately undergoes dramatic change. Think of the message I would send to my field: *If group therapy could help Arthur Schopenhauer, the arch pessimist and most dedicated misanthropist of the ages, then group therapy could help anyone!*

Later, looking back on the finished novel, I realized that it might be a good teaching tool for training group therapists, and in many sections of the fifth edition of my group therapy textbook, I refer student readers to various pages of the novel where they might read dramatic portrayals of therapy principles.

I wrote the novel in an unusual manner, alternating chapters depicting the meetings of the therapy group with a psychobiography of Schopenhauer. I suspect many readers have been puzzled by this format and, even in the midst of writing, I knew it made for an awkward amalgam. Nevertheless, I believed that a résumé of Schopenhauer's life would help the reader understand Philip, Schopenhauer's double. But that's only part of the reason: I confess that I had become so fascinated with Schopenhauer's work, life, and psyche that I couldn't pass up the opportunity of speculating on his character formation. Nor could I resist exploring the ways in which Schopenhauer had anticipated Freud and set the stage for psychotherapy.

I believe this book is the best demonstration of effective group therapy I have written. Julius was the therapist I had always endeavored to be. In the book, however, he develops an untreatable malignant melanoma. Despite his illness, he continues to find meaning, even near his death, by enhancing the lives of all the members of his group. He is open, generous, focused on the here-and-now, and gives all his remaining energy to helping the members explore their relationships with each other and learn about themselves.

Selecting the novel's title was unusually painless: as soon as *The Schopenhauer Cure* coasted into my mind, I embraced it. I liked its double entendre: Schopenhauer the person is offered a cure, and Schopenhauer the thinker offers a cure to all of us.

Twelve years after publication, the novel is very much alive. A Czech film company is working on a film version. *The Schopenhauer Cure* also anticipated the field of clinical philosophy, as I have learned from leaders in that discipline.

Several years ago at the annual convention of the American Group Psychotherapy Association in San Francisco, a large audience of group therapists watched Molyn Leszcz, a former student of mine and coauthor of the fifth edition of my textbook on group therapy, lead a half-day meeting of actors playing the group members in the novel. My son Ben selected the actors, directed the production, and played one of the characters. The actors had no script, but they were instructed to imagine themselves in a therapy group, to stay within their character, and to interact spontaneously with the other members. I was the discussant for segments of the interaction. Another of my sons, Victor, edited a film of the event and has made the video available on his educational website. It was a great delight for me to sit back and watch my imagined characters interact in the flesh.

CHAPTER THIRTY-FIVE
STARING AT THE SUN

My sister, Jean, died as I was writing this book. Seven years older than I, Jean was a gentle soul and I loved her dearly. During our adult lives she lived on the East Coast, I on the West, but we always phoned one another weekly, and whenever I was in Washington I stayed with her and her husband, Morton, a cardiologist, who was always generous and welcoming.

Jean developed aggressive dementia and at my last visit to Washington, a few weeks before she died, she no longer recognized me. Because I felt I had already lost her, I was not shaken by the news of her death—not consciously. Instead, I welcomed it as a release for her and her family, and the following day Marilyn and I flew to Washington to attend her funeral.

I had intended to begin my eulogy by telling a story about our mother's funeral in Washington fifteen years earlier. On that occasion, I tried to honor my mother by baking *kichel*, an old-world pastry, to be served at the family gathering after the funeral. My *kichel* looked good, and smelled wonderful, but, alas, were entirely tasteless: I had followed her recipe but forgotten to put in the sugar! Jean was always gracious and generous and my point in telling this story was to highlight my sister's sweetness by saying that, if I were baking *kichel* for *her*, I could never have forgotten the sugar. But, though I had arrived at the funeral feeling composed and unaware of deep grief, I broke down completely during my remarks, and returned to my seat without finishing.

My seat was in the front row, close enough to touch my sister's plain wooden casket. When gusts of strong wind arose and buffeted the cemetery, I saw, out of the corner of my eye, my sister's casket begin to shake. Despite all my rationality, I could not get the bizarre thought out of my mind that *my sister was trying to get out of her casket*, and I had to fight the instinct to bolt from the gravesite. All the experience I've had with death, all the patients I've escorted to the very end, all my supreme detachment and rationality in prose about the topic of death—all of it evaporated in the presence of my own terror.

This incident shocked me. I had been trying for decades to understand and ameliorate my personal anxiety about death. I had played these fears out in my novels and stories and projected them onto fictional characters. In *The Schopenhauer Cure*, Julius, the group leader, announces that he has been diagnosed with a fatal illness, and the group members attempt to console him. One member of the group, Pam, tries to offer comfort by citing a passage from Vladimir Nabokov's memoir, *Speak, Memory*, describing life as a spark between two identical pools of darkness—the one before birth and the one after death.

Immediately, Philip, the Schopenhauer clone and acolyte, responds in his usual condescending manner, saying, "Nabokov undoubtedly lifted the idea from Schopenhauer, who said that after death we will be as before our birth and then proceeded to prove the impossibility of there being more than one kind of nothingness."

Pam, furious with Philip, says, "You think Schopenhauer once said something vaguely similar. Big fucking deal."

Philip closes his eyes and begins reciting: "'A man finds himself, to his great astonishment, suddenly existing after thousands and thousands of years of nonexistence; he lives for a little while: and then, again, comes an equally long period when he must exist no more.' I quote from Schopenhauer's essay, 'Additional Remarks on the Doctrine of the Vanity of Existence.' Is that vague enough for you, Pam?'"

I cite this passage because of what it did *not* include: namely, that Schopenhauer's and Nabokov's statements both trace back to Epicurus, an ancient Greek philosopher who held that the primary source of human misery was our omnipresent fear of death. To ease that fear, Epicurus developed a series of potent secular arguments for the students in his school in Athens and stipulated that they learn them just as they might memorize a catechism. One of these arguments was the renowned "symmetry argument" positing that *our state of nonbeing* after death *is identical to our state before our birth*, and yet the thought of our "pre-being" state is never associated with anxiety. Philosophers throughout the ages have attacked this argument, and yet to my mind it is beautiful in its simplicity and still holds considerable power. It has offered comfort to many of my patients, and to me as well.

As I read more about Epicurus's arguments to dispel death terror, a bombshell of an idea for my next book occurred to me and held me enthralled for a great many months. Here's the idea. A horrific nightmare terrorizes a man: In a forest at nightfall he is pursued by some terrifying beast. He runs until he can run no farther; he stumbles, feels the creature pouncing upon him, and realizes this is his death. He awakens screaming, heart pounding, soaked in sweat. He jumps out of bed, quickly dresses, bolts from his bedroom and from his home, and sets off to find someone— an elder, a thinker, a healer, a priest, a doctor—anyone who can help with this death terror.

I imagined a book consisting of eight or nine chapters, each beginning with the same first paragraph: the nightmare, the awakening, and the setting out to seek help for his death terror. Yet each chapter would be set in a different century! The first would take place in the third century BC in Athens, and the dreamer would rush to the Agora, the section of Athens where many of the important schools of philosophy were located. He would walk past the Academy, founded by Plato and now led by his nephew, Speusippus; past the Lyceum, the school of Aristotle; past the schools of the Stoics and the Cynics; and finally would reach his destination, the Garden of Epicurus, where, at sunrise, he would be permitted to enter.

Another chapter might be set in the time of St. Augustine, another during the Reformation, another in the late eighteenth century at the time of Schopenhauer, another in the days of Freud, perhaps another at the time of Sartre or Camus, and perhaps others in a Muslim and a Buddhist country.

But one thing at a time. I decided to write the entire episode in Epicurus's Greece in 300 BC, and then turn to each of the later time periods. For months I researched the details of daily life in Greece in that era, the clothing, the type of breakfast, the customs of daily life. I studied ancient and current historical and philosophical texts, read novels set in ancient Greece (by Mary Renault and others), and eventually arrived at the sad realization that the research required to write this and the chapters in the other time periods would consume the rest of my life. With great regrets I abandoned the project. It's the only book I've ever started and did not finish.

I nstead, I decided to discuss the work of Epicurus in a nonfiction book on death anxiety, and that book gradually morphed into *Staring at the Sun*, published in 2008. *Staring at the Sun* traces my thoughts about death that emerged from my clinical practice with healthy as well as terminally ill patients. The book's title comes from a seventeenth-century maxim by François de La

Rochefoucauld: "*One cannot stare straight into the face of the sun or death.*" Though I use the maxim for my title, I challenge its truth in the text by emphasizing that much good may come from staring directly at death.

I illustrate that idea not only with clinical but also with literary vignettes. For example, Ebenezer Scrooge in Dickens's *Christmas Carol* begins the story as a miserly, isolated creature, but by the end he is a kind, generous, and beloved man. Whence the transformation? Dickens gave Scrooge a strong dose of existential shock therapy when the Ghost of Christmas Yet to Come allows Scrooge to view his own gravesite and read his name on the headstone.

Throughout *Staring at the Sun*, the confrontation with death serves as an *awakening experience*, one that teaches us how to live more fully. Therapists sensitized to this process see it often. As I mentioned earlier, in my clinical practice I often suggest that patients draw a line on a sheet of paper and imagine that one end of the line represents their birth and the other end their death. I ask them to indicate where they are now situated on the line, and meditate on that for a few moments. The film *Yalom's Cure* begins with my voice suggesting this exercise.

During my training as a psychiatrist, I never once heard death discussed in therapy seminars or in case discussions. It was as though the field still followed the advice of Adolf Meyer, the longtime dean of American psychiatrists: "Don't scratch where it doesn't itch"—in other words, don't raise troublesome topics unless the patient does, especially in areas that might be beyond our capacity to assuage. I've taken the contrary position: since death itches all the time, there is much to be gained by helping patients explore their posture toward it.

I agree entirely with the Czech existential novelist Milan Kundera, who wrote that the act of forgetting offers us a foretaste of death. In other words, what terrifies us about death is not only loss of the future but also loss of the past. As I reread my own books, I often fail to remember the faces and names of the patients I have written about: I've disguised them so well I cannot recognize who they were. I ache sometimes to think of all the intimate and wrenching hours I spent with individuals who are now lost to memory.

I believe that death anxiety lies behind the presenting complaints of many patients. Consider, for example, the discomfort that accompanies big birthdays (age thirty or forty or fifty), which remind us of the inexorable passage of time. I saw a patient recently who described several nights of terrifying nightmares. In one, an intruder had threatened her life; in another, she had felt herself falling through space. She mentioned that her fiftieth birthday was approaching, and she dreaded the party her family was giving. I urged her to explore all the connotations of being fifty. She said that she felt fifty was truly old and recalled how old her mother had looked at fifty. Both her parents had died in their late sixties, and thus she knew she was now two-thirds through her life. Before we met, she had never spoken openly about how she might die, about her funeral, or about her religious beliefs, and though our sessions were painful, I believe that demystifying the process ultimately offered her relief. Death anxiety lurks in many of our milestones—in the empty nest syndrome, retirement, the midlife crisis, and high school and college reunions—as well as in our grief at the deaths of others. I believe that most nightmares are driven by death anxiety that has escaped its corral.

Now, as I write these lines, ten years after writing *Staring at the Sun*—ten years closer to my own death—I don't believe I could write as dispassionately about the subject as I did then. In the past year, I have not only lost my sister, but also lost three of my oldest and closest friends—Herb Kotz, Larry Zaroff, and Bob Berger.

Larry and Herb were my classmates in college and medical school. We were anatomy partners in dissecting a cadaver and roomed together during our internships. The three of us with our wives vacationed together in many places: the Poconos, the Eastern Shore of Maryland, the Hudson Valley, Cape May, and Napa Valley. We loved the days and nights we spent together talking, biking, playing games, and sharing meals.

Larry had a long career as a cardiac surgeon in Rochester, New York, but then, after thirty years of practice, switched fields, obtaining a PhD in the history of medicine at Stanford. In his final years he taught literature to undergraduates and medical students before dying suddenly of a ruptured aortic aneurism. In my brief eulogy at his funeral, I tried to add a lighter note by describing a vacation trip the six of us had taken in the Poconos at a time when Larry was in his bad-clothes phase and had worn a beaten-up, wrinkled T-shirt to a fancy restaurant. We all harangued him about his appearance until he stood up and left the table. He returned ten minutes later looking quite dapper: he had just bought the shirt off our waiter's back! (The waiter, fortunately, had a spare one in his locker.) Though I wanted to lighten the atmosphere with this tale at the funeral, I choked up and struggled to get the words out.

Herb, who had trained as a gynecologist and then as an oncologist, gradually developed dementia. He lived his last years in a state of such confusion and physical pain that I felt, as with my sister, that I had lost him long before he died. I was too ill with the flu to travel to Washington, DC, for his funeral, but sent my remarks with a friend to be read at the graveside.

I felt relief for him and for his family, and yet, at the precise time of his funeral, I grew agitated, took a brief walk in San Francisco, and unexpectedly broke into tears, recalling a scene I hadn't thought of in many years. When Herb and I were in college and medical school, we had often played pinochle on Sundays with his Uncle Louie, a bachelor who lived with Herb's family. Louie, an endearing man with a tendency toward hypochondriasis, always started the evening by announcing that he wasn't sure he could play well that night because there was "something wrong upstairs," pointing to his head. That was the cue for each of us to whip out our brand new stethoscopes and blood pressure cuffs and, for a five-dollar fee, take his blood pressure, listen to his heart, and pronounce him healthy. Louie was such a good player that we didn't hang on to our five dollars very long: almost always, by the end of the evening, he had recouped his money and then some.

I loved those evenings. But Uncle Louie is long dead, and now, with Herb gone as well, I experienced a staggering loneliness as I realized I no longer had a witness to that scene of so long ago. It now existed only in my mind, somewhere in the mysteries of my crackling neural circuits, and when I died it would vanish entirely. Of course, I've known these things *in the abstract* for decades, and emphasized them in books and lectures and many therapeutic hours, but I am *feeling* them now, feeling that when we perish, every one of our precious, joyful, unique memories vanishes with us.

I'm also grieving Bob Berger, my dear friend of over sixty years, who died a few weeks after Herb. After a cardiac arrest, Bob was unconscious for several hours before being resuscitated, and during a brief interval of lucidity he called me on the phone. Jocular as ever, he rasped, "I bring you a message from the other side." That was all he said: his condition quickly worsened. He slumped back into a coma and died two weeks later.

Bob and I first met in Boston in my second year of medical school. Though we subsequently lived on different coasts, we remained lifelong friends, and kept in touch frequently by phone and visits. Fifty years after our first meeting, he asked me to help him write about his life as an adolescent when the Germans overran his native Hungary. He told me about passing as a Christian and participating in the Resistance during the Nazi occupation of Budapest. He related hair-raising stories, one after the other. For example, at the age of sixteen, he and a fellow Resistance fighter, on motorcycle, had followed lines of Jews who had been tied together and were being forced to walk through the woods to the Danube, where they were to be thrown into the river and drowned. There was no hope of saving any of the captives, but Bob and his friend drove by and threw grenades to kill the Nazi guards. Later, when Bob was away for a few days, trying, unsuccessfully, to find his mother, their landlord had turned his roommate, another close friend, over to the Nazis, who had dragged him into the street and pulled down his pants. When they saw he was circumcised, they shot him in the abdomen and left him to die, warning onlookers to offer no help, not even a drink of water. I heard such horrific tales, one after another—all for the first time—and at the end of the evening I said to him, "Bob, we've been so close. We've known each other for fifty years. Why have you never told me any of this before?" His answer stunned me: "Irv, you weren't ready to hear it."

I didn't protest. I knew he was right: I *hadn't* been ready to hear it, and I must have conveyed that to him in a multitude of ways. I had long avoided any type of exposure to the Holocaust. I was horrified, as a teenager, when, shortly after the Allies liberated the concentration camps, the newsreels showed the few survivors, looking like human skeletons, and the mountains of corpses everywhere, being moved by bulldozers. Decades later, when Marilyn and I went to see *Schindler's List*, she drove separately, knowing that I would most likely bolt before the end of the film. And I did. For me it was a predictable formula. If I saw or read anything graphic about the horrors of the Holocaust, I would be swept by a storm of feelings: terrible sorrow, unbearable rage, crippling agony, to think of what the victims must have experienced, and to think of myself in their place. (It was sheer luck that I had been safe in America rather than in Europe, where my father's sister and her entire family, and my uncle Abe's wife and four children, were murdered.) I never expressed my feelings explicitly to Bob, but he had picked them up in many ways: he told me that, though I had listened to some of his other wartime stories, I had never once asked him a question.

A half-century later, Bob had a horrendous experience in a Nicaraguan airport when someone attempted to kidnap him. He was heavily traumatized and it was shortly afterward that he contacted me and asked me to write about his life experience during his adolescence in Nazi-occupied Budapest. We spent a great many hours together discussing the kidnapping and all the memories it revived of the wartime years.

I braided his adolescent life experiences together with an account of our friendship into a novella, *I'm Calling the Police*, published in the United States as an ebook. In Europe eight countries published it in paperback. The title is taken from a particularly hair-raising incident in the novella. Though it had been over sixty years since the end of the war when the book was published, Bob so feared the Nazis that he balked at having his real name on the book jacket. I reminded him that any living Nazis would be in their nineties and harmless, but he insisted on using a pseudonym—Robert Brent—for the English and Hungarian versions. Only after a sustained campaign did he relent and agree to have his real name on seven of the translations, including the German one.

I have often marveled at Bob's courage and tenacity. As an orphan, he came from a displaced persons (DP) camp to the United States after World War II speaking not a word of English. After attending less than two years at Boston Latin High School, he was accepted to Harvard, where he not only performed well enough to get into medical school, but also played varsity soccer—and all of this when he was completely alone in the world. Later he married Pat Downs, a physician, the daughter of two physicians, and the granddaughter of Harry Emerson Fosdick, the eminent pastor of the interdenominational Riverside Church in Manhattan. Bob asked her to convert to Judaism before their marriage and Pat agreed. In the conversion process, Pat told me, things were proceeding well until the rabbi announced that Jewish dietary laws banned the eating of shellfish, including lobster. Having spent much of her early life in Maine, Pat was stunned. She had eaten lobster all her life and felt this was too much, a potential deal-breaker. The rabbi, perhaps because of Pat's eminent grandfather, was so eager to bring her into the fold that, after consulting with a consortium of rabbis, he made a rare exception: she, alone of all Jews, would be permitted to eat lobster.

Bob chose to train as a heart surgeon—he told me that the only time he felt entirely alive was when he held a beating heart in his hand. He had an extraordinary career as a cardiac surgeon, became professor of surgery at Boston University, wrote over five hundred research and clinical papers in professional journals, and was on the brink of doing the world's first heart transplant before another surgeon, Christiaan Barnard, beat him to the punch.

A t the end of 2015, after suffering the loss of my sister and of my three close friends, I had several weeks of the flu, with loss of appetite and weight loss, and then an acute bout of gastroenteritis, most likely food poisoning, with vomiting and diarrhea that left me dehydrated. My blood pressure was so dangerously low that my son Reid drove me from San Francisco to the Stanford emergency room, where I remained for a day and a half. I received seven liters of intravenous fluid, and my blood pressure slowly returned to normal. As I awaited the results of an abdominal CT scan, I had, for the first time, a strong sense that I might be dying. My physician daughter, Eve, and my wife stayed with me, offering comfort, and I tried to soothe myself by drawing upon a thought I had often invoked in my work with patients: the greater the sense of unlived life, the greater the terror of death. This equation calmed me as I considered how few regrets I have about the life I've lived.

After discharge from the hospital I weighed only 139 pounds—about 20 pounds under my average weight. Sometimes the hazy memory of my medical education creates problems. In this instance, I was haunted by a medical maxim: *If the patient has significant weight loss of unknown cause, think of an occult cancer.* I imagined my abdomen laced with metastatic lesions. During this time I comforted myself with a thought experiment suggested by Richard Dawkins: Imagine a laser-thin spotlight moving inexorably along the immense ruler of time. Everything that the beam has passed is lost in the darkness of the past; everything ahead of the spotlight is hidden in the darkness of that yet to be. Only that which is illuminated by the laser-thin spot of light is alive and aware. That thought always brings me solace: it makes me feel lucky to be alive at this moment.

I sometimes think the very act of writing is my effort to dispel the passage of time and inevitable death. Faulkner put it best: "The aim of every artist is to arrest motion and hold it fixed so that at some point a stranger reads it and it comes back to life again." I believe that thought explains the intensity of my passion to write—and to never stop writing.

I take very seriously the idea that, if one lives well and has no deep regrets, then one faces death with more serenity. I have heard this message not only from many dying patients but also from great-souled writers such as Tolstoy, whose Ivan Ilych realized he was dying so badly because he had lived so badly. All my reading and life experiences have taught me the importance of living in such a manner that I would die with few regrets. In my later years, I have made a conscious effort to be generous and gentle with everyone I encounter, and I proceed into my later eighties with a reasonable degree of contentment.

Another reminder of my mortality is my email. For more than twenty years I've been receiving a good amount of fan mail each day. I attempt to respond to each letter—I think of it as my form of daily Buddhist lovingkindness meditation. It gives me joy to think that my work offers something to those who write me. But I am also aware, as the years go by, of the ever-increasing numbers of email—a rush that is fueled by the knowledge that I shan't live too much longer. Increasingly, this message is entirely explicit, as in this email that came a few days ago:

> . . . I wanted to write to you a long time ago, but thought that
> you would get overwhelmed with emails and would not have the
> time to read them all; however I thought I would email you any-
> way. As you say yourself, your age is advanced and you may not
> be around for much longer and then it would be too late.

Or in another that arrived the following day:

> . . . To put it bluntly, and I think you will appreciate this, I real-
> ize you will no longer be here at some point. I don't want to take
> your existence for granted and regret not contacting you when it's
> too late. . . . It would mean a lot to me to have an exchange with
> you because most people I know are not interested in discussing
> death, nor have they made their own personal connection with
> the fact that they will die.

Sometimes, in recent years, I have started lectures by acknowledging the size of the audience and saying, "I'm aware that,
as I age, audiences grow larger and larger. And of course that is
wonderfully affirming. But if I put on my existential spectacles I
see a darker side and I wonder, why such a rush to see me?"

CHAPTER THIRTY-SIX
FINAL WORKS

I was a teenager when I first heard Einstein's response to quantum theory: "God doesn't play dice with the universe." Like most science-minded adolescent boys, I revered Einstein and was astounded to hear that he believed in God. The fact called into question my own religious skepticism, and I sought an explanation from my junior high school science teacher. His answer: "Einstein's God is the God of Spinoza."

"What does that mean?" I asked. "Who is Spinoza?" I learned that Spinoza was a seventeenth-century philosopher and pioneer of the scientific revolution. Though he often referred to God in his writing, his Jewish community had excommunicated him for heresy when he was twenty-four, and many, if not most, scholars regard him as a closet atheist. It would have been dangerous, my teacher told me, for Spinoza to express skepticism about the existence of God in the seventeenth century, and he protected himself by frequently employing the term "God." However, whenever Spinoza uses the word "God," most scholars understand him to mean *the orderly laws of nature*. I picked out a life of Spinoza from the library's A–Z biography section and, though I didn't understand much of it, I resolved that someday I would learn more about Einstein's hero.

About seventy years later, I came across a book that rekindled my interest. I learned how, after Spinoza's excommunication from Judaism, he had refused to attach himself to any religious community. Instead he had worked as a glass-grinder making lenses for spectacles and telescopes, lived frugally in isolation, and composed philosophical and political tracts that changed the course of history. That book was *Betraying Spinoza* by Rebecca Goldstein, a novelist and philosopher. One by one I had devoured her extraordinary novels, but it was *Betraying Spinoza*, part philosophy, part fiction, and part biography, that set my mind on fire. The thought of writing a novel about Spinoza percolated in my brain, but I felt entirely stymied. How could I write a novel about a man who had lived mostly in his thoughts, whose life was solitary and without intrigue or romance, spending his adulthood in rented rooms, grinding lenses and scribbling with quill and ink?

Fortuitously, I was invited to Amsterdam to address an association of Dutch psychotherapists. Though, as I have aged, I rarely look forward to overseas travel, I welcomed this opportunity and agreed to give a workshop with the proviso that they arrange a Spinoza day, during which a knowledgeable guide would accompany my wife and me to Spinoza sites in the Netherlands: his birthplace, various residences, his grave, and, most important of all, the small Spinoza museum, the Spinozahuis, in the small town of Rijnsburg. So, after a daylong presentation in Amsterdam, Marilyn and I and our guides—the president of the Dutch Spinoza Society and a well-informed Dutch philosopher—set out on our mission.

We visited the Amsterdam neighborhood where Spinoza spent his early life, saw the houses in which he later dwelled, and took the same barge rides on the canal that he had taken. I now had numerous visual details of Spinoza's Holland, but I was no closer to formulating the narrative necessary for a novel. All that changed when I visited the Spinozahuis. At first I was disappointed to find that the museum held none of Spinoza's personal effects. Instead, I saw a replica of the lens-grinding equipment he would have used, and a portrait painted after his death. Moreover, our guide informed me that the portrait may not have been accurate, because no likenesses of him were made during his lifetime. All the paintings of Spinoza were based on written descriptions.

Then I turned to the museum's major attraction: Spinoza's personal library of 151 sixteenth- and seventeenth-century books. I had been looking forward to holding books that Spinoza's fingers had touched, hoping that his spirit would inspire me. Although the public was not permitted to touch the books, I was granted special permission. As I held one reverently in my hands, my guide drifted over to my side and gently said, "Pardon me, Dr. Yalom . . . perhaps you know this . . . but Spinoza's hands never touched this book, or, indeed, any of the books in the library: these books are not the *actual physical* books owned by Spinoza."

I was stunned. "What do you mean? I don't understand."

"After Spinoza's death in 1677, Spinoza's tiny estate could not cover the costs of his funeral and burial, and his one possession of value, his library, had to be auctioned off."

"But these books here, these ancient books?"

"The auctioneer was exceedingly punctilious. For the auction he wrote an extremely detailed description of each book—the date, publisher, city, binding, et cetera. Two hundred years after his death, a wealthy patron provided funds to reconstitute Spinoza's entire library, and the buyers faithfully followed the auctioneer's book descriptions in their purchases."

Though I was interested in all that I saw and heard, none of it was the stuff of a novel. Discouraged, I turned to leave, but at that very moment, I overheard the word "Nazis" used in a conversation between our guides and the museum guard. "Why the Nazis? What were they doing in this museum?" They told me an amazing story. Shortly after the Nazis occupied Holland, a troop of ERR soldiers appeared at the museum, closed and sealed it, and confiscated the entire library.

"So this library again had to be reconstituted?" I asked. "And that means these books are *twice* removed from the touch of Spinoza's fingers?"

"No, not at all," my guide reassured me: "To everyone's amazement, the entire collection stolen by the Nazis, minus only a few volumes, was found after the war hidden in a sealed salt mine."

I was astonished and bursting with questions. "The ERR—what does that stand for?"

"Einsatzstab Reichsleiter Rosenberg—the task force of Nazi leader Alfred Rosenberg, the man in charge of looting Jewish possessions throughout Europe."

My heart began to race. "But, why? Why? Europe was in flames. Why would they bother to confiscate this small village library when they could loot all those Rembrandts and Vermeers?"

"No one knows the answer to that," my guide replied. "The only clue we have is a sentence in the report written by the officer in charge of the raid—it was given as evidence at the Nuremberg trials. Now it is in the public domain and you can easily bring it up on the Internet. It says in effect that the Spinoza library contains works of great importance for the exploration of the Spinoza problem."

"Spinoza problem?" I asked, growing even more intrigued. "What does *that* mean? What kind of problem did the Nazis have with Spinoza? And why would they preserve all the books in this library rather than burning them like everything else Jewish throughout Europe?"

Like a mime duo, my hosts hunched their shoulders and showed their palms—they had no answers.

I left the museum with an intriguing and unsolved puzzle! Manna from heaven for a famished novelist! I got what I came for. "I've got a book now," I told Marilyn. "I've got a plot and a title!" and, as soon as I returned home, I began writing *The Spinoza Problem*.

Before long, I developed an entirely plausible explanation for the Nazis' "Spinoza problem." I learned in my reading that Goethe, the literary idol of all Germans, including the Nazis, was fascinated by Spinoza's work. In fact, Goethe had mentioned in one of his letters that he carried Spinoza's *Ethics* in his pocket for an entire year! Surely this must have presented an enormous problem for a Nazi ideologue: How could Germany's greatest writer have been so devoted to Spinoza, a Portuguese-Dutch Jew?

I decided to intertwine two life narratives—that of Benedict Spinoza, the seventeenth-century Jewish philosopher, and that of Alfred Rosenberg, a pseudo-philosopher and Nazi propagandist. As a fiercely anti-Semitic member of Hitler's inner circle, Rosenberg had ordered the confiscation of Spinoza's library, and it was Rosenberg who ordered that the books be saved rather than burned. In 1945 at the Nuremberg trials, Rosenberg was sentenced to death by hanging along with eleven other top-ranked Nazis.

I began by writing alternating chapters—Spinoza's life set in the seventeenth century and Rosenberg's in the twentieth—and developed a fictional connection between the two characters. Soon, however, it became too cumbersome to keep shifting back and forth between two eras and I decided to write the entire Spinoza story first, then Rosenberg's afterward, and then finally interlaced the two stories with the necessary sanding and polishing to ensure a snug fit.

Writing narratives set in two different centuries greatly increased the necessary research, and *The Spinoza Problem* took more time than any other book I've published (with the exception of *Existential Psychotherapy*). But I never considered it work: on the contrary, I was stimulated and eager to get to my reading and writing every morning. I read, not without difficulty, Spinoza's major works, commentaries on those works, and many biographies, and then, to unravel remaining mysteries, solicited advice from the Spinoza scholars Rebecca Goldstein and Steven Nadler.

I spent even more time researching the birth and development of the Nazi Party and Alfred Rosenberg's role in it. Though Hitler respected Rosenberg's ability and assigned him to important positions, he greatly preferred the company of Joseph Goebbels and Hermann Göring. Rumor has it that Hitler once hurled Rosenberg's major work, *The Myth of the Twentieth Century*, across the room, shouting, "Who can understand this stuff!" Rosenberg was so pained that Hitler did not love him as much as the others that he sought psychological help on more than one occasion, and I used an actual psychiatric report in my novel.

Unlike my other novels, *The Spinoza Problem* is not a teaching novel, but psychotherapy still plays an important role: the inner world of each of my two main characters is laid bare in ongoing discussions with a confidant. Spinoza confides in Franco, a friend who at times takes a therapist-like role, and Rosenberg has several psychotherapy sessions with an invented psychiatrist, Friedrich Pfister. In fact, Franco and Pfister are the only important characters I fictionalized: all others are historical figures.

Unfortunately, *The Spinoza Problem* had little appeal for American readers, but it did find an appreciative audience abroad: in France it was awarded the 2014 Prix des Lecteurs. In 2016 I received an email from Hans van Wijngaarden, a Dutch colleague, informing me that a likeness of Spinoza painted during his lifetime had just been discovered in a 1666 painting by Berend Graat. Gazing into Spinoza's soulful eyes, I much regretted not having seen this painting before I wrote the novel. Perhaps I would have felt even more personally connected to him, as was the case earlier after seeing portraits of Nietzsche, Breuer, Freud, Lou Salomé, and Schopenhauer.

More recently, Manfred Walther sent me his 2015 scholarly article titled "Spinoza's Presence in Germany During the Nazi Era," which describes Spinoza's enormous influence not only on Goethe but also on such eminent German philosophers as Fichte, Hölderin, Herder, Schelling, and Hegel. Had I seen this while writing the novel, it would have augmented my argument that Spinoza was, indeed, a major problem for the Nazis' anti-Jewish campaign.

My next project, *Creatures of a Day*, required no laborious research. I had only to raid, one last time, my "ideas for writing" file. The procedure was straightforward: I read and reread the clinical incidents in this file until one seemed to quiver with energy, and I then proceeded to build my story around it. Many of the stories are of single consultations, and many describe older patients dealing with issues of later life, such as retirement, aging, and confrontation with death. As with all my writing (aside from *The Spinoza Problem*), my target audience is still the young therapist needing guidance in the art of psychotherapy. As always, I sent my patients the final draft and obtained written permission—aside from two deceased patients who I knew would have given permission; I took care to disguise their identities even more deeply.

The title *Creatures of a Day* comes from one of the meditations of Marcus Aurelius: "All of us are but creatures of a day: the rememberer and the remembered alike." In the title story I describe a therapy session in which I learn that a patient has withheld important information from me, for fear of damaging my favorable image of him. As I explored his longing to persist in my mind, a longing so strong that it jeopardized his own therapy, I thought of Marcus Aurelius, whose *Meditations* I then happened to be reading. I walked over to my desk and showed him my copy of *The Meditations* and suggested he might find the book useful, because one meditation stressed the transient nature of existence and the idea that each of us is but a creature of a day. My story contains a subplot involving a second patient, to whom I also suggested reading Marcus Aurelius.

Not uncommonly when I am in the midst of reading and relishing the work of an outstanding thinker, something arises in a therapy session that leads me to recommend that particular author to my patient. More often than not, this suggestion is a total fiasco, but in this true story (there are no fictional events in *Creatures of a Day*), both patients embraced the book. Ironically, neither valued the particular message I had in mind but found other wise counsel in Marcus Aurelius.

Nor is this unusual. The patient and the therapist are fellow travelers, and it is not uncommon for the patient to see and be nourished by sights along their journey that entirely escape the therapist.

CHAPTER THIRTY-SEVEN

YIKES! TEXT THERAPY

For over fifteen years I led a supervision group of practicing therapists in San Francisco. During our third year we accepted a new member, an analyst relocating in San Francisco after a long career back east. The first case she presented to the group was a patient living in New York, whom she was continuing to meet via phone sessions. Phone sessions! I was appalled! How can one possibly do decent treatment without actually seeing the patient? Wouldn't the therapist miss all the nuances—the mingled glances, the facial expressions, the smiles, the nods, the handshakes at departure—so absolutely essential to the intimacy of the therapeutic relationship?

I told her, "You can't do long-distance therapy! You can't treat someone who is not in your office." God, what a prig I was! She held her ground and insisted that the therapy was proceeding quite well, thank you very much. I doubted it and continued to eye her suspiciously for several months until I conceded that she knew exactly what she was doing.

My opinion about long-distance therapy evolved further about six years ago when I received an email from a patient pleading for help and requesting therapy by Skype. She lived in an extremely isolated part of the world where no therapist was available within five hundred miles. In fact, because of an overwhelmingly painful rupture in a relationship, she had deliberately chosen to immigrate to such a remote place. She felt so raw that, if she lived nearby, I'm certain she would not have been willing to meet me, or any other therapist, face-to-face in an office. I had never done therapy via Skype before, and, given my doubts about the method, I hesitated. But since there was no other option for her, I finally decided to accept her for video therapy (but without mentioning this to any of my colleagues). For over a year, she and I met via Skype weekly. With her face filling my computer screen, I began to feel close to her, and within a very short time, the thousands of miles separating us seemed to evaporate. At the end of our year together she had made much progress in therapy, and since then I have seen a great many patients from such faraway countries as South Africa, Turkey, Australia, France, Germany, Italy, and the UK. I now believe there is little difference in outcome between my live therapy and my video therapy. However, I do make a point of selecting patients carefully. I do not use this medium for severely ill patients in need of medication and possible hospitalization.

Three years ago, when I first heard about text therapy, in which therapists and clients communicate entirely by texting, I was once again repelled. THERAPY BY TEXTING! YIKES! It seemed a distortion, a dehumanization, a parody of the therapy process. It was a step too far! I wanted nothing to do with it and moved back into my full prig mode. Then Oren Frank, the founder of Talkspace, the largest online text-therapy program, called and told me his company was now offering therapy groups that met via texting and asked me to consult with his therapists.

TEXTING THERAPY GROUPS! Once again I was shocked. A group of individuals who never saw one another (to maintain anonymity, their faces were never shown on the monitor, but were represented by symbols) and communicated entirely by text—this was too much! I could not imagine group therapy working via texting, but I agreed to participate, almost entirely out of curiosity.

I observed a few of the groups and this time I was right. The group therapy I witnessed turned out to be too cumbersome, and the project was soon abandoned. Instead, the company then concentrated entirely on using texting for individual therapy. Soon other text-therapy companies opened up in the United States and several other countries, and three years ago, I agreed to supervise therapists who were responsible for Talkspace staff training.

Now in my eighties, I rarely read journals or travel to attend professional conferences in my field, and I feel increasingly out of touch with new developments. Even though texting seemed the epitome of impersonality and the very opposite of my highly intimate approach to therapy, I sensed that texting was to play a significant role in the future of therapy. As a way of combatting personal obsolescence, I elected to keep current with this rapidly expanding method of delivering psychotherapy.

The platform's format offers clients the opportunity to send and receive texts (daily if desired) with a therapist for a modest fixed monthly fee. The use of such therapy is expanding exponentially and, at this writing, Talkspace, the largest of the US companies, engages over a thousand therapists. Many such platforms are opening in other countries—three companies in China have contacted me, each claiming to be the largest Chinese Internet therapy company.

The innovation evolved quickly. Soon Talkspace offered not only text therapy, but also the possibility for clients and therapists to leave voice messages to one another. Then, a short time later, the client was offered the option of meeting via live videoconference. Soon only 50 percent of the sessions were via texting, 25 percent by phone-messaging, and 25 percent by videoconference. My expectation was that there would be an inevitable sequence, that clients would use texting only during the initial phase of therapy and gradually progress to audio, and then finally to video—the real stuff. But how wrong I was! That was not what happened! Many clients prefer texting and decline phone and video contact. That seemed counterintuitive to me, but I soon learned that many clients felt safer with the anonymity of texting, and, moreover, that younger clients were extremely comfortable with texting: they grew up with texting and often prefer texting to phone contact with their friends. As of now it appears that text therapy will continue to play a robust role in the future of our field.

For some time I continued to feel dismissive of text therapy: it appeared to me like a feeble facsimile of the real thing. As I examined the work of supervisees, I was certain this modality did not offer the kind of therapy I offered my patients. Gradually, however, I have come to understand that, though it is not the same therapy offered in face-to-face encounters, *it does offer something important to clients*. Without doubt, many clients value text therapy and undergo change. I urged Talkspace to launch some careful outcome research, and the initial findings indeed support the presence of significant change. I've read patients' comments in their texts expressing how much they value the process. One patient texted that she had printed out some of her therapist's words and pasted them to the refrigerator door in order to review them regularly. If clients have a panic attack in the middle of the night, they can immediately text their therapist. Though the therapist will not read the text for hours, there is still a *sense* of immediate contact. Furthermore, clients can easily review their entire therapy, every word they have told their therapist, and thus gauge how much progress they have made.

The supervision of therapists using text therapy feels different from supervision of traditional therapists. For one thing, when I supervise the work of a text therapist, I do not have to rely on the therapist's sometimes unreliable recollections of what transpired in the hour; instead, I have available the entire transcription of everything, every word that passed between therapist and patient—there is nothing hidden from the supervisor's eyes.

Lastly, I've so strongly urged text-therapy practitioners under my supervision to be attentive to the human, empathic, genuine nature of the client-therapist relationship that an odd, paradoxical result has occurred: in the right hands of well-trained therapists, the texting approach may offer a more personal encounter than face-to-face meetings with therapists who rigidly follow mechanized behavioral manuals.

CHAPTER THIRTY-EIGHT
MY LIFE IN GROUPS

I have led a great many therapy groups over the decades—groups of psychiatric outpatients and inpatients; patients with cancer, bereaved spouses, alcoholics, and married couples; and medical students, psychiatric residents, and practicing therapists—but I have also been a member of many groups, even now, in my mid-eighties.

The one that looms largest in my thoughts is a leaderless group of therapists that, for the past twenty-four years, has been meeting every two weeks for ninety minutes in one of the members' offices. One of our fundamental ground rules is total confidentiality: what transpires in our group must stay in the group. So these paragraphs will be the first time I've disclosed anything about this group, and I write not only with the members' permission but also with their encouragement: none of us wants this group to die. Not that we seek immortality, but we all want to encourage others to have the vital, enriching experience we have had.

One paradox of life as a therapist is that we are never alone while working, and yet many of us experience deep isolation. We work without a team—without nurses, supervisors, colleagues, or assistants. Many of us ameliorate such loneliness by scheduling luncheons or coffee meetings with colleagues, or attending case discussions, or through seeking supervision or personal therapy, but for many of us, those remedies do not reach deep enough. I have found that meeting regularly in an intimate group of other therapists is restorative; the group offers comradeship, supervision, postgraduate learning, personal growth, and, occasionally, crisis intervention. I strongly encourage other therapists to create a group such as ours.

Our particular assemblage was born one day, over twenty years ago, when Ivan G., a practicing psychiatrist whom I had met when he was a resident at Stanford, phoned to invite me to join a support group to meet regularly in a medical office building close to the Stanford Hospital. He listed the names of the other psychiatrists who had thus far agreed to join—I knew almost all of them, some of them very well, since I had taught them when they had been psychiatry residents.

Joining such a group felt like a huge commitment: not only was it a ninety-minute meeting every other week, but it was also to be an ongoing group without a specified ending. So I knew when I accepted that it might be a long-term commitment, but none of us could have foreseen that we'd still be meeting twenty-two years later. In all these years, aside from a rare conflict with a major holiday, we have never canceled a meeting, and no one has ever missed a meeting for a trivial reason.

I myself had never been a member of an ongoing group, even though I had often envied my group patients. I, too, longed to be a member of a therapeutic group, to have a circle of trusted confidants. I knew from previous experience as a group leader how helpful it was to the members.

For six years I had once led a therapy group for therapists, and I had observed, week in and week out, the benefits it offered participants. Molyn Leszcz, coauthor of the fifth edition of my textbook on group therapy, was a Fellow at Stanford in 1980. He had come to Stanford to learn about group therapy, and as part of his training, I asked him to co-lead that group for a year. Ever since, even decades later, he and I reminisce about what we saw and felt during those meetings. I ended that group with much regret when I left for a sabbatical in London. For one thing, it was the only group I have led that resulted in a marriage. Two members began a relationship with each other and married shortly after the group ended. Thirty-five years later I saw them at a lecture, and they were still happily married.

So despite some discomfort at joining a group that included my former students, I signed on—not without anxiety: I, like many of the other members, felt uneasy revealing my vulnerability, my shame, and my self-doubts to colleagues and former students. I reminded myself that I was all grown up, and would probably survive the embarrassment.

Our early months were spent deciding what type of group we should be. We didn't want to discuss cases, though all of us wanted to have that option. Ultimately, we decided to become an all-purpose support group—in other words, a leaderless therapy group. One thing was clear at the outset: though I had the most experience with groups, I was *not* to be the group leader, and no one has ever regarded me as such. To avoid slipping into any kind of leadership role, I forced myself to be particularly self-revealing from the start. In my years of practice I've learned that, if one is to profit from such an experience, one must take risks. (In fact, in recent years I've generally made that point to my patients in our initial individual session, and often refer back to it whenever I see them resisting the work.)

We began with eleven members, all male, all psychotherapists (ten psychiatrists and one clinical psychologist). In the early stages two members dropped out, and a third had to leave for medical reasons. For the past twenty-two years, the group has been remarkably cohesive: not a single member has voluntarily dropped out, and the attendance has been outstanding. I personally have never missed a meeting when I have been in town, and the other members also give the group priority over all other activities.

When I am upset by an interaction with my wife or children or colleagues, or stymied in my work, or troubled by powerful positive or negative feelings toward a patient or acquaintance, or rattled by a nightmare, I have always looked forward to discussing it at the next meeting. And, of course, any uncomfortable feelings existing between members of the group were always dealt with in depth.

Perhaps there are other ongoing leaderless groups of therapists committed to scrutinizing process as well as the lives and psyches of the members, but none have come to my attention, certainly not one that has survived so long. During these two decades we have experienced the deaths of four members as well as dementia in two members that forced them to retire. We have discussed the death of spouses, remarriage, retirement, family illness, problems with children, and relocation into a retirement community. In every instance we have remained committed to honest scrutiny of ourselves and each other.

For me, what has been most remarkable has been the persistence of novel encounters. For over five hundred meetings, I continue to discover something new and different about my co-members and myself every single meeting. Perhaps the most difficult experience for all of us was to have observed in great detail the onset and development of dementia in two beloved members. We faced many dilemmas. How open should we be about what we saw? How should we respond to the grandiosity or denial that accompanies dementia? And, even more pressing, what to do if we felt the member should no longer be seeing patients? Each time this has occurred we responded by strongly pressuring the member to consult with a psychologist and undergo neuropsychological testing, and in each instance the consultant exercised her authority to order the member to stop seeing patients. Like most people in their eighties, I worry about dementia myself, and on three or four occasions have been informed by the group that the incident I had just related was one I had already described earlier. Mortifying though it is, I was grateful for the group's dedicated honesty. Somewhere in the back of my mind, however, there lurks a dread that one day some group member will insist I get neuro-psychological testing.

When one of our younger members stunned us by telling us that he had just been diagnosed with untreatable pancreatic can-cer, we remained fully present with him as he openly and coura-geously discussed all his fears and concerns. Toward the end of his life, when he was too ill to travel, we held a meeting at his home. The entire group attended his memorial.

Each time a member died, we added a new member to keep our size relatively constant. We all attended the wedding of one member, which was held at the home of another member, and yet a third member conducted the wedding ceremony. The group also attended two other weddings and the Bar Mitzvah of a member's son. On another occasion the entire group visited the residen-tial center where a member suffering from severe dementia was confined. Many times we discussed adding female members, but since we always added just a single member at a time, most of us thought a woman would feel uncomfortably outnumbered. In retrospect, I think we erred in this decision. My hunch is that the group would have been even richer had we begun with both males and females.

I've always been active in the group, and early in its course I would often be the one, when the group seemed to be unengaged and avoidant of deeper issues, to make a process comment—that is, to remark on the group's overconcern with safe, superficial issues; after the first few years, however, others have taken that role as frequently as I have. We've offered help to one another on a number of different levels. Sometimes we work on deeper character issues, or on members' proclivities toward sarcasm, be-littling remarks, guilt at taking up too much time, fear of expo-sure, or shame, and sometimes our focus is just to offer support and let a member know we stand close to him. Recently I arrived quite shaken up after a car accident the week before. Since the accident, I'd felt anxious driving and was beginning to question whether, at my age, I should still be behind the wheel. Another member told me that he had had a significant accident a few years earlier and had been shaken up for six months. He thought of it as a minor posttraumatic stress syndrome. Reframing it in that manner proved to be very useful to me, and I drove home feeling calmer, but still driving cautiously.

I am also a member of Pegasus, a writing group for medical doctors founded in 2010 by a good friend, Hans Steiner, the former head of the Stanford Department of Child Psychiatry. Our group of ten physician-writers meets monthly for two-hour evening meetings in which we discuss each other's writing. The evenings end with dinner supplied by the one whose work has been critiqued. This group read many of the pages of this book, liked the first third far more than the rest, and urged me to put more of my own inner life into the text.

Several books and shorter pieces from group members have been published, including *A Surgeon's War* by Henry Ward Trueblood—an amazing memoir describing the life of a trauma surgeon on the front lines during the Vietnam War. We do regular public readings at Stanford of new work by our members, and I have participated in these readings several times.

Pegasus has expanded, and at the present time there are four Pegasus groups made up of physicians and several medical students. On a few occasions the poets in our group have done public readings of poems inspired by artistic pieces—for example, paintings at the recently opened Stanford Anderson Collection, or musical performances by the St. Lawrence String Quartet, the Stanford resident musical group. We also offer grand rounds in psychiatry each year, offer a competition for student writing with a cash award, and sponsor an annual visiting professorship in the medical humanities.

I attend yet another monthly event, the Lindemann Group, named after one of the founding members, Erich Lindemann, an influential psychiatrist who was a longtime professor of psychiatry at Harvard and, in his last few years, at Stanford. I first joined the group at its founding in the 1970s and attended monthly meetings for years. At each of the two-hour evening meetings of eight to ten therapists, one of them presents a current problematic case. I much enjoyed the camaraderie for many years until Bruno Bettelheim moved to Stanford and joined the group. He felt that, because of his seniority, the meeting should consist of members presenting cases to him. Neither I nor anyone else could disabuse him of this idea, and when we came to an impasse, several of us dropped out. Many years after Bruno's death, I was invited to rejoin, and I have cherished the group since then.

Each member presents a case in his or her own style. At one recent meeting, a member chose to use psychodrama and assigned group members parts to play (the patient, the wife, the therapist, other members of the family, an observing commentator, etc.). At first it seemed silly and off the point, but by the end of the meeting we all felt very stuck and unable to offer help to the patient—that is, we felt exactly like the presenting therapist in his work with his patient. It was an unusually powerful and graphic method of conveying his therapeutic dilemma.

The group in which I am most closely entwined is my family group. I've been married to Marilyn for sixty-three years, and rarely does a day pass that I do not thank my good fortune for having such an extraordinary life partner. Yet, as I have so often said to others, one doesn't find a relationship: one creates a relationship. Over the decades, both of us have worked hard to create the marriage we have today. Whatever complaints I've had in the past have evaporated. I've learned to accept her few failings—her indifference to cooking, to sporting events, to bicycling, to science fiction, to science per se—but all these complaints are minor. I feel fortunate to have lived with a walking encyclopedia of Western culture who can immediately answer most of the historical or literary questions I pose.

Marilyn, too, has learned to overlook my failings—my intractable household messiness, my refusal to wear neckties, my adolescent infatuation with motorcycles and convertibles, and my feigned ignorance of how to operate the dishwasher and washing machine. We have arrived at a mutual understanding that I could not have anticipated as a young, impetuous, and often insensitive lover. Our major concerns now lie with each other's well-being and the fear of what will happen when one of us dies before the other.

Marilyn is a scholar with an inquiring mind, and she is particularly steeped in European literature and art. Like me, she is an eternal student and reader. Unlike me, she is outgoing, gregarious, and socially skilled—as attested by her many friendships. Though we are both passionate about writing and reading, our interests don't always overlap, and I think that's for the best. I am drawn to philosophy and science, particularly psychology, biology, and cosmology. Aside from a Wellesley botany course, Marilyn has had no science education whatsoever and is entirely clueless about the modern technical world. I have to bargain hard to get her to accompany me to the planetarium and aquarium at the California Academy of Sciences, and, once there, she is eager to leave for the de Young art museum across the park, where she will spend ten minutes examining a single painting. She is my gateway to the world of art and history, but sometimes I'm beyond help. Though I'm hopelessly tone-deaf, she continues trying to awaken my musical sensibility, but when I'm driving alone and there is no baseball game, I often turn the radio dial to bluegrass.

Marilyn loves good wine, and for years I pretended to have a taste for it. But recently I've given up all pretenses and openly admit that I dislike the taste of alcohol in any form. Perhaps there is a genetic component: my parents also disliked alcoholic drinks, except for an occasional glass of beer and sour cream, a Russian concoction they often drank in the summer.

Fortunately, thank God, Marilyn is not a religious believer, but she has a secret yearning for the sacred, whereas I am a dedicated skeptic and align myself with the likes of Lucretius, Christopher Hitchens, Sam Harris, and Richard Dawkins. We love films, but selection is often a challenge: she vetoes anything with violence or the slightest aroma of lowlife. For the most part, I agree with her, but when she's away I'll indulge in a con-man film or a Clint Eastwood western. And when *she's* alone, the TV remains fixed at the cable French channel.

Her memory is good—too good at times: she remembers films so clearly that, even decades later, she balks at seeing many old films a second time, whereas I gladly watch old films, which seem sparkling new to me since I've forgotten almost all of their plots. Her favorite author, hands down, is Proust. He is too precious for me; I tend toward Dickens, Tolstoy, Dostoevsky, and Trollope. Among contemporary writers I read David Mitchell, Philip Roth, Ian McEwan, Paul Auster, and Haruki Murakami, while she would vote for Elena Ferrante, Colm Tóibín, and Maxine Hong Kingston. We both love J. M. Coetzee.

Despite having four children, Marilyn never missed a year of teaching. We were dependent on young au pairs from Europe and daily household help. Like most people reared in California, our children have chosen to stay here, and we feel fortunate to have them all nearby. We gather often as a family and generally have summer vacations together, most frequently in Hanalei on the island of Kauai. The 2015 photo on the next page shows us with our children and grandchildren. It was posted only for a few days before Facebook removed it for indecency. (If you look hard, you'll note my daughter-in-law discreetly nursing my youngest grandson.)

Our family life includes a lot of games. I played tennis for years with each of my three sons at a neighborhood tennis

Entire family in Hanalei, Hawaii, 2015.

court—those are some of my fondest memories. I taught Reid and Victor chess at an early age and they both became strong players. I enjoyed taking them to tournaments from which they always emerged with a gleaming trophy. Reid's son, Desmond, and Victor's son, Jason, are also strong players, and we rarely have a family get-together without one or two chess games in progress.

Other games are much in evidence at family gatherings. There is Scrabble with my daughter, Eve, who is always the reigning champion. But most of all, I've enjoyed our medium-stake poker games and my regular pinochle games with Reid and Ben, using the same rules and stakes I played with my father and Uncle Abe.

At times Victor entertains us with magic tricks. In high school he was well-known as a prankster, and during his adolescence he was a professional magician performing at both adult and children's functions. Anyone who attended his Gunn High School graduation ceremony will remember the sight of Victor solemnly marching down the aisle to receive his diploma when suddenly the mortarboard on his head burst into flame. The ceremony was interrupted with "oohs" and "aahs" and a huge burst of applause. I was as stunned as anyone else and begged him to tell me how he did it. As a dedicated magician, he had steadfastly refused to reveal any of his professional secrets, even to his pleading father, but on this one occasion he took pity on me and told me the secret of the burning mortarboard: a hidden aluminum foil basin in the brim of the hat, a reservoir of lighter fluid, a tiny match, and voilà! A flaming mortarboard. (Do not try this at home.)

I was so absorbed in teaching and writing and financially supporting my family that now, looking back, I feel I missed a great deal. I regret not spending more individual time with each child. At my friend Larry Zaroff's memorial ceremony, one of his three children described a treasured family tradition in which their father spent much of each Saturday with one of his three children in turn. They had lunch together, one-on-one talks, and a visit to the bookstore where each chose a book. What a lovely tradition! As I listened, I found myself wishing I had entered more deeply into each of my children's lives. If I had another go-round, I'd do it differently.

Marilyn was the primary parent on a daily level and put off most of her writing until the children were grown. After her required academic publications, she began to write for a broader public, following my lead. She published *Blood Sisters: The French Revolution in Women's Memory* in 1993, and since then she has authored seven other books, including *A History of the Wife*, *Birth of the Chess Queen*, *A History of the Breast*, *How the French Invented Love*, *The Social Sex*, and *The American Resting Place* with our son Reid, who is a fine art photographer. Each of her books was a great adventure for me. We are always each other's first reader. She credits my fascination with women's breasts for inspiring *A History of the Breast*, a cultural study of how women's bodies have been viewed and represented throughout history. Yet my favorite is *Birth of the Chess Queen*, a book in which she traced the evolution of a piece that did not exist on the board for hundreds of years and first appeared around the year 1000 as the weakest piece on the board. Gradually she assumed more power as European queens grew more potent, and attained her present status as the game's strongest piece at the end of the fifteenth century, during the reign of Queen Isabella of Spain. I've attended a great many of Marilyn's readings at bookstores and universities and watched her with enormous pride. At present she is near completion of another book, *The Amorous Heart*, that will explore how the heart became a symbol for love.

Despite our strong work ethic, Marilyn and I have been firmly implanted within our family, fulfilling the roles of parents and grandparents for more than sixty years. We have tried to make our home a welcoming place not only for our children, but also for our friends and our children's friends. Our house has hosted a great many weddings, book parties, and baby showers. Perhaps we felt this necessity even more than most people, since we left our own families of birth behind on the East Coast and have created a new network of family and friends in California, with roots into the future rather than the past.

Though we have traveled considerably in our lives—to many European countries, to a great many tropical islands in the Caribbean and Pacific, to China, Japan, Indonesia, and Russia—I find that, as I age, I grow more and more reluctant to leave home. The jet lag is more potent than in earlier years, and frequently I fall ill on long trips. When it comes to traveling, Marilyn, chronologically only nine months my junior, often seems twenty years younger. When invited to lecture now in a distant country, I invariably decline, often proposing a videoconference instead. I limit my travel to Hawaii and sometimes to Washington, DC, and New York, and to Ashland every year for the Oregon Shakespeare Festival.

In an interview shown in the 2014 film documentary *Yalom's Cure*, our daughter, Eve, candidly told the filmmakers that Marilyn and I always put our relationship first—that is, above our relationship to our children. My instinct was to protest, but I believe she was right. Eve said that she had put her children first, but then added, wistfully, that her marriage did not last beyond twenty-five years. In post-film discussions with audience members, several viewers noted that our marriage appeared so strong and so enduring, whereas all four of our children had divorced. I responded that I suspect some historical factors are at play: 40 to 50 percent of contemporary US marriages end in divorce, whereas among my contemporaries divorce was very rare. During my first twenty-five or thirty years of life, I never knew a divorced person. In the discussions with film audiences about our children's divorces, Marilyn always wanted to call out, "Hey, three of our children have remarried and have great second marriages."

Following each of the divorces, Marilyn and I endlessly discussed what we might have done wrong. Are parents responsible for the breakdown of their children's marriages? I'm sure that many parents have asked themselves that same unanswerable question. Divorce is generally a painful experience for everyone involved. Marilyn and I shared our children's sadness, and to this day we are intimately involved with all of our children and grandchildren and are heartened by the support they give each other.

THE AUTHOR WITH HIS WIFE, MARILYN, IN SAN FRANCISCO, 2006.

CHAPTER THIRTY-NINE
ON IDEALIZATION

Ever since my book *The Theory and Practice of Group Psychotherapy* was adopted as a textbook forty-five years ago, I've had a loyal following among students and therapists. They are my primary audience and I never expected to have a wider readership. So I was both surprised and thrilled when my collection of therapeutic tales, *Love's Executioner*, became a bestseller in America and was widely translated. It always gladdened my heart when friends wrote telling me they have seen it displayed at airports in Athens or Berlin or Buenos Aires. Later, when my novels reached foreign readers, I relished the copies of exotic editions: Serbian, Bulgarian, Russian, Polish, Catalan, Korean, Chinese versions arriving in the mail. Only gradually have I accepted (but never fully understood) that the great majority of my readers come from other countries and know my books in another language.

Marilyn was dismayed for many years to note that the one major country that entirely ignored me was France. She had been a Francophile ever since she started French classes at the age of twelve, and especially after her junior year in France with the Sweetbriar College program. I tried repeatedly to improve my French with several different teachers, but was so inept that even my wife concluded it was simply not my sport. In 2000, however, a new French publishing company, Galaade, made an offer for the French translation rights to the seven books I had written up to that time. Galaade published one of my books each year thereafter, and I soon had a sizable French readership.

In 2004, Galaade staged a public event at the Marigny Theatre in Paris on the Right Bank (now the Theatre at St. Claude). I was to be interviewed (via an interpreter, of course) by the publisher of *Psychologies*, a popular French magazine. The theater is a grand old structure with a large orchestra, two balconies, and a majestic stage once graced by the great French actor Jean-Louis Barrault. When I arrived for the event, I was amazed to discover that it was sold out, and I noted, in wonderment, the long line of folks waiting outside. As soon as I entered the theater, I spotted a huge red velvet throne in the center of the stage, where I was expected to sit and address the multitudes. That was too much! I insisted they switch the throne for something less exalted. When the crowd filed in, I recognized a large coterie of Marilyn's French-speaking friends, who for years could neither converse with me nor read my books. The interviewer asked just the right questions, I told many of my best stories, the translator was miraculous, and the evening could not have gone better. I could almost hear Marilyn purring as her friends realized I wasn't such an idiot after all.

In 2012, a Swiss filmmaker, Sabine Gisiger, approached me about making a documentary based on my life. It seemed an odd proposition, but when I attended a showing at the Mill Valley Film Festival of *Guru*, her excellent film about Rajneesh, the manipulative cult leader who led a commune in Oregon, I grew more interested. When I asked her why she had selected me as the subject of a film, she responded that she had felt soiled by her work on Rajneesh and had resolved to make a film about a "decent person." *Decent person*—that won me over.

We began a period of shooting that lasted more than two years, with Sabine as director, Philip Delaquis as producer, and their marvelous sound and film technicians. The crew made several visits to our home in Palo Alto, to Stanford, and to our family vacations in Hawaii and the South of France, and soon the entire cast felt like part of our family. I was filmed in many situations— while speaking publicly, bicycling, swimming, snorkeling, playing Ping-Pong, and once while soaking in our hot tub with Marilyn.

All along I wondered who on earth would want to see a film showing all these mundane aspects of my life. I had no financial investment in the film, but, having grown close to the filmmaker and the producer, I worried about the money they were going to lose. In the end, when my entire family and several close friends saw a private showing of an early version in San Francisco, I was relieved: Sabine and her film editor had done an excellent job winnowing down many dozens of hours into a coherent seventy-four-minute film. Over my protests, it was titled *Yalom's Cure*. Still, I puzzled why anyone outside my immediate family and friends would have the slightest interest in seeing it. Moreover, I felt self-conscious and exposed. Though I've come to identify myself with my writing and consider my books, especially the stories and novels, to be major chapters of my adult life, the film takes little note of me as a writer and focuses instead on my quotidian activities. And yet, to my surprise, the film proved successful in Europe, ultimately playing in fifty cinemas to several hundred thousand spectators.

In the autumn of 2014, when it opened in Zurich, the filmmaker asked Marilyn and me to attend the world premiere. Though I had resolved not to travel overseas anymore, this was an invitation I could not refuse. We flew to Zurich and attended two showings, the first for an invited audience of therapists and dignitaries, and the second for a general audience. At the end of each showing I responded to questions and felt highly exposed, especially at the shots of Marilyn and me in the hot tub, even though only our heads and shoulders were visible. But I was thrilled by

PARISCOPE COVER, MAY 20, 2015.

the scenes of a family vacation in which our granddaughter Alana and our grandson Desmond compete in a dancing contest. Another granddaughter, Lilli Virginia, a professional songwriter and singer, is heard singing as the film ends.

When it opened in France a few months later, Marilyn flew to Paris for the premiere and spoke to the theater audience after the film. She was thrilled to see our faces on the front page of *Pariscope*, a popular weekly guide to happenings in Paris.

A few months later the film opened in Los Angeles but, in contrast to Europe, it generated little interest. Despite a favorable review in the *Los Angeles Times*, it closed after only a few days.

In conjunction with our earlier trip to Zurich for the film's opening, I had accepted an offer to speak in Moscow. The incentive was an unusually generous fee and a flight from Zurich to Moscow on a private jet. That flight turned out to be a story unto itself. There were only four passengers: Marilyn, me, a former patient whom I had seen for only one session many years before, and my former patient's close friend, a Russian oligarch, who owned the plane. I was seated next to the oligarch, with whom I had a most genial conversation throughout the flight. He came across as a thoughtful, soulful individual, troubled by a few unhappy areas in his life. I empathized with his travails but, out of politeness, did not press too deeply. Only much later did I learn that the (unstated) purpose of the flight was for me to offer some therapy to this beleaguered man. If only I had known, if only someone had been more direct, I would have been more focused on helping him.

The host for my lecture was the Moscow Institute of Psychoanalysis, a large training university, and the venue was a site often used for rock concerts. The sponsors had planned to have simultaneous translation with 700 headphones available, but 1,100 people showed up, causing such chaos that the host abandoned the idea of simultaneous translation. He requested the return of the headphones and instructed a very anxious translator to translate live.

As I began my talk and noted that no smiles greeted any of my jokes, I realized there was a serious translation problem. Later my host told me that the unnerved translator needed about fifteen minutes to settle down, but thereafter did a fine job. Afterward the conference sponsors staged a dramatic performance, in Russian, of "Arabesque," one of the stories in *Creatures of a Day*, about a Russian ballerina. Two extraordinarily beautiful actors dressed in exotic costumes dramatized the story, witnessed by a silent old man (I assume myself) sitting in the corner. The background of the action was a large film screen that projected an artist's hand and brush in the act of creating beautiful, surreal designs in oil. At the end of the event both Marilyn and I had a marathon book signing.

Once in Moscow I accepted an unusual invitation to discuss existentialism with a group of bank officers for an hour and a half. We met in a beautiful large room on the top floor of a skyscraper. About fifty were in attendance, among them the bank president, one of the few who spoke English. I, of course, knew not a word of Russian, and translation made the discussion cumbersome. The audience seemed profoundly uninterested in existentialism and asked no questions. I assumed they were disinclined to engage in a free discussion in the presence of their managers, and I tried hard to explore this, but to no avail. The bank president sat in the front row riveted to his iPad, and after twenty minutes he interrupted our session to announce that the European Union had just levied even more damaging sanctions on Russia, and he would like us to use our remaining time to discuss their concerns about this turn of events. I was all for this, since there was obviously little enthusiasm for existentialism, but, once again, there was only silence. Once again I expressed my concern that members might be unwilling to voice opinions with their managers present, but, try as hard as I could, I could find no way to break the impasse. My work ended up with little to show for it aside from my fee, which was paid in a curious fashion. I was told I would receive it the next day at a dinner party the university was giving in my honor. The following evening, after dessert, someone surreptitiously handed me a plain unmarked envelope full of US currency. I assumed I was paid in this mysterious manner as a favor to me, on the (false) assumption that I would then avoid paying taxes on the income, but it's also possible that for some reason the bank may have been looking for ways to get rid of extra cash.

As I have grown older I have tried to avoid long flights and have come to prefer appearances via videoconference. This entails going to a local videoconference office near my home and addressing the audience and responding to questions for approximately ninety minutes. I've done dozens of videoconference presentations since I decided to stop traveling overseas, but a recent one, in May 2016, for Mainland China, was the most unusual. Three psychiatrists in China interviewed me for ninety minutes, while an interpreter, who had flown to San Francisco for the occasion, sat by my side and translated their questions and my responses. The following day my sponsors told me that the

THE AUTHOR WITH HIS WIFE, MARILYN, AT THE KREMLIN, 2009.

interview was seen by a large audience, but I was staggered when they emailed me a photo of the interviewers and a precise count: there had been 191,234 viewers.

When I expressed my surprise and disbelief at the size of the audience, my Chinese sponsor replied, "Dr. Yalom, like most Americans, you don't truly appreciate the vastness of China."

Every day, without fail, I receive emails from readers from many parts of the world, and I make a point of responding to each letter, generally with something as simple as "Thank you for writing" or "I'm very glad that my work is meaningful for you." I'm careful to mention on the person's name so that the writer can be certain I've actually read his or her letter and am personally writing a response. This takes a good bit of time, but I feel I'm doing something similar to the daily lovingkindness meditation practiced by my Buddhist friends. Almost daily I get a request for a consultation from some part of the world, either by Skype or from individuals offering to fly to California to meet with me. The other day a man wrote asking if I would be able to Skype with his mother, a retired psychotherapist, on her one hundredth birthday.

Along with fan mail, readers sometimes send gifts, and our house is adorned with objects from Greece, Turkey, Iran, and China. But the most striking gift came from Sakellaris Koutouzis, a well-known Greek sculptor living and working on the small island of Kalymnos. I received an email from him requesting my address and informing me that he had enjoyed my books and was in the process of making a plaster bust of me from photographs he had found on the Web. I looked him up on the Internet and learned he was an accomplished sculptor, whose pieces were on display in different cities throughout the world. I insisted on paying the shipping costs, but he refused. A month later a larger-than-life-size bust arrived at my doorstep in a huge wooden box. It now sits in our house and is such a remarkable likeness that I feel spooked every time I look at it. Often I, or my children, adorn it with glasses, neckties, or one of my many hats.

THE AUTHOR WITH A SCULPTURE OF HIM
BY SAKELLARIS KOUTOUZIS, 2016.

Much as I try to deflect such tokens of renown, I have no doubt they have enhanced my sense of self. I also believe that my seniority, gravitas, and reputation increase my effectiveness as a therapist. Over the past twenty-five years the majority of my patients have contacted me because they have read some of my writing, and they arrive at my office with a strong belief in my therapeutic powers. Having met well-known therapists in my life, I have some sense of how such encounters can leave their mark: I can still see the crevices of Carl Rogers's face. Fifty years ago, I requested a conversation with him and flew down to Southern California to spend an afternoon. I had sent him some of my work, and I remember him telling me that though my group therapy textbook was well-done, it was my Ginny book (*Every Day Gets a Little Closer*) that he regarded as very special. And the faces of Viktor Frankl and Rollo May remain so clear in my mind's eye that if I had artistic talent (I don't) I could render them accurately from memory.

So, because of my reputation, patients reveal secrets they have never told anyone else, even previous therapists, and if I accept them nonjudgmentally and empathically, my interventions are likely to carry more weight simply because of their preconceptions about me. Recently, during the same afternoon, I saw two new patients who were familiar with my work. The first, a retired therapist, drove to my office from her home several hours away. She was worried about her tendency to hoard (in only one room of her home) and her obsessional behavior: upon leaving home, she would drive less than a block before returning home to see whether the door was locked and the stove turned off. I told her I didn't think these were going to be cleared up in brief therapy with me, nor were they significantly interfering with her life. I considered her a well-integrated person, someone who had an excellent marriage and was dealing with the difficult task of searching for meaning after retirement. She was pleased to hear that I thought she did not need therapy. The following day she emailed me these words:

*I just wanted to let you know how much I enjoyed and valued
our consultation last Thursday, it meant a great deal to me. I felt
your support and validation that I'm doing well, am happy and
content with my life and really appreciate your comment I do not
need any therapy. And I left your office feeling less anxious and
more confident and accepting of myself. I felt that it was a true
gift. That's pretty darn good for just one session!*

Later, the same afternoon, a middle-aged South American
man, visiting a friend in San Francisco, came for a single consultation. He spent almost the entire hour speaking of his concerns
about his sister, who has fought anorexia nearly all her life. After
the death of his parents, he was so heavily burdened by the expenses of her medical and psychiatric care that he was never able
to marry and have a family. I asked why he, rather than other
members of his large family, had taken on the entire burden of her
care. Then, with a great deal of anxiety and hesitation, he told me
a story he had never before shared with anyone.

He is thirteen years older than his sister, and one day, when
she was two and he fifteen, his parents left his sister in his care
for several hours while they and his older siblings attended a wedding. During their absence he had a long erotic phone conversation with a girlfriend (whom his parents greatly disliked and had
expressly forbidden him to contact). During this conversation his
sister crawled out the open front door and fell down several steps,
suffering very considerable bruising of her body and face. When
his parents returned, he had to confess everything—the worst
moment of his life—and, though his sister's injury was slight and
the bruising faded in a few days, he had harbored, all these years,
a secret fear and conviction that her anorexia was caused by that
fall. Moreover, in the twenty-five years since his sister's injury, this
was the first time he had ever disclosed this experience to anyone.

Using my deepest and most formal voice I told him that I had
listened carefully to what he had told me about his sister and, after

considering all the evidence, I now pronounced him innocent. I assured him that he had paid his dues for his episode of negligence, and reassured him there was no way in which her fall could have caused anorexia. I also suggested he explore this in therapy when he returned to his country. He wept with relief, declined my suggestion to pursue therapy, and assured me he had gotten precisely what he wanted. He left my office with a much lighter step.

These one-shot consultations, in which I recognize the patient's efforts and strengths and offer my blessings, owe their success in large part to the power with which the patient imbues me.

Not too long ago a woman recounted one of the saddest events of her life. In her late adolescence, just before leaving home for college, she took a long train ride with her eminent but very distant father. She had so looked forward to time alone with him, but was devastated when he opened his briefcase and spent the entire ride working, without speaking a word to her. I responded that our therapy offered an opportunity to replay that event. She and I (an older prominent man) would take a multi-hour therapy trip, but we would travel differently: she would have full permission, even encouragement, to ask questions, register complaints, and express feelings. And I would make sure to respond and reciprocate fully. She was moved and ultimately helped by such an approach.

And the impact of all this attention and applause upon my own sense of self? At times I feel heady and at other times disquieted, but generally I keep my balance. Every time I meet with colleagues in my support group or in my case discussion group, I am aware that they, excellent clinicians in practice for decades, are every bit as effective in their work as I am in mine. So I don't take the adulation to heart. All I can do is take my work seriously and be the best therapist I can be. I remind myself that I am being idealized and that we humans, all of us, crave a wise, all-knowing, white-haired elder. If I've been chosen to fit that slot, well, I happily accept the position. Someone has to do it.

CHAPTER FORTY
A NOVICE AT GROWING OLD

A s a child, I was always the youngest kid—youngest in my class, on the baseball team, on the tennis team, in my bunk at camp—but now, wherever I go, I am the oldest—oldest at a lecture, a restaurant, a book reading, the cinema, a baseball game. Recently I attended and spoke at a two-day continuing medical education conference for psychiatrists sponsored by the Stanford Department of Psychiatry. When I looked at the audience of colleagues from around the country, I saw only a few gray-haired folks and not one with white hair. I wasn't just the oldest; I was the oldest by far! Listening to the program of sixteen other lectures and discussions made me even more aware of my age and the changes in the field since I began the practice of medicine in the 1950s. All the current developments—the new psychopharmacology for schizophrenia and bipolar disorders and depression, the new generation of drug trials in progress, high-tech treatments for sleep disorders, eating disorders, and attention deficit disorder—much of this has passed me by. I recalled myself as a promising young faculty member who took great pride in keeping abreast of every new development. Now, I felt lost in many of the presentations, none more so than when listening to a lecture on transcranial magnetic stimulation of the brain, which described methods of stimulating and inhibiting critical centers in the brain far more efficiently and precisely than can be done with medication, and without side effects. Was this to be the future of my field?

When I first entered residency in 1957, psychotherapy was the very core of psychiatry, and my passion for exploring it was shared by almost all of my colleagues. But now, in the eight presentations I attended at this conference, there was only scant mention of psychotherapy.

I have read very little in psychiatry these past few years. I often pretend this is due to visual problems—I've had surgical procedures on both of my corneas, as well as bilateral cataract operations—but that's a lame excuse. I could have kept abreast by reading professional material on the large font on my Kindle. The truth—slightly embarrassing to admit—is that I am no longer interested. When I start to feel guilty about this, I comfort myself by saying that I have put in my time, and that, at eighty-five, I should be free to read whatever I wish. Then, I add, "Besides, I'm a writer and need to stay abreast of contemporary literary currents."

When it was my turn to address the audience at the Stanford conference, I did not lecture, and had no slides to show—unlike the other speakers. In fact—and here follows a huge first-time confession—*I have never made or used a slide in my life!* Instead, a Stanford colleague and close friend, David Spiegel, skillfully and genially interviewed me about my career and evolution as a therapist. This is a comfortable format for me, and the time flowed so quickly that I was startled when the session ended. As the audience stood and applauded, I had the disquieting sense they were saying farewell.

Because there are few psychiatrists practicing at my age, I often ask myself: *Why are you still seeing patients?* It's not for economic reasons; I have enough money to live comfortably. It's that I love my work too much to let it go before I have to. I feel privileged at being invited into the intimate lives of so many people, and after so many decades, I think I may be getting good at it.

Perhaps, in part, this is a result of getting good at selecting my patients. For the past several years I've done time-limited therapy: I tell patients at our first session that I will see them for a maximum of one year. As I approached eighty, I began to wonder how long my mind and memory would remain intact. I didn't want patients to become overly dependent on a man who might soon be retiring. Moreover, I've found that setting a termination date at the outset generally increases the efficiency of treatment and plunges patients more quickly into the work. (Otto Rank, one of Freud's early disciples, made that same observation over a hundred years ago.) I am careful not to accept a patient if it appears unlikely that we can make considerable progress in a year, and I refer patients who are more severely ill and in need of psychotropic medication to other psychiatrists. (Because I've not kept abreast of new research, I stopped prescribing medication several years ago.)

Since I have helped so many people deal with aging, I thought I was well prepared for the losses looming ahead, but I find it far more daunting than I had imagined. The aching knees, the loss of balance, the early-morning back stiffness, the fatigue, the fading vision and hearing, the skin blemishes, all these catch my attention but are minor compared to the fading of memory.

On a recent Saturday, my wife and I went out for a walk and lunch in San Francisco, and upon returning to our apartment I realized that I had neglected to take my keys with me. We had to wait outside for a couple of hours before the return of a neighbor who had a duplicate set. That evening we attended a play, *The Unheard of World*, by Fabrice Melquiot, about an imaginative vision of the afterlife. It was produced by my son Ben and staged by FoolsFURY, his dramatic group. Marilyn and I had agreed to discuss the play with the audience after the performance, she from a literary perspective and I from a philosophical and psychiatric one. Although my remarks seemed satisfactory to the audience, I realized, in the middle of my presentation, that I had forgotten an important and interesting point I had wished to discuss. I kept speaking on automatic pilot while frantically burrowing in my mind for the lost idea. After ten more minutes or so, it suddenly popped into awareness and I made my point. I doubt if the audience knew of the frantic internal chase for my lost material, but during those ten minutes, as I was speaking to the audience, I heard a phrase circling in my mind, "That's it—the time has come. I've got to stop giving public talks. Remember Rollo." I was referring to a scene I described earlier about Rollo May at an advanced age giving an address in which he described the same episode twice. I had vowed never to put an audience through the spectacle of my senility.

The following day, I returned a rental car to the agency (my car had been in the shop). It was after hours, and the agency was closed. I followed the posted instructions: I locked the car and deposited the keys in the locked drop box. But only a few minutes later I discovered that I had left my bag containing my wallet, keys, money, and credit cards in the car. I finally had to call AAA to come and open the car to retrieve my bag.

Though this was an unusually bad siege of crumbling memory, milder lapses happen almost every day now. Who is that man smiling and approaching me? I know him, I'm certain, but his name, oh, his name? And what was the name of that restaurant Marilyn and I used to go to near the beach at Half Moon Bay? The name of that short funny comedian in the movie *Throw Momma from the Train*? On what street is the San Francisco Museum of Modern Art? What is the name of that odd form of therapy that rests on nine different personality types? And the name of the psychiatrist I used to know who originated transactional analysis? I recognize familiar faces, but the names evaporate—some return, and some disappear immediately after each reminder.

Yesterday I had lunch with a friend, Van Harvey, a few years older than I (yes, there are still a few of those around). He suggested I read a novel called *The Glass Room* by Simon Mawer, and I suggested he try *Winter* by Christopher Nicholson. A few hours later our emails crossed, each asking the other: "What was the name of that novel you recommended?" Of course, I should carry a notepad. But remembering to bring the notepad—ah, there's the rub.

Lost keys, eyeglasses, iPhones, phone numbers, and the location of parked cars—this is my daily fare. But losing both my apartment and automobile keys was extreme and probably related to the insomnia I had experienced the night before. I am certain I know the cause of the insomnia. That evening I had seen a French film, *Amour*, that depicts the ordeal of an aging loving husband who helps his ailing wife die. The couple resembled Marilyn and me, and the film haunted me all night long. *Amour* is a superb film, but take my advice: see it before you reach your eighties.

I've worried for a long time that my aging memory may force me to give up seeing patients, so, to forestall retirement, I make heavy use of a computer dictating program: after each session I never fail to dictate a one- or two-page summary of each hour, and I take great care always to read the summary just before I see the patient again. For that reason I always schedule at least twenty minutes between patients. Moreover, for the past few years, I see no more than three patients a day. When a patient from the deep past emails me, I often draw a blank at first, but reading a few sentences of my old notes usually opens up the spigot for the entire story.

But there is one bright side to memory loss: forgetting plotlines of many books enables me to obtain pleasure in rereading them. I find fewer and fewer contemporary novels that I enjoy, and so I turn back to my "favorites" lined up in my bookcase: *A Hundred Years of Solitude*, *Grendel*, *Great Expectations*, *The Adventures of Maqroll*, *Bleak House*, *Midnight's Children*, *Aunt Julia and the Scriptwriter*, *Daniel Deronda*, *Silas Marner*, and *The Way of All Flesh*, many of which I can read as though for the first time.

In *Staring at the Sun*, I describe the concept of "rippling" as a way to assuage anxiety about death. Each of us creates, often without our knowledge, concentric circles of influence that may affect others for years to come, even for generations. The effect we have on others is passed on much as the ripples of a pond go on and on, until they are no longer visible but still continue at a nano level. As John Whitehorn and Jerry Frank have rippled into me, I believe I have rippled into my students and readers and patients, and especially into my four children and eight grandchildren. I still remember my tears of joy when my daughter, Eve, phoned to tell me she had gotten into medical school, and last year my tears flowed again when I learned that her daughter, Alana, had been accepted into Tulane University School of Medicine. And this past Christmas, I sat down with Adrian, my three-year-old grandson, for our first game of chess.

THE AUTHOR GIVING HIS GRANDSON, AGE
THREE, A FIRST CHESS LESSON, 2016.

A conundrum: When shall I retire? I am often called upon to help patients deal with that very decision. Not long ago, I worked with Howard, a successful, highly intelligent hedge fund manager in his mid-eighties, whose wife insisted he seek therapy because he couldn't stop working long hours glued to his computer screen. Living on the West Coast, he had to rise at 4:30 a.m. to monitor the stock market, and he stayed at the screen all day. Even though he had worked for years to perfect a computer program to do his work, he felt he owed it to his investors never to stray far from the monitor. His three partners, two younger brothers and a lifelong friend, rarely missed their daily nine holes of golf, and Howard felt that he had to work for all of them. He knew that he and his wife and three daughters had far more money than they could spend, but he couldn't stop. It was his duty, he said. He couldn't entirely trust the computer program he'd designed to make trades. Yes, he agreed he was addicted to watching the rise and fall of the ticker tape, yet he knew no other way to live. And moreover, he winked at me, it's a blast to win big on the market.

"Imagine your life without work, Howard. What would it be like?"

"I admit I am terrified about stopping."

"Try to imagine this life without work."

"I know where you're heading. I admit it makes no sense. I admit I'm scared to stop. What would I do all day long? There's only so much traveling and sightseeing possible. All the interesting sites—you name them—I've seen them all."

I pushed him harder: "I wonder if you feel that work keeps you alive, that without work you'd drift into the final stages of life—senility and death. Can we together find some way to disentangle life and work?"

He listened intently and nodded. "I will think about these issues."

I doubted that he would.

I am a novice at being eighty-five and, like Howard, struggle with being old. Sometimes I accept the idea that retirement should be a time of rest and peace, a time of contented reflection. Yet I also know there are unruly feelings from my very early life that continue to create turbulence and threaten to surface if I slow down. Earlier I cited lines from Dickens: "For, as I draw closer and closer to the end, I travel in a circle nearer and nearer to the beginning." Those words haunt me. More and more, I sense some forces tugging me back to my beginnings. The other night, Marilyn and I attended the FoolsFURY Factory Festival in San Francisco—an event sponsored every two years by my son Ben's company—in which twenty small theaters from around the country presented their work. Before the show we stopped for a quick bite at Wise Sons, a small Jewish deli that seems to have stepped right out of the 1940s Washington, DC, of my childhood. The walls of the deli are almost entirely covered with family pictures—groups of soulful, wide-eyed, frightened refugees arriving at Ellis Island from Eastern Europe. The photographs transfixed me: they resembled those of my own extended family. I saw a sad young boy, who could have been me, delivering his Bar Mitzvah speech. I saw a woman who I first thought was my mother. I felt a sudden—and novel—rush of tenderness for her and felt mortified and guilty for having criticized her in these pages. Like my mother, the woman in the photo seemed uneducated, frightened, hardworking, and just trying to survive and raise her family in a strange new culture. My life has been so rich, so privileged, so safe—largely because of the hard work and generosity of my mother. I sat there in this deli weeping as I looked into her eyes and the eyes of all those refugees. I've had a lifetime of exploring, analyzing, and reconstructing my past, but I'm realizing now there is a vale of tears and pain in me I may never be done with.

Since I took early retirement from Stanford in 1994 my daily schedule has remained the same: I write for three to four hours every morning, usually six or seven days weekly, and five times a week I see patients later in the day. I've lived for over fifty years in Palo Alto, and my office is a separate building fifty meters from my home. About thirty-five years ago I bought a flat on Russian Hill in San Francisco with a beautiful view of the city and bay, and I see patients there on Thursday and Friday afternoons. Marilyn joins me Friday evenings and we generally spend weekends in San Francisco, a city that I find endlessly interesting.

THE AUTHOR IN HIS PALO ALTO OFFICE, 2010.

I chide myself about my faux retirement. "How many eighty-five-year-old psychiatrists are working as hard as I do?" Am I, like my patient Howard, continuing to work in order to stave off senility and death? Such questions jolt me, but I have my arsenal of answers. "I still have a lot to offer. . . . My aging makes me more able to understand and comfort people my age. . . . I am a writer and intoxicated by the writing process, so why give it up?"

Yes, I confess: I have terrible qualms about arriving at this last paragraph. I've always had a stack of books waiting in the back of my mind to be written, but no longer. Once I finish this work, I feel certain there are no more books waiting for me. My friends and colleagues groan when they hear me say this. They've heard it many times before. But I fear this time is different.

I always ask my patients to explore regrets and urge them to aspire to a regret-free life. Looking back now, I have few regrets. I've had an extraordinary woman as my life partner. I have loving children and grandchildren. I've lived in a privileged part of the world with ideal weather, lovely parks, little poverty or crime, and Stanford, one of the world's great universities. And I receive letters every day reminding me that I've been helpful to someone in a distant land. Hence, the words of Nietzsche's Zarathustra speak to me:

"Was *that* life? Well then once again!"

ACKNOWLEDGMENTS

I am grateful to many who have assisted me in this venture. The members of Pegasus, my monthly group of Stanford doctors who write, critiqued several chapters. And special thanks to the founder of this group, Hans Steiner, and to my friend Randy Weingarten, a psychiatrist and poet, who proposed the chapter title "A Novice at Growing Old." My thanks to my patients who have permitted me to describe incidents from therapy. In order to protect their confidentiality I have changed all names and deeply disguised all identifying details while attempting, at the same time, to convey certain truths of each encounter. My patients continually educate and inspire me. I was extremely fortunate to have Sam Douglas and Dan Gerstle as editors. Thanks to David Spiegel and, as always, to my literary agent Sandra Dijkstra and her associate, Andrea Cavallaro, who offered enthusiastic support from start to finish. Lifelong friends Julius Kaplan and Bea Glick helped jar my memory, as did my four children and eight grandchildren. And, most of all, to my beloved wife, Marilyn, who helped me recall events of long ago and served as my in-house editor-in-chief.

IRVIN D. YALOM is an emeritus professor of psychiatry at Stanford University and practices psychiatry in San Francisco and Palo Alto. He is the author of many books, including *Love's Executioner*, *The Gift of Therapy*, *When Nietzsche Wept*, and *The Schopenhauer Cure*. He and his wife, the author Marilyn Yalom, have four children and eight grandchildren. They live in Palo Alto, California.